D0204756

The Words and Music of George Harrison

THE PRAEGER SINGER-SONGWRITER COLLECTION

The Words and Music of George Harrison

Ian Inglis

James E. Perone, Series Editor

PRAEGER

AN IMPRINT OF ABC-CLIO, LLC
Santa Barbara, California • Denver, Colorado • Oxford, England

ML
420
.H167
I54
2010

Copyright 2010 by Ian Inglis

All rights reserved. No part of this publication may be reproduced,
stored in a retrieval system, or transmitted, in any form or by any
means, electronic, mechanical, photocopying, recording, or otherwise,
except for the inclusion of brief quotations in a review, without
prior permission in writing from the publisher.

Library of Congress Cataloging-in-Publication Data
Inglis, Ian, 1948-
  The words and music of George Harrison / Ian Inglis.
    p. cm. — (Praeger singer-songwriter collection)
  Includes bibliographical references and index.
  ISBN 978-0-313-37532-3 (hard copy : alk. paper) — ISBN 978-0-313-37533-0
(ebook) 1. Harrison, George, 1943–2001—Criticism and interpretation. I. Title.
  ML420.H167I54 2010
  782.42166092—dc22   2009050180

ISBN: 978-0-313-37532-3
EISBN: 978-0-313-37533-0

14 13 12 11 10   1 2 3 4 5

This book is also available on the World Wide Web as an eBook.
Visit www.abc-clio.com for details.

Praeger
An Imprint of ABC-CLIO, LLC

ABC-CLIO, LLC
130 Cremona Drive, P.O. Box 1911
Santa Barbara, California 93116-1911

This book is printed on acid-free paper ∞

Manufactured in the United States of America

For Christopher

University Libraries
Carnegie Mellon University
Pittsburgh, PA 15213-3890

Contents

Series Foreword

Although the term "singer-songwriter" might most frequently be associated with a cadre of musicians of the early 1970s such as Paul Simon, James Taylor, Carly Simon, Joni Mitchell, Cat Stevens, and Carole King, the Praeger Singer-Songwriter Collection defines singer-songwriters more broadly, both in terms of style and time period. The series includes volumes on musicians who have been active from approximately the 1960s through the present. Musicians who write and record in folk, rock, soul, hip-hop, country, and various hybrids of these styles are represented. Therefore, some of the early 1970s introspective singer-songwriters named here will be included, but not exclusively.

What do the individuals included in this series have in common? Some have never collaborated as writers, whereas others have, but all have written and recorded commercially successful and/or historically important music *and* lyrics at some point in their careers.

The authors who contribute to the series also exhibit diversity. Some are scholars who are trained primarily as musicians, whereas others have such areas of specialization as American studies, history, sociology, popular culture studies, literature, and rhetoric. The authors share a high level of scholarship, accessibility in their writing, and a true insight into the work of the artists they study. The authors are also focused on the output of their subjects and how it relates to their subject's biography and the society around them; however, biography in and of itself is not a major focus of the books in this series.

Given the diversity of the musicians who are the subject of books in this series, and given the diversity of viewpoint of the authors, volumes in the series differ from book to book. All, however, are organized chronologically around the compositions and recorded performances of their subjects. All of the books in the series should also serve as listeners' guides to the music of their subjects, making them companions to the artists' recorded output.

James E. Perone
Series Editor

Acknowledgments

I am indebted, in differing ways, to various groups of people for their advice and assistance during the preparation and writing of this book. They include my colleagues in the Department of Media at the University of Northumbria for their support through a busy academic year, my peers in the international popular music studies network for their encouragement and enthusiasm, and my family—Annette, Eleanor, Christopher, and Susannah— each of whom celebrates living in a rock 'n' roll household with all the energy and spontaneity that the music contains.

I wish also to acknowledge the part played over many years and in many places by those people whose company and conversation have (often unwittingly) helped to shape my perceptions of popular music. They include Norman Barr, Sue Davies, Russ Jackson, Phil Booth, Pete Smith, Greg Hoare, Kevin Sheridan, Phil Burns, Sue Fleming, Derek Layder, Sandy Wolfson, Gary Burns, Sheila Whiteley, Derek Scott, Lee Barron, and Ian Brown. While the errors and omissions in this book remain my own, the principles of enjoyment and exploration which guide it are, I hope, a testament to their friendship.

Introduction

George Harrison was born on February 25, 1943, in a small, two-bedroom house in Wavertree, a working-class area of Liverpool. For many families in wartime Britain, including George's—his parents, Harold and Louise, and their three other children, Louise, Harold, and Peter—it was a time of cautious optimism. The threat of an invasion had receded, Mussolini's troops had surrendered at Tripoli, the Red Army had liberated Stalingrad from German occupation, Germany's Afrika Korps had been destroyed at El Alamein, and U.S. forces were pouring into North Africa. Just a few weeks earlier, Winston Churchill had announced to the House of Commons: "It is not the end. It is not even the beginning of the end. But it is perhaps the end of the beginning."

But for George Harrison, it was the beginning of an extraordinary journey that would take him from the terraced streets of Liverpool and a school career characterized by rebellion and failure, through the unprecedented global exuberance of Beatlemania, to a profound humanitarianism and yearning for spiritual enlightenment, and a final withdrawal into quiet and reflective privacy. And, for more than forty years, these changes were mirrored in the words and music he created, as a Beatle and as a solo performer.

In 1948, the five-year-old Harrison was enrolled as a pupil at Dovedale Road Primary School. Although neither had any recollection of ever meeting, John Lennon was also a pupil there, three years ahead of him, alongside George's brother Peter. When in 1954 George moved on to the Liverpool Institute, he was in the year below Paul McCartney. They often caught the same bus to school and, particularly after the emergence of skiffle—a peculiarly British amalgamation of jazz, blues, and folk traditions, whose principal exponent was Lonnie Donegan[1]—became friendly through their common interest in the music.

The simplicity of skiffle, with its basic three-chord style and rudimentary instrumental lineup (guitar, banjo, tea-chest bass, and washboard), inspired many thousands of aspiring young musicians around the country to participate in music for the first time. In the summer of 1956, after Donegan's recording of "Rock Island Line" sold more than three million copies in the United States and United Kingdom, one such group that formed in Liverpool was the Rebels, fronted by George and his brother Peter. Another was the Quarry Men Skiffle Group, formed by six friends (John Lennon, Pete Shotton, Eric Griffiths, Rod Davis, Len Garry, and Colin Hanton) from Quarry Bank High School; its leader, Lennon, invited Paul McCartney to join in June 1957, after the two had been introduced by mutual friend Ivan Vaughan.[2] In March 1958, at McCartney's encouragement, he issued the same invitation to Harrison, who had impressed him with his ability to reproduce Duane Eddy's guitar work on "Raunchy."[3] While their original impetus to perform had stemmed from skiffle, the three were drawn together through their increasing preference for American rock 'n' roll; their admiration for Elvis Presley, Little Richard, Chuck Berry, Larry Williams, Carl Perkins, and Buddy Holly was to be the defining influence on their musical output over the next few years.[4]

Through changes of name (Johnny and the Moondogs, the Silver Beetles), personnel (Stuart Sutcliffe, Pete Best), management (Allan Williams, Brian Epstein), and location (Liverpool, Hamburg), the three were able to make occasional demo recordings and informal tapes from 1958 onward and, with Pete Best on drums, were the backing group at a recording session with singer Tony Sheridan in Hamburg in 1961. After being turned down by most of the major British record companies (Decca, Pye, Columbia, HMV), they eventually secured a recording contract in July 1962 with Parlophone—a label best known for the comedy records by Peter Ustinov, the Goons, Flanders and Swann, and Peter Sellers, all of which had been produced by George Martin. The lineup of the Beatles was finally completed by the arrival of drummer Ringo Starr in August 1962, to complement the nucleus of Lennon (rhythm guitar), McCartney (bass guitar), and Harrison (lead guitar). Their first official single release, in October 1962, was "Love Me Do"/"P.S. I Love You," which was a minor chart hit in the United Kingdom.

The group's British breakthrough came in 1963, when they enjoyed four #1 singles ("Please Please Me," "From Me to You," "She Loves You," and "I Want To Hold Your Hand") and two #1 albums (*Please Please Me* and *With the Beatles*). The pattern was repeated in the United States and around the world in 1964; at one point in March, they famously occupied the top five places in the *Billboard* singles charts and the top six places in the Australian singles charts. The term "Beatlemania" was coined to describe the scenes of mass hysteria that accompanied their appearances, and the group dominated, and directed, popular music throughout the decade. When, in August 1966, they controversially decided to abandon touring in order to concentrate on studio recording, their popularity remained undiminished. After Epstein's death in August 1967, they established their own production and management company, Apple. The Beatles effectively disbanded in 1970 to pursue solo careers, but the group remains universally recognized as the most distinctive and familiar icon of the 1960s.

Faced with the perfectly tuned commercial sensibilities of McCartney's songwriting and the force of Lennon's creative impulse, it is not surprising that Harrison's own attempts at composing should have been overlooked. The tracks on the group's singles were exclusively reserved for Lennon–McCartney compositions and, on the Beatles' first few albums, his contributions as lead vocalist tended to be limited to songs they had written for him ("Do You Want to Know a Secret," "I'm Happy Just to Dance with You"), cover versions of rock 'n' roll standards ("Roll Over Beethoven," "Everybody's Trying to Be My Baby"), and adaptations of pop songs by U.S. girl groups ("Chains," "Devil in Her Heart"). Harrison's first composition to appear on a Beatles album was "Don't Bother Me" on *With the Beatles* in 1963. He composed no songs on the next two albums, but in 1965, *Help!* and *Rubber Soul* each contained two of his original compositions.

This practice quickly became a policy, and for the rest of the Beatles' recording career, Harrison was allowed no more than two or three songs per album, much to his disappointment. It was not until 1968 that his songs were included on the group's singles: "The Inner Light" and "Old Brown Shoe" were both B sides, and in 1969, "Something" was released as a double A side with "Come Together." When the group broke up, Harrison wasted little time in exploiting the large number of unrecorded songs he had written, and the triple album *All Things Must Pass* was, by common consent, the most immediately impressive of all the post-Beatles solo recordings; its first single, "My Sweet Lord," quickly became one of popular music's greatest anthems. The following year, his organization of the Concert for Bangla Desh to raise funds for refugees in that country established him as one of popular music's earliest political campaigners, and the interplay between his status as a rock star and the scope of his humanitarian and spiritual concerns would characterize his music for the rest of his life.

Throughout the 1970s and 1980s, Harrison released a steady stream of albums and singles; from 1976 onward, these were on his own Dark Horse label. While their commercial success was intermittent and unpredictable, the body of work demonstrated beyond a doubt the pleasure and satisfaction he gained from having the personal freedom to write, record, and produce songs that were not governed, or measured, by the constraints of chart success. Many contained observations and reflections about events and people in his own life—death, friendship, separation, remarriage. Although his most successful hit single in this period was a cover version of Rudy Clark's "Got My Mind Set on You," two songs in which he returned to the subject of the Beatles themselves ("All Those Years Ago" and "When We Was Fab") provided eloquent insights into the nature of his relationship with his former colleagues. Having successfully emerged from the shadows of Lennon and McCartney, Harrison was able to effectively control his own career and to direct it along routes chosen *by* him rather than *for* him. Some of these were nonmusical: his executive role in Handmade Films helped to sustain British cinema at a time of crisis, producing some of the country's most memorable movies of the 1980s.

In the 1990s, Harrison continued to collaborate professionally (as performer or composer or musician) with the Beatles and others, culminating in the formation of the Traveling Wilburys and the Beatles' *Anthology* project. The early diagnosis of cancer in 1997 and his attempted murder at his home in Henley-on-Thames in 1999 thereafter dissuaded him from further musical activity. He died in November 2001. His final recordings were released on the album *Brainwashed* in 2002; it was hailed as a mature and thoughtful collection of songs, and an appropriate end to his career as one of the century's most celebrated musicians.

SCOPE AND ORGANIZATION

In order to fully appreciate the words and music of George Harrison the solo performer, it is necessary to acknowledge the words and music of George Harrison the Beatle. Not only did those songs provide the foundation on which much of his later output was built, but unlike Lennon and McCartney, whose songs for the group were written in varying degrees of collaboration, Harrison nearly always composed alone. In this sense, his development as a singer-songwriter definitively started within the confines of the group, and it would be perverse to omit those compositions.

The vast majority of Beatles songs were recorded and released in sequence, and it is sensible to discuss them chronologically. However, there are a few exceptional cases where some tracks were not made available until many years after their production. Where this is the case, I have chosen to consider them in the order in which they were recorded. In doing so, I hope to present a trajectory that reveals Harrison's natural evolution as a composer and performer within the group, rather than one which leaps between decades in an attempt to follow the often idiosyncratic and confusing consequences of marketing decisions.

However, because of the multiplicity of formats and labels around the world on which the Beatles' music was released, the alternative album titles used in different territories, the differences in track listings between U.S. and U.K. releases, and an abundance of compilations and reissues, there have been disagreements about the most accurate manner in which to approach their musical history. For example, the Beatles released thirteen albums in the United Kingdom (on Parlophone and Apple) from 1963 to 1970; by contrast, twenty-three albums appeared in the United States (on Vee-Jay, Capitol, United Artists, and Apple) over the same period. In an attempt to resolve these conflicting histories, I will consider Harrison's contributions within the Beatles as they appeared on the group's original U.K. albums and singles. The principal justification for my decision is that this is the pattern commonly accepted as the "authorized version" of the group's recording history—although, for ease of comparison, information is also provided in the text about the U.S. releases. It may also serve as a small reminder that—despite his fascination with Indian music, culture, and religion, his working relationships with many of North America's finest musicians, his marriage to Olivia Arias, and the lengthy periods of time spent at his holiday homes in Australia and Hawaii—Harrison remained, as much of his music confirmed, a stubbornly British artist.

Harrison's post-Beatles output is presented according to the conventional logic of his U.S. releases. Like many of his contemporaries—Neil Young, Bob Dylan, John Lennon, Van Morrison, Paul Simon—Harrison generally chose to record and release songs as he wrote them, album by album, and his solo career contains relatively few promotional, sequential, or geographical discrepancies. Each collection of songs provided, in the main, a statement of his priorities, aspirations, thoughts, and motivations at a specific time. This, of course, is one of the principal distinctions between the singer-songwriter who seeks to present an authentic, individual body of work and the pop performer who searches for a compilation of attractive, but unrelated, songs to fill each new album.

Only Harrison's "official" recordings are considered here. There exist, particularly from the Beatles era, a considerable number of "bootleg" recordings, but I have decided to exclude these, for a number of reasons. First, they are not universally available. Second, detailed information on their origins, locations, and personnel is often in dispute. Third, many are little more than rehearsals or works-in-progress, revisited and completed at a later time. And fourth, the quality of some of the recordings is so poor that it is difficult to make a valid assessment of their overall significance.

Similarly, I have not included detailed analyses of the many occasions on which Harrison contributed to the recordings of other performers (as composer, musician, or producer), some of which involved merely the briefest and most tenuous of associations. Although they may be of passing interest, only a few play a significant part in his musical career. Where this is so,

I have discussed them, but, for the most part, my emphasis is on the songs that he wrote and recorded himself.

I have also resisted the temptation to expand my account of Harrison's songs by including examinations of the album covers and music videos that accompany them. The significance of both these formats in the transformation of popular music from a purely aural medium into an aural-visual one has been reflected in the increasing literature devoted to each of them.[5] And there is little doubt that they can offer fascinating insights into Harrison's motivations and intentions. The four toppled gnomes on the front cover of *All Things Must Pass*, the presence of Ringo Starr in the "When We Was Fab" video, the inert mannequins gazing vacantly at a crowded television screen in the *Brainwashed* CD booklet, and the cast of surreal, fantasy figures in the video for "Crackerbox Palace" are among the many intriguing examples that run through Harrison's output. But a comprehensive analysis of such clues would fill another book. More importantly, they are essentially temporary signifiers, useful rather than essential, with the potential to detract from, as well as add to, musical meaning.

It should be noted that the information in the discography relates to the primary medium (CD or vinyl) through which the music was made available at the time of release. Furthermore, it excludes subsequent reissues, added "bonus tracks," promotional copies, alternate mixes, and re-presentations of existing material. It represents Harrison's music, as it was originally and intentionally created, in its purest historical form.

I have not set out to provide a biography of George Harrison. However, from his first Beatles song, "Don't Bother Me," written while he was ill and confined to bed in a hotel room in 1963, to "Brainwashed," the last track on his final album, in which he reflected on the dishonesty of the education he had endured as a child, it is impossible to separate the music from the man. His songs provided commentaries, clarifications, and conclusions to the situations in which he found himself, in a way that is true of very few other musicians. Although my focus is on the songs themselves, the personal and social contexts in which they were created are, therefore, inevitably woven into their analysis.

The Quiet One

Numerous theories have been advanced to account for the remarkable success in Britain of the Beatles in 1963. They began the year still relatively unknown, playing out a final engagement at the Star Club in Hamburg, before returning home to Liverpool. By the end of the year, they had, in addition to selling millions of singles and albums, completed four nationwide tours, starred in the *Royal Variety Show*, hosted their own fifteen-part weekly radio series *Pop Go the Beatles*, topped the bill on ITV's *Sunday Night at the London Palladium*, approved the monthly publication of *The Beatles Book*, been named as the Variety Club's Show Business Personalities of the Year, contracted to make their U.S. debut on CBS-TV's *The Ed Sullivan Show*, performed to more than 100,000 fans over sixteen sellout nights at London's Astoria Theatre in *The Beatles Christmas Show*, negotiated a three-picture contract with United Artists, and established their own music publishing company, Northern Songs.

It was, by any standards, a tale of dramatic and overwhelming proportions. Explanations for the group's phenomenal achievements ranged across the managerial strategy of Brian Epstein, the studio skills of George Martin, the songwriting abilities of John Lennon and Paul McCartney, the sorry state of popular music at the time, the rise of the "baby boomer" generation, the complex attractions of the "Mersey sound," a breakdown in parental and adult authority, and the consequences of the increasing power and presence of television. When the group repeated its success in the United States the following year, the national gloom that followed the assassination of President John F. Kennedy was included as an additional factor.

However, as the group's impact and influence rapidly spread beyond the traditional territories of popular music, more and more attention was focused on the specific personalities of the four Beatles themselves, and shorthand consensual descriptions of them began to be employed, first by a hungry news media, then by a fascinated public. Lennon was seen as the cynical, sarcastic leader; McCartney the handsome, romantic charmer; Ringo Starr the sad-faced clown. The part allocated to George Harrison was that of the "boy next door," the quiet, thoughtful Beatle whose undemonstrative exterior was in sharp contrast to the obvious visibility of the other three.[1] The depictions quickly became familiar stereotypes, particularly after the release of the group's first movie, *A Hard Day's Night* (1964), in which they conformed rigidly to those perceived roles, as re-created for them by director Richard Lester and screenwriter Alun Owen.[2]

This conventional imagery began to blur into perceptions of their music, and there, too, Harrison seemed content at the time to accept a secondary position within the Beatles. Having relentlessly practiced his guitar-playing for many years, often until his fingers bled,[3] he appeared satisfied with his role as lead guitarist and occasional vocalist. Indeed, he regularly expressed no interest in songwriting, other than to admit to it as a vague possibility for the future.[4] But, in fact, this apparent lack of ambition did not quite tally with the contribution he had made to the group before 1963. Of the fifteen tracks recorded by the Beatles at their (unsuccessful) audition for Decca in January 1962, he was the lead vocalist on four ("The Sheikh of Araby," "Take Good Care of My Baby," "Three Cool Cats," and "Crying, Waiting, Hoping"), which compared favorably to Lennon's four and McCartney's seven.[5]

Although the majority of songs at the Decca audition included, at Epstein's insistence, a majority of "safe" cover versions,[6] with just three original titles ("Like Dreamers Do," "Hello Little Girl," and "Love of the Loved," all composed by Lennon–McCartney), it has often been forgotten that some of the very earliest Beatles compositions were, in fact, cowritten by Harrison. In July 1958, shortly after he had joined the Quarrymen, the group (Lennon, McCartney, Harrison, pianist John Lowe, and drummer Colin Hanton) recorded two tracks at local electrician Percy Phillips's domestic sound recording service in Liverpool. One was a cover of Buddy Holly's "That'll Be the Day"; the other was a Harrison–McCartney composition, "In Spite of All the Danger."[7] In May 1961, the group's first professional studio recording, produced by German band leader Bert Kaempfert in Hamburg, was the Harrison–Lennon instrumental "Cry for a Shadow."[8] And in 1977, the release of *The Beatles Live at the Star Club in Hamburg, Germany, 1962* confirmed his role as lead singer across a range of tracks ("Roll Over Beethoven," "Lend Me Your Comb," "Reminiscing," "Nothin' Shakin' (But the Leaves on the Trees)," "Everybody's Trying to Be My Baby," "Sheila") in the early 1960s. As permanent lead guitarist, regular vocalist, and occasional cocomposer, the position Harrison occupied within the group was, quite clearly, anything but secondary.

It is therefore important to emphasize from the outset that his journey as a composer was much longer than has often been assumed. The music he wrote and performed during his years with the Beatles was not separate from, but rather an integral part of, his overall output.

With the Beatles

As the very first authentic Beatles recording and the only Harrison–McCartney composition in existence, "In Spite of All the Danger" presents an intriguing portrait of two very different composers, struggling to define their respective styles at the start of their careers. Drawing all too clearly on their musical influences at the time, the song combines elements of rudimentary blues, doo-wop, and country. The tempo is slow, even sluggish, and there is little to signal the arrival of a fresh, new talent. Harrison's tentative, stumbling guitar intro is matched by an equally hesitant vocal delivery from Lennon, who, as the group's leader, automatically assumes the role as lead singer. However, the song's lyrics are surprisingly frank; instead of naively predicting a lifetime of unending love, the singer is aware that relationships contain risks and that happiness cannot be guaranteed. Nevertheless, in spite of the danger, disappointment, and heartache that may come his way, he offers to "look after you . . . [and] do anything you want me to" on one condition: "if you'll be true to me." It is, perhaps, an early indication of the subtle and wide-ranging thematic variations that the Beatles consistently introduced to their love songs.[9] The song was eventually released thirty-seven years after its original recording, on *Anthology 1*.

During the Beatles' second visit to Hamburg in the spring of 1961, they were recruited to provide instrumental and vocal backing for British singer Tony Sheridan, during a Polydor recording session produced by Kaempfert. They had occasionally backed Sheridan on stage and were familiar with many of the songs he recorded, including "My Bonnie," "Why," "Nobody's Child," and "Sweet Georgia Brown." However, they were quick to take advantage of their time in the studio to record two numbers by themselves: "Ain't She Sweet" and the Harrison–Lennon instrumental "Cry for a Shadow"—the latter named (perhaps ironically) after Cliff Richard's backing group, the Shadows, which was Britain's most successful instrumental group of the late 1950s and early 1960s and had cemented the four-piece template of lead guitar, bass guitar, rhythm guitar, and drums that the Beatles and others adopted. It is a competent and polished track that manages to re-create in uncanny detail the sound of the Shadows themselves; in particular, Harrison convincingly imitated the fluent, vibrato style of lead guitarist Hank Marvin. The two groups freely expressed their mutual admiration, and for a while it was even rumored that they might record together.[10] "Cry for a Shadow" was released by Polydor in the United Kingdom on the *My Bonnie* EP in July 1963; in the United States, it first appeared on the MGM album *The Beatles with Tony Sheridan and Their Guests* in February 1964.

Producer George Martin's decision to include "Don't Bother Me" on the Beatles' second U.K. album, *With the Beatles*, in November 1963 aroused no great comment. The song was written by Harrison to pass the time in a Bournemouth hotel room during the group's summer season at the resort, when he was confined to bed after a bout of illness.[11] Its insistent and repetitive use of jagged chord patterns distances it from the more accessible pop melodies of Lennon–McCartney, and its blunt lyrics reflect the impatience and frustration of the convalescent who simply wants to be left in peace: "Go away, leave me alone, just stay away." Harrison's achievement is to recast these lyrics from a commentary on his own situation to a scenario in which he laments not the misfortune of his illness, but the absence of his lover: "Since she's been gone I want no one to talk to me." There is little optimism in the double-tracked vocal, and the song is distinguished by a sense of unease and uncertainty. Given his later demands for privacy and his complaints about the persistent public intrusions into his personal life, the plea in the title could apply equally to his post-Beatle career. In the United States, the track was included on *Meet the Beatles*, the first of the group's Capitol albums, in January 1964.

Although "You Know What to Do" was recorded by the Beatles in 1964, it remained unheard for more than thirty years, until it was finally made available on *Anthology 1*. Harrison's enthusiastic performance of the jaunty, country-influenced ballad shows Lennon's pervasive influence in its phrasing, intonation, and nasal vocal. In addition, the lyrics echo the frank expressions of romantic intent that run through many of Lennon's early songs, including "Hello Little Girl" and "Please Please Me." Many of the rhyming schemes are predictable ("only" and "lonely"; "every day" and "every way"), but there is a shared simplicity between words and music that is immediately attractive. However, although Harrison constantly reminds the girl that she knows "what to do," he never reveals exactly what this might be; his deliberate oversight anticipates the playfulness with which he approaches love in later songs with the Beatles such as "If I Needed Someone" and "You Like Me Too Much."

Through 1963 and 1964, perceptions of Harrison's contribution to the Beatles' success contained little or no recognition of his role as a songwriter. "Don't Bother Me" had been his only composition on the group's first four albums, and the enormous popularity of the seemingly endless supply of songs written by Lennon and McCartney made it highly unlikely that this position would change. This might explain why the deal that Harrison was able to agree with Northern Songs at the start of 1965 was much more favorable than that negotiated by Lennon and McCartney.

The history of Northern Songs is a complex tale: the major facts, however, are that when it was established in February 1963, Dick James Music (the publishers of the earliest Lennon–McCartney songs) owned half of the company; the other half was jointly owned by Brian Epstein's company NEMS and the two songwriting Beatles. As the scale of their songwriting abilities began to dawn on Lennon and McCartney, they established Maclen as a subdivision of Northern Songs in order to reclaim some of the autonomy they felt they had surrendered; Harrison was keen to follow the same path, and did so in 1965 with the creation of Harrisongs. However, whereas Maclen's contract stipulated a comprehensive 50–50 split with Northern Songs, the contract with Harrison's company gave him an 80–20 split on publishing royalties from record sales, a 70–30 split on receipts from overseas publishing, and a 67–33 split of all performing and broadcast fees.[12] As Harrison was at this stage still an unproven songwriter, such a generous arrangement seemed relatively unimportant. For Harrison, however, it represented a boost to his confidence and a spur to his ambitions; and as if to emphasize his new standing, the next three Beatles' albums departed from the pattern of the previous four by including seven of his songs.

"I Need You" is the first of his two songs on *Help!* and was allegedly written with some uncredited assistance from Lennon.[13] Harrison's plea is to the girl who has left him without warning. The unexpected nature of her decision is revealed in the casual way in which it is introduced—"[You] said you had a thing or two to tell me"—which is a hallmark of the Beatles' ability to root the dramatic and the emotional in the routine of everyday life. In contrast to the guarded and sullen outlook of "Don't Bother Me," he openly admits his unhappiness and pleads with her to return. Although he readily confesses his bewilderment, it is not a hopeless situation; the upbeat tempo, warm backing harmonies, innovative use of the wah-wah pedal on electric guitar, and confident double-tracked lead vocals carry with them a real sense of hope. When he urges her to "please come on back to me," there is little doubt that she will. In contrast to the melodic flexibility of Lennon and McCartney, its rhythmic and tonal structures clearly identify this as a Harrison song,[14] but it is also, indisputably, a Beatles song.

Like several Lennon–McCartney songs from the same album ("The Night Before," "Another Girl," "I've Just Seen a Face"), "You Like Me Too Much" presents love as a game that should not be taken too seriously. It may be punctuated by fluctuating moods, teasing, warnings, and temporary departures, but these apparent setbacks are quickly overcome. Harrison wryly acknowledges that he may be at fault in these disputes and notes that his girlfriend's threat to leave him is "all that I deserve." However, this is not an arrogant male boasting of his domination (as exemplified in the Rolling Stones' "Under My Thumb"), but a playful exchange of affection. The lyrics affirm that they will, in fact, never part, and the reason is simple, as he astutely declares: "You like me too much, and I like you."

The barrelhouse piano introduction locates the song in the tradition of vaudeville entertainment, and the unpretentious phrases and everyday vocabulary—"it's nice," "I really do," "I couldn't stand it"—reinforce his message that a relationship can be *fun*. The Beatles were at the peak of their global popularity in 1965, and it was perhaps inevitable that their collective buoyancy and exhilaration should find its way into their songs. The melody is very similar to Lennon–McCartney's "I Don't Want to Spoil the Party" and is a timely reminder that Harrison was, at this stage, still learning his craft and absorbing influences from his two more prolific partners. In the United States, "You Like Me Too Much" appeared on *Beatles VI*.

When the Beatles met Bob Dylan at New York's Delmonico Hotel in August 1964,[15] it marked the beginning of an active and reciprocal relationship between the two most original and creative forces in popular music.[16] The impact on Harrison was especially profound.[17] In addition to providing him with a friend and colleague with whom he would compose, record, and perform over the next thirty years, it was to decisively shift the form and content of the lyrics he wrote. "Think for Yourself," on *Rubber Soul*, is the earliest song to betray that influence. In it, Harrison is severing connections with a former acquaintance, announcing the end of their relationship and signaling what this means for the future: "Think for yourself, 'cos I won't be there with you." He accuses the person of lying and causing "more misery" and urges her (or him) to "think more" and to "rectify" previous misdeeds. It is a withering attack, reminiscent of the sentiments in Dylan's "Positively 4th Street," also recorded and released in 1965. Harrison's blunt "I left you far behind" and Dylan's curt "It's not my problem" could be spoken by the same voice. The deliberately exaggerated Liverpudlian pronunciation of "there" (to rhyme with "her" rather than "hair") is one of the first examples of a tendency he retained throughout his recording career. The track is propelled by McCartney's growling fuzz-bass, which helps to maintain a persistent mood of menace. At the same time, the song's debt to Lennon is also apparent, both in its musical contours (which refuse to depart from movement around a single repeated chord) and its vocabulary (which repeats the explicit accusations and warnings contained in "Run for Your Life").

Dylan's presence also can be traced on "If I Needed Someone" from the same album. Harrison's D-chord-based melody and his use of a twelve-string Rickenbacker were inspired by two Byrds songs, "Bells of Rhymney" and "She Don't Care about Time." The Byrds, of course, had been spectacularly successful in 1965 with their electric folk-rock versions of Dylan's "Mr. Tambourine Man" and "All I Really Want to Do." Harrison's sparkling guitar and the song's gorgeous three-part harmonies support a bright, attractive melody, but there is a tough and unexpected cynicism in his lyrics,[18] especially in the offhand way in which he holds out to the girl the possibility of a relationship: at the moment, he is "too much in love" with someone else to consider it, but if, in the future, he has "some more time to spend," then he might just get in touch. Again, there is no arrogance in what he says, just a straightforward statement of fact. It is a dismissive offer, but the only one he is prepared to make. A cover version of the song was a minor hit in Britain for the Hollies. In 1969, Graham Nash of the Hollies and David Crosby of the Byrds were united in Crosby, Stills, and Nash, thus bringing the connections full circle. The track was excluded from the U.S. release of *Rubber Soul* in 1965, but appeared the following year on *Yesterday and Today.*

"12-Bar Original" was the working title of an instrumental track recorded during the *Rubber Soul* sessions, but not released until 1996 on *Anthology 2.* Jointly credited to Lennon, McCartney, Harrison, and Starr and using the riff from John Lee Hooker's "Dimples" as its starting point, it elaborates the familiar twelve-bar pattern, with Harrison's electric guitar to the forefront. Although he often expressed his admiration for blues performers, Harrison seldom worked with them, preferring instead the company of rock 'n' rollers such as Carl Perkins and Roy Orbison, and this venture into blues is therefore all the more interesting for its rarity.

Revolver has often been cited as the album on which Harrison came of age as a songwriter.[19] Not only was he allowed three of the fourteen songs, but his composition "Taxman" was selected as the opening track. Long regarded as the Beatle who was most concerned with financial matters,[20] he used the song to vent his anger and frustration at what he saw as the unfairness of Britain's internal revenue system, which claimed a huge amount of the group's earnings: "There's one for you, nineteen for me . . . be thankful I don't take it all." His stringent double-tracked vocal is supported by a memorable lead guitar contribution from McCartney and Starr's unusually forceful drumming. Although the melody is simple and repetitive, the lyrics are complex and precise; their succinct description of a tax regime specifically points the finger of blame at two prime ministers of the 1960s, Harold Wilson and Edward Heath, and the song's closing message from the taxman—"You're working for no one but me"—conclusively demonstrates Harrison's cynicism.

Although the instrument had first been played by Harrison on "Norwegian Wood," the thirty-five-second sitar introduction to "Love You To" was a decisive sign of the musical and spiritual trajectory that would become such an important part of his life. Indian musician Anil Bhagwat was recruited to play on tabla, and it is the combination of sitar and tabla that defines the track. Harrison's lyrics combine sourness ("There's people standing 'round who'll screw you in the ground") with a blasé rationality ("I'll make love to you if you want me to") and remind us that in a world of material dissatisfaction and moral disharmony, there is always the solace of sexual pleasure. Such unsophisticated sentiments may be at odds with the delicacy of the Indian instrumentation, but are a natural continuation of the sardonic humor of "Taxman" and the casual, matter-of-fact approach to relationships evident in "You Like Me Too Much" and "If I Needed Someone."

At first hearing, "I Want to Tell You" appears to return to more familiar lyrical and instrumental territories. The track is often read as a conventional love song, in which Harrison reveals his uncertainty in the face of a tentative romance.[21] But it also exists as a commentary about our inability to effectively communicate with others and the way in which thoughts and words can impede, rather than assist, the creation and maintenance of meaningful relationships. Harrison's twentieth-century understanding of the dilemma may be expressed in more direct language—"My head is filled with things to say . . . when I get near you, the games begin to drag me down"—but his underlying concern with the barriers between self and others echoes many of the themes that have occupied philosophers from the pre-Socratic period through to the present day. The conflict between what Harrison wants to do and what he is able to do is reinforced musically: the mood of tension created by the song's harshly ascending verses and unvarying piano riff is only partly defused by the song's gentler descending chorus.

Harrison met the Indian musician Ravi Shankar in June 1966. They quickly formed a close friendship and were keen to explore the bridges between Eastern and Western musical forms.[22] Shankar agreed to give the Beatle sitar lessons, and the improvement in his playing was evident on "Within You Without You," Harrison's one song on *Sgt. Pepper's Lonely Hearts Club Band*, released the following year. No other Beatles are present on the track; Harrison's vocal and sitar are backed by a variety of Indian musicians from the North London Asian Music Circle and an octet of British violinists. The lengthy instrumental tabla solo in 5/4 time shows his eagerness to break away from the routine rhythms of rock 'n' roll, while the words, based on a conversation with his close friend and fellow musician Klaus Voormann, draw attention to the inability of people to recognize the folly of material selfishness: "We were talking about the space between us all . . . and the people who gain the world and lose their soul." The answer, he tells us, is not to entertain false ideas about our own importance, but to realize that every one of us is actually "very small." The lyrics are given greater depth by the double meaning of *without*—"in the absence of" and "outside"—each of which is perfectly applicable to the song's sentiments. Unlike Harrison's allotted compositions on the group's previous albums, "Within You Without You" is not an additional or peripheral track but a song whose presence is absolutely central to the form and content of the musical project.[23] In some ways, it can be seen as Harrison's first completely independent piece of work; even the dubbed laughter at the end of the track is his suggestion.

The features of Indian music that appealed to Harrison cannot be easily separated from the religious and philosophical contexts in which he discovered them. For him, the non-Western sounds and styles he employed were chosen not simply for their unusual musical properties but also because they were symbolic of the ancient, indigenous culture from which they came. However, the facets of Indian music that found their way into Harrison's compositions showed that he fully understood some of the form's most basic characteristics: its all-pervasive drone; its construction around the polarity between rhythm and melody (rather than Western music's construction around the polarity between harmony and melody); and patterns of notes added to, or subtracted from, a recurring phrase. While some popular musicians restricted themselves to temporary flirtations with the sound (Traffic's "Paper Sun") and others used Western instruments to mimic the sound (Steely Dan's "Do It Again"), Harrison was virtually unique in his perseverance and commitment to the original source.[24]

The second half of 1967—the six months between the releases of *Sgt. Pepper* and *Magical Mystery Tour*—was marked by a number of events that were important for Harrison and the Beatles: his trip to Haight-Ashbury in August left him disillusioned with the mundane reality of San Francisco's hippie community; the group's attendance at the Maharishi Mahesh Yogi's weekend seminar on transcendental meditation at Bangor in North Wales (largely as a result of Harrison's encouragement) was interrupted by the news of Brian Epstein's death; the group's newly established company, Apple, announced itself to the world with the opening of its boutique (and administrative office) in Baker Street, London; McCartney was a member of the organizing committee of the world's first major outdoor rock festival, in Monterey, California; the first edition of *Rolling Stone* (with a photograph of Lennon on its front cover) was published; and Harrison was invited by film director Joe Massot to compose the score for his forthcoming movie *Wonderwall*.

In the midst of this period of innovation and experiment, the Beatles produced, directed, wrote, and acted in the fifty-minute film *Magical Mystery Tour*, which was premiered in the United Kingdom on BBC-TV during the Christmas holiday. The accompanying soundtrack release contained six new tracks, one of which was Harrison's composition "Blue Jay Way." Named after a street in Los Angeles where he had rented a house and written while waiting for friends to arrive, the song is colored by an extraordinary sense of yearning and melancholy that belies its apparently trivial lyrics. Harrison's emotional, almost childlike, plea to his friends ("Please don't be long, please don't you be very long"), the persistent Indian-like drone of his Hammond organ, and Lennon and McCartney's ethereal supporting vocals combine to create an unusually atmospheric and strangely moving song. The use of a drone as an anchorage point for vocal and instrumental improvisation became increasingly popular in the late 1960s, especially among British folk performers such as Fairport Convention and the Incredible String Band, but its use here is one of the earliest examples of the technique. An alternative reading of the lyrics, in line with the contemporary advice attributed to Timothy Leary—"Turn on, tune in, drop out"—asserts that what Harrison really intends to say is "please don't belong."

"Flying" was only the Beatles' second instrumental release, and the first composition to be officially credited to all four members. The effectiveness of its simple, gentle melody is largely achieved by Lennon's Mellotron and Harrison's relaxed guitar, amplified by a restrained vocal chorus, and the casual, spiraling fadeout sweetly recalls the tranquil promise and lazy hedonism of that year's Summer of Love.

The Beatles' lack of interest in the cartoon film *Yellow Submarine* (dir. George Dunning, 1968) was evident in their decisions not to provide the speaking voices for their characters nor to compose any songs for the soundtrack. As a result, the film's four "new" songs, two of which were attributed to Harrison, were in fact all unused tracks that had been recorded, and effectively discarded, several months earlier.[25] "Only a Northern Song" can lay valid claim to being the group's first "postmodern" song; its self-referential topic (the song is about itself), its multiple quotations from other sources (tape effects, overdubbed conversation), its fragmentary and disjointed structure, its lack of narrative resolution, and even its title (Northern Songs was the name of the Beatles' publishing company) are all presented with deliberately ironic intent. Harrison's lyrics mock both the listener and himself: "You may think the band are not quite right, but they are: they just play it like that." Perhaps, too, the song contains references to the complaints he frequently made when performing live with the Beatles to tens of thousands of fans who came to scream at the group rather than to listen to its music.[26] The observation that "it doesn't really matter what chords I play" is a precise summation of those dispiriting episodes. Its accelerated bass line adds to the sense of unease, and its surreal, collage-like design directly anticipates the aural confusion that would run through Lennon's "Revolution 9" the following year.

In contrast, "It's All Too Much" abounds in exuberant optimism. Beginning with a jolt of extended feedback that signals the song's psychedelic roots, it describes the awareness of universal oneness achieved through Harrison's experiments with LSD and meditation.[27] The references to "the love that's shining all around here" and his experience of "floating down the stream of time" are concise representations of the emerging counterculture's philosophical foundations. But it may best be described as Harrison's version of "All You Need Is Love," with which it shares some startling stylistic and structural similarities. Both were recorded in June 1967, and both display the blissful aspirations that defined the Summer of Love. "All You Need Is Love" includes a reprisal of lyrics from "She Loves

You," features a trumpet extract from Bach's "Brandenburg Concerto," and fades out with the repeated mantra "Love is all you need." "It's All Too Much" includes a reprisal of lyrics ("with your long blonde hair and your eyes of blue") from the Merseys' hit single "Sorrow," features a trumpet extract from Jeremiah Clarke's "Prince of Denmark's March," and fades out with the repeated mantra "Too much, too much." Rather like the French Impressionists of the late nineteenth century—Manet, Monet, Renoir, Bazille, Sisley—who painted individual versions of the same scenes around Paris and Argenteuil, Lennon and Harrison are, in these two songs, presenting alternative accounts of the same subject.

Although he was by now a regular supplier of songs to the group's albums, none of Harrison's songs had yet been released on a single. In March 1968, George Martin and the other Beatles agreed that the "The Inner Light" should be the B side of "Lady Madonna." Harrison had created the instrumental track with various Indian musicians at EMI's studios in Bombay during his recording of the film score for *Wonderwall*. The lyrics are adapted from Sanskrit scholar Juan Mascaro's translation of a poem in Lao-Tse's *Tao Te Ching*, and it is the extraordinary synthesis of separate musical and lyrical traditions (in this case, Indian instrumentation, Chinese philosophy, and Western popular music) that distinguishes the song. Harrison's uncharacteristically warm vocal weaves in and around the delicate, almost fragile, melody to deliver a simple testimony to the power of meditation, which affirms that real understanding comes from internal, not external, sources: "Without going out of my door, I can know all things on earth."

The similarity between this song's insight that "the further one travels, the less one knows" and his realization in "It's All Too Much" that "the more I learn, the less I know" show that Harrison's immersion in Indian philosophy was, at this time in his life, one of the most important components of his role as a Beatle. In early 1968, when the Beatles spent two months at the Maharishi's ashram in Rishikesh, he was, by all accounts, the most serious in his devotion to meditation,[28] and the most eager to retain an active involvement with its teachings, long after Lennon, McCartney, and Starr had lost interest.

The only British performer to have demonstrated a similar immersion in religious activity had been Cliff Richard, whose announcement of his conversion to Christianity in 1966 excited only passing interest from a largely indifferent public. By contrast, Harrison's spiritual journey was seen as a serious and important development that reflected popular music's increasing maturity. When, in the years that followed, similar statements of faith were made by Pete Townshend, Carlos Santana, John McLaughlin, Cat Stevens, and Bob Dylan, Harrison's example certainly helped to shape the response to them; what he, and the Beatles, had managed to overturn was the paternalistic assumption that popular musicians had no role other than to stand on stage and sing their hit songs.

However, although his return from India abruptly marked the end of his attempts to overtly incorporate Eastern musical styles and instrumentation into the group's songs, the lyrics of Harrison's four tracks on *The Beatles* (also known as *The White Album*) continued to consider the spiritual questions that had first attracted him. "While My Guitar Gently Weeps" is a commentary on a world in which love is "sleeping" and actions are "controlled." While he hopes that "with every mistake, we must surely be learning," it is a forlorn hope; he and his guitar can only weep at the state of hopelessness and lost opportunities he sees around him. The use of multiple rhyming schemes ("diverted . . . perverted . . . inverted . . . alerted"), rather than the standard reliance on rhyming couplets, is a strategy learned from Dylan, who regularly employed it to great effect in songs such as "All I Really Want to Do" ("analyze . . . categorize . . . finalize . . . advertise"), "Subterranean Homesick Blues" ("manhole . . . candle . . . sandals . . . scandals . . . handles") and "Visions of Johanna" ("showed . . . corrode . . . flowed . . . road . . . owed . . . loads . . . explodes"). Harrison's light, double-tracked voice is regretful rather than accusing, and his control of the dramatic, undulating melody adds to the confidence with which the song is performed. Significantly, his invitation to Eric Clapton to provide the lead guitar solo on the track was the first occasion that an outsider had been allowed to take part in a Beatles recording session; it also signaled the beginning of an intimate working relationship between the two that would continue throughout his career. *The Beatles* has been regarded as an album that lacks cohesiveness and unity,[29] but "While My Guitar Gently Weeps" is one of its most accomplished and mature songs.

Interestingly, in May 2009, the British Library added to its public collection a previously unseen lyric written and discarded by Harrison, whose meter is identical to that employed in "While My Guitar Gently Weeps." The scrap of paper was discovered by Hunter Davies, who had originally kept it as a souvenir of the time he spent with the Beatles when preparing their authorized biography in 1967.[30] It utilizes the anapestic tetrameter rhythmic form, in which one stressed syllable is followed by two unstressed syllables. The eight lines (in two four-line verses) tell of Harrison's disgust with those whose selfishness, arrogance, and jealousy prevent them from doing good in the world. Their thoughts and behavior are "obscene," and they remain indifferent to the hurt and suffering they inflict on others. Even so, he holds out the possibility of salvation. Although it sometimes appears that they "haven't a hope," he remains certain that "that isn't true."

While there is no firm evidence of Harrison's intent, the similarity (not only in meter, but in sentiment and vocabulary) to the final version of "While My Guitar Gently Weeps" is so marked that it is almost certainly a first draft of the eventual lyrics—and not, as others have fancifully suggested, a poem about Lennon.[31]

By contrast, "Piggies" displays all the features of a song written in haste: a forgettable melody, simplistic words, unnecessary sound effects, and a heavy-handed message. Harrison's use of three different vocal textures— a naturalistic introduction, a distorted middle, and a multitracked conclusion—have no obvious connection with the song's musical progression and are largely superfluous. His depiction of self-centered capitalist consumers as "piggies crawling in the dirt" who deserve "a damn good whacking" may be well intentioned, but lacks any subtlety or charm. The song's title has a twin motivation. Most obviously, it draws from George Orwell's novel *Animal Farm*, in which mass revolution leads to the formation of a totalitarian state, whose self-appointed leaders—the pigs—seek to protect their position by declaring that "all animals are equal, but some are more equal than others." But it also references the way in which "pigs" was widely used in the emerging counterculture as a general term of abuse for the police. The following year, the song acquired darker associations when it was cited (along with several other tracks from the album, including "Revolution 1" and "Helter Skelter") as providing a bizarre lyrical justification used by Charles Manson to instruct his "family" of followers to carry out the Sharon Tate/Leno LaBianca murders in Los Angeles.[32]

Like an increasing number of Harrison's songs, "Long Long Long" invites two readings. One is to see it as a straightforward love song, in which his sentiments are expressed simply and movingly: "I'm so happy I found you . . . how I love you." The other interpretation is to understand that "you" is in fact God, and that Harrison is rejoicing in his discovery of a deity to guide him through the vicissitudes of life after he has wasted "so many tears." The chord pattern repeats Dylan's "Sad Eyed Lady of the Lowlands," but that song's mournfulness is replaced here by the calm and peaceful acceptance of a life that is now fulfilled. The soothing, Hammond organ–led melody is interrupted by some unexpectedly fierce drumming, but Harrison's quiet voice manages to retain the impression of an exquisite, if fragile, love. Like "While My Guitar Gently Weeps," it stands out among the noise and chaos of much of the rest of *The White Album*.

"Savoy Truffle" might not be one of the album's more memorable songs, but its subject matter—a warning to Clapton that chocolates will damage his teeth—is a striking, and bizarre, example of the way in which Harrison was now willing to compose songs about topics that would have been unthinkable for popular musicians only a few years earlier.[33] The words are taken directly from the names of the assortment to be found in a box of Good News chocolates: "crème tangerine, montelimar, coffee dessert, coconut fudge, ginger sling." Yet, despite its forceful tempo, strong brass section, aggressive delivery, and inventive lyrics, the song cannot overcome its secondary status. Indeed, its presence on the album raises the question of whether it was included not because of its musical quality, but merely to satisfy Harrison's demand for his allotted number of compositions.

A throwaway piece of studio jamming from these sessions was eventually released on *Anthology 3* in 1996 and is credited to all four Beatles. "Los Paranoias" cannot begin to be considered as a finished track; it is little more than a brief, Latin-tempo improvisation, in which McCartney's spontaneous lyrics keep pace with some rudimentary acoustic guitar and percussion work.

In the summer of 1969, "Old Brown Shoe" became the second of Harrison's compositions to appear on the B side of a Beatles single. The song (and its A side, "The Ballad of John and Yoko") was recorded and released in less than six weeks, and it boasts the pace and enthusiasm of a live performance or studio jam session. The rolling, boogie rhythm is reminiscent of Dylan's "Subterranean Homesick Blues," and the lyrics deal with the uncertainty of love and the ambiguous positions in which we find ourselves. The singer wants "a short-haired girl who sometimes wears it twice as long"; he admits he may seem "imperfect" and confesses that he changes "faster than the weather." Relationships, he tells us, are confused and confusing. Nevertheless, his love is unequivocal, and his hope is that he may, with his lover's help, escape from "this zoo." While it may not be so direct, it is, in some ways, the same kind of plea for understanding and guidance found in Lennon's "Help!" Harrison's reference to the singer who wears "rings on every finger" is an affectionate nod to Starr and one example (among many) of the way in which all the Beatles were happy to acknowledge each other in their songs.

Although *Let It Be* was the last Beatles album to be released, it was actually recorded over several weeks from January to March 1969, some months before the sessions that produced *Abbey Road*. On "I Me Mine," Harrison returns to the persistent problems of egoism, greed, and selfishness that surround us. The repetitive melody only adds to the impression that such attitudes are constant and ever-present. Wherever and whenever he goes, he hears the cries of "I," "me," and "mine"—not just from a few people, but from "everyone"; not just occasionally, but "all through your life." Given the internal divisions that were about to tear the Beatles apart, the song (which was prompted by Harrison's consideration of absolute and relative values while taking LSD) is not merely a general observation on the state of mankind but a barbed attack on the inability of the four personalities within the group to see the merit of any other ambitions than their own.

The jaunty, country blues guitar introduction and slide guitar solo (played by Lennon) announce from the outset that "For You Blue" contains no profound humanitarian or political insights. Instead, it is an unashamed love song to Harrison's wife, Pattie Boyd, whom he had met during the filming of *A Hard Day's Night* and married in January 1966, in which he assures her that "I loved you from the moment I saw you." Her "sweet and lovely" personality makes her irresistible; the song's conclusion tells her (and us) that he now loves her "more than ever." The simplicity of the song's four verses, set to a twelve-bar blues form, is a refreshing sign that, notwithstanding his search for spiritual and intellectual enlightenment, Harrison can still choose to write an uncomplicated and enjoyable love song. Its directness, and his obvious enjoyment, reinforce the sincerity of his words.

Abbey Road, the group's final album, saw the Beatles temporarily put the personal and professional differences that had been increasing since Epstein's death to one side, to present a compelling collection of songs that perfectly reflected their musical personalities. The raw power of Lennon's compositions is matched by the pop craftsmanship of McCartney's contributions. More importantly, the two tracks by Harrison confirm that his songwriting apprenticeship is over. Both are exquisite; not only do they illuminate this album, but they are equal to any of the two-hundred-plus songs written and recorded by the group over the previous eight years.

Among Beatles songs, "Something" is second only to "Yesterday" in the number of cover versions it has generated. Famously described by Frank Sinatra as the greatest love song of the last fifty years,[34] it was also Harrison's first song to be single-released as a (joint) A side, with "Come Together." The title—and the opening line—were borrowed from "Something in the Way She Moves," an album track by James Taylor, whom the Beatles had signed to Apple in 1968. Its emotional impact lies largely in its unaffected statement of Harrison's love for Boyd (who seems to be unique in her ability to inspire memorable songs: "Layla" and "Wonderful Tonight" were also written for, or about, her). When listening to Harrison's words, it is as though we are eavesdropping on his private thoughts.[35] In addition, there is a clear and mutual confidence in the reciprocal nature of their love; he muses that she "attracts me like no other lover" and "all I have to do is think of her," but he is equally aware that she feels the same, that "somewhere in her smile, she knows." There are no ripples of doubt. When asked if his love for her might increase, his reply—"I don't know, I don't know"—is not an indication of uncertainty, but a wry reflection that his love is already so complete that it may simply be impossible for it to become any greater. His gentle vocal and the undulating melody reinforce the uncomplicated message conveyed in his words. "Something" is a calm and assured testament to Harrison's position, as both a husband and a musician.

There is little doubt that the creation of "Something" and its public reception were huge boosts to Harrison's confidence and marked a decisive turning point in his development as a songwriter. During the recording of *Abbey Road*, he was more assertive than he had ever been, regarding any suggested improvements—particularly from McCartney—as unwarranted intrusions and flatly resisting any attempts to modify his words or music.[36] After its release, he independently announced that all future albums by the

Beatles would contain an equal number of compositions by himself, McCartney, and Lennon; he also, for the first time, speculated about releasing a solo album in order to clear the backlog of unused songs that he had written in recent years.[37]

"Here Comes the Sun" was written on a spring day at a time when the Beatles were increasingly embroiled in legal and financial arguments that would eventually bring about their disintegration. The delicate acoustic introduction immediately provides a ray of hope, a possible escape, from the administrative quagmire that Apple had become. He admits that "it's been a long, cold, lonely winter," but feels that now "the ice is slowly melting." The repeated chorus and the gently ascending chords celebrate all that Harrison hopes for at this moment: clarity, friendship, growth, warmth, rebirth, the banishment of gloom.

The song's final words are not, like some of his previous lyrics, pessimistic or cynical, but are those of an optimist looking to the future: "Here comes the sun, it's alright." It is a prophetic statement. The Beatle would shortly evolve into the ex-Beatle and, in the same way that the end of winter and the appearance of the spring sun encourage hopes and ambitions for the summer, so too the inevitable demise of the Beatles provided the opportunity for Harrison to free himself from the constraints of living in the shadows of Lennon and McCartney, to pursue the personal and musical ambitions that had become so important to him, and to announce himself to the world as a singer-songwriter of great depth, originality, and sensitivity.

WITHOUT THE BEATLES

The Beatles' decision to stop touring after August 1966 reflected their frustration at the tedium of live performance and their desire to replace the limitations of the stage with the opportunities of the studio. However, it brought with it an unintended consequence, in that it suddenly provided each of them with a resource they had not enjoyed for several years: time. It was a resource they exploited in varying ways, particularly in the possibilities it offered for musical collaborations outside the group. John Lennon's new alliance with Yoko Ono dominated much of his professional (and emotional) activities, as demonstrated in the flow of singles ("Give Peace a Chance," "Cold Turkey," "Instant Karma") and albums (*Two Virgins, Life with the Lions, Wedding Album, Live Peace in Toronto*) by the Plastic Ono Band. Paul McCartney, who had composed the soundtrack of *The Family Way* (dir. Roy Boulting, 1966) was keen to extend his services, as producer and/or writer, to a widening collection of musicians, including the Black Dyke Mills Band, Cilla Black, Peter and Gordon, Badfinger, the Bonzo Dog Band, and Mary Hopkin.

George Harrison's first musical activity outside the Beatles came with his composition of the score for *Wonderwall* (dir. Joe Massot, 1968). The

movie is an archetypal example of the "swinging London/psychedelic sixties" films that were produced in the second half of the decade. Its central
character is Collins, an absent-minded and eccentric scientist. When he dis-
covers a hole in the wall of his apartment through which he can secretly
observe his next-door neighbor—a model called Penny Lane (!)—he finds
his own dull and lonely life increasingly disrupted, as he is irresistibly
drawn to the glamorous, colorful, and unpredictable world she inhabits.
After intervening to prevent her attempted suicide, he not only saves her
life but also liberates himself in the process.

   Wonderwall had been filmed in London over the summer of 1967, and,
after showing Harrison the footage, director Joe Massot invited him to
supply an accompanying soundtrack. What Harrison created was an assured
and varied collection of music that reflected his own influences and interests and perfectly complemented the juxtaposition of the exotic and the ordinary that Massot's film depicted. Eager to introduce cinema audiences to
the Indian music that had so entranced him, Harrison visited EMI's Bombay studios in the winter of 1967–1968, where he recorded, with local
musicians, some of the nineteen instrumental pieces to be inserted into the
film at strategic points. But, recognizing that it would be inappropriate to
overwhelm moviegoers with a soundtrack constructed solely from Eastern
traditions, he balanced those interludes with a selection of conventional
pop and country-based tracks completed in the familiar surroundings of
Abbey Road studios with the assistance of an eclectic set of (mostly
uncredited) friends such as Eric Clapton, Peter Tork (of the Monkees), the
Fool (the Dutch trio who had designed the inner sleeve for *Sgt. Pepper*),
and the Remo Four (from Liverpool). Under his scrupulous supervision,
the result was a satisfying and assured blend of music that belies Harrison's
inexperience as a composer of film music; Massot himself was surprised at
the accuracy with which it illustrated and enhanced the images on screen.[38]

   The titles of many of the tracks are indicative of the scenes they accompany in the film ("In the Park," "On the Bed," "Dream Scene") or are
descriptions of the sounds themselves ("Tabla and Pakavaj," "Singing
Om"). Although the album—*Wonderwall Music*—is, first and foremost, a
soundtrack, several of the pieces stand alone as memorable pieces of music
outside the context of the film. "Microbes," which introduces the movie,
is a beautiful example of Harrison's ability to create forlorn, mournful,
yearning soundscapes. Despite its title, "Greasy Legs" is a delicate and
charming composition. "Love Scene" is a mature and comfortable contribution. "Cowboy Music" is exactly that: a steady, relaxed tune, whose use
of steel guitar and harmonica recalls the soundtracks of the countless western movies with which Harrison had grown up in the 1940s and '50s.
"Drilling a Home" also springs from the same cinematic history; its jangle
piano instantly recreates the mood of a crowded saloon in a frontier
town, or a Laurel and Hardy or Keystone Cops pursuit. "Skiing" is a

straightforward example of contemporary rock, built around a repeated riff. The ascending and descending melody of "Party Seacombe" and its combination of different sounds is very like "Flying" from *Magical Mystery Tour.*

Harrison's role on *Wonderwall Music* is strictly limited to that of composer and producer. He neither sings nor plays on it, and yet it can be, and often is, regarded as his first solo work. The film attracted only small audiences at the time of its release and has largely disappeared from public view. Undoubtedly, some of that negative reception continues to color the perception of the album—the first to be released on the group's new Apple label, in November 1968—and it is often neglected in assessments of Harrison's career. But it provides a fascinating summary of the myriad patterns of musical activity whose fusions stimulated the growth of psychedelic, underground, and progressive scenes in the late 1960s, and it is a key moment in the development of his preparations for life after the Beatles.

Significantly, Harrison was also responsible for one of Apple's earliest single releases. He had written "Sour Milk Sea" in Rishikesh, to celebrate his faith in transcendental meditation, and gave the song to Jackie Lomax, who had been the lead singer with Liverpool group the Undertakers in the early 1960s. To enhance Lomax's version, Harrison not only produced the song but also assembled a backing group comprising himself (rhythm guitar), McCartney (bass), Clapton (lead guitar), Ringo Starr (drums), and Nicky Hopkins (piano). Their aggressive rock tempo and Lomax's powerful voice (not unlike that of Robert Plant, or Terry Reid, who was Jimmy Page's first choice to be lead vocalist with Led Zeppelin) are somewhat at odds with Harrison's thoughtful lyrics, which speak of the value of meditation: People may "fool around with every different cult," but none of them—apart from meditation—can guarantee awareness or "illumination." His advice is delivered with a touch of impatience: we should be prepared to take responsibility for the problems in our lives, and to "do it soon." The command to "get out of Sour Milk Sea" is unambiguous: admit your shortcomings, pull yourself together, look for a solution. Historically, the track can be seen as an early prototype of heavy metal, particularly in the interplay between drums and lead guitar and its relentless sequence of musical climaxes. Despite Apple's extensive promotion, which centered around a packaged presentation of "Our First Four" (the Beatles' "Hey Jude," Mary Hopkin's "Those Were the Days," the Black Dyke Mills Band's "Thingumybob," and Lomax's "Sour Milk Sea" were given a simultaneous release to announce the label in August 1968), the song failed to chart.

Similar advice is contained in "Badge," cowritten with Clapton for inclusion on Cream's final album, *Goodbye.* The members of Cream— Clapton, Jack Bruce (bass), and Ginger Baker (drums)—came from jazz/ blues backgrounds, and the song's deliberate rhythm is notably "heavier" than in the songs Harrison recorded with the Beatles. After their previous albums, *Fresh Cream*, *Disraeli Gears*, and *Wheels of Fire*, Cream was widely seen to epitomize the increasing sophistication of popular music, and the generic transformation from pop into rock. The fact that Harrison should not only write a song for the group but also appear on the track was a clear affirmation of his elevated musical status.

"Badge" begins with a clutch of random and inconsequential memories from a shared past: "the times you drove in my car"; "our kid" (northern English slang for "my brother"); "the swans that live in the park." But this superficial innocence is shunted aside when Harrison's words abruptly warn the listener to "pick yourself up from the ground." And as the lyrics of the final verse make clear, this is not just a general suggestion for all to consider but a specific message aimed at one person in particular: "a girl who looks quite like you [who] cried away her life." By lulling the listener into a false sense of security through its easy compilation of affectionate anecdotes, the song's true purpose, when revealed, is that much more effective: life may appear to be pleasant and unproblematic, but its inherent unpredictability demands caution. Musically, the song follows the same pattern. The first half is built around an insistent, and apparently purposeless, bass riff; the introduction of Harrison's chiming arpeggio signals a sudden transition to a second half of much greater urgency, whose musical momentum is dominated by Clapton's lead guitar.

Clapton misread Harrison's handwriting, mistaking "bridge" for "badge," which explains the irrelevance of the song's title and its absence from the lyrics. In keeping with the dictatorial and inflexible attitude that so enraged the Beatles and George Martin,[39] EMI refused to allow any of its artists to appear on recordings issued by rival record companies, which meant that Harrison's participation had to be disguised under the nom de plume "L'Angelo Misterioso."

Perhaps encouraged by the ease with which he had created the soundtrack for *Wonderwall*, Harrison undertook a second individual project in the following year. When the Beatles had formed Apple in 1968, they had also approved the establishment of Zapple, a specialist label intended to provide an outlet for spoken-word recordings, poetry, and other experimental works. Recordings of discussions, conversations, and readings with Allen Ginsberg, Pablo Picasso, Norman Mailer, Henry Miller, William Burroughs, and Charles Bukowski were planned; invitations were also extended to Mao Tse-Tung, Eldridge Cleaver, Indira Gandhi, and Fidel Castro.[40] Ultimately, only two albums were ever released: Lennon and Ono's *Life with the Lions* and Harrison's *Electronic Sound*, both of which were issued in May 1969.

The spirit of eclecticism and experiment that irradiated the late 1960s and led to a blurring—sometimes a dismantling—of traditional boundaries was increasingly apparent in the worlds of art, literature, film, and performance.[41] Musically, too, there were similar shifts. The adoption of Indian styles—of which Harrison was, of course, a leading agent—has already been discussed. But there were other, equally significant reformulations, including the fusion of folk song and rock to form folk rock, and, a little later, of country and rock to form country rock; the introduction of the "concept album"; the synthesis of the drug and musical cultures that created psychedelic music; the emergence of the "rock opera"; and the incorporation of European classical music and British popular music to create progressive rock. Alongside these, the work of musicians such as Karlheinz Stockhausen and John Cage, whose minimalist compositions and electronically produced sounds had been gaining wider audiences through the 1950s, was beginning to interest those popular musicians for whom the studio, rather than the stage, was a principal point of reference.

The Beatles' desire to embrace these new ideas was initially, and publicly, demonstrated in "Tomorrow Never Knows" and "Revolution 9." Other tracks, including "What's the New Mary Jane" and "Carnival of Light," were to remain unheard for years but, for Harrison in particular, the opportunity to indulge himself in the studio, after years of touring, was a temptation he did not wish to resist. Unfortunately, indulgence slipped into self-indulgence. *Electronic Sound* is nothing more than a random, unmanipulated collection of noises and effects created on his newly acquired Moog synthesizer. To attempt to explain the nineteen-minute "Under the Mersey Wall" and the twenty-five-minute "No Time or Space" as evidence of artistic exploration, or to describe them as avant-garde or as examples of contemporary musical solidarity, as some critics have suggested,[42] is to give the tracks a status they do not deserve. There is no evidence of structure or balance, no statement of direction or intent, no sense of texture or depth to the sounds. At best, Harrison can be accused of inexperience; at worst, of pretentiousness. Either way, *Electronic Sound* is a pointless and rather embarrassing blot on his musical career, and one that he was understandably reluctant to discuss in later years.[43]

In his poem *Little Gidding*, T. S. Eliot wrote that "to make an end is to make a beginning." In the few months after April 1970, when the world's news media carried confirmation of the end of the Beatles, the group's songwriters reacted in different ways. McCartney used the sleeve notes of his solo album, *McCartney*, to make it clear that his association with the Beatles had ended. In the lyrics of "God," on the *John Lennon/Plastic Ono Band* album, Lennon announced that "the dream is over." While the two of them were desperate to take every opportunity—in their songs and in interviews—to criticize the other's failings,[44] only Harrison seemed to understand that the group's demise also marked a new beginning. He was no longer an enthusiastic and promising understudy to Lennon and McCartney, but their equal.

As the Beatles' lead guitarist, Harrison had been responsible for ornamenting the vast majority of Lennon–McCartney compositions with some of popular music's most potent chords and riffs ("A Hard Day's Night," "I Feel Fine," "Day Tripper").[45] His five-year marriage had provided a point of anchorage against the recent turbulence of the Beatles and Apple, his commitment to Indian religion and philosophy had deepened his suspicions of a world based around the acquisition of material possessions, and his friendships with Dylan, Clapton, and Shankar had strengthened his confidence as a lyricist and a musician. His confidence had been boosted by the completion of his two album projects, and the professional satisfaction he had gained from seeing his songs recorded by Cream and Lomax had led to a number of additional compositions written (or cowritten) for others, including Billy Preston ("Sing One for the Lord"); Doris Troy ("Ain't That Cute," "Give Me Back My Dynamite," "Gonna Get My Baby Back," "You Give Me Joy Joy"); and Ashton, Gardner, and Dyke ("I'm Your Spiritual Breadman").[46] Attracted by their blend of Southern soul and rock 'n' roll, Harrison had even performed on stage again, as a member of the shifting lineup of Delaney and Bonnie and Friends, at some of the dates on their European tour in December 1969. In addition, he had combined spiritual and musical activities through his role as producer, arranger, and guest performer on the Radha Krishna Temple's recordings of "Hare Krishna Mantra" and "Govinda." His ten-year career as Beatle George, "the quiet one," had ended, and a thirty-year career as George Harrison, singer-songwriter, was about to begin.

In the Spiritual World

Transitions from one style, or form, of popular music to another are rarely sudden (although the international success of the Beatles themselves in 1963–1964 had provided an exception to that rule). However, by 1970, it was abundantly clear that the long tradition of the professional song-writer had been effectively usurped by the new supremacy of the singer-songwriter, who was motivated less by a requirement to produce hit singles for others than by a desire to create highly personal musical statements. Many of the more memorable albums released in that year testified to the significance of that tendency: Simon and Garfunkel's *Bridge over Troubled Water*, Van Morrison's *Moondance*, Neil Young's *After the Goldrush*, Joni Mitchell's *Ladies of the Canyon*, James Taylor's *Sweet Baby James*, and Cat Stevens's *Tea for the Tillerman*. But none possessed the startling impact of George Harrison's appropriately named *All Things Must Pass*, a lavishly boxed triple set—popular music's first by a solo performer[1]—that would top the album charts in the United States and United Kingdom, sell more than six million copies around the world, produce a single that has to date sold more than ten million copies, and elevate "the third Beatle" into a position that, for a time at least, comfortably eclipsed that of his former bandmates.

ALL THINGS MUST PASS

On an album on which Bob Dylan's influence can be recognized at a number of levels,[2] it is appropriate that the opening track is a song Harrison cowrote with Dylan. "I'd Have You Anytime" is a gentle, relaxed love song, enhanced by some of Harrison's most supple guitar work. He urges his lover to "let me into your heart," yet his confident tone suggests that this is not a desperate plea but a reassuring conversation between two people who have already given their love. The element of reciprocity that distinguished the declaration of love in "Something" is there in the simple statement that "all I have is yours, all you see is mine." Harrison was twenty-seven years old, and the song and its promise of love are indisputably those of a mature adult, sure of what he wants. While few would suggest that the song is one of Harrison's (or Dylan's) most memorable compositions, its true significance is that it marked the first formal collaboration between the two.

"My Sweet Lord" begins with a casually strummed acoustic introduction, which is then joined by one of rock music's most familiar electric riffs. This, Harrison's most famous song, is a powerful and emotional homage to God and a joyous affirmation of faith. However, the lyrics are not directed at a specific manifestation of a single faith's deity, but rather to the concept of one god whose essential nature is unaffected by particular interpretations and who pervades everything, is present everywhere, is all-knowing and all-powerful, and transcends time and space. Indeed, that universality is one of the major reasons why the song is so effective. All of us—Christian, Hindu, Muslim, Jew, Buddhist—can address our gods in the same way, using the same phrase. "My" emphasizes the personal nature of the relationship; "sweet" indicates his benevolence and kindness; "Lord" reveals that we are his servants. The switch between the calls of "Hallelujah" and "Hare Krishna" in the backing vocals is a deliberate attempt to show that the religious beliefs they celebrate are, in fact, the same.[3]

The extraordinary impact and enduring popularity of "My Sweet Lord" stem in part from its evident lack of artifice. Harrison's announcement that he wants to "see" and "know" the Lord provides the impetus for the song's two verses. But beneath this apparent simplicity, his lyrics attempt to reconcile the long journey to salvation (and the sacrifices it will inevitably entail) with an understandable impatience for a rapid outcome. As his vocal becomes increasingly impassioned, Harrison's restlessness grows, but the frustration is born of eagerness rather than dissatisfaction. While the call-and-response chorus increases the sense of communal excitement, the timely reappearance of his slide guitar and coproducer Phil Spector's swelling production reiterate the track's rock pedigree. As a result, "My Sweet Lord" can be heard as a prayer, a love song, an anthem, a contemporary gospel track, or a piece of perfect pop.

Harrison insisted that the inspiration for the song came from the Edwin Hawkins Singers' version of "Oh Happy Day," which had been a worldwide hit in 1969.[4] However, a few weeks after the release of the album, he was sued for professional plagiarism by Bright Tunes, the publishers of the Chiffons' 1963 song "He's So Fine." A lengthy court case eventually ruled that two musical motifs in Harrison's composition were virtually identical to phrases in the Chiffons' song (written by Ronnie Mack), and he was ordered to pay more than half a million dollars in damages. Nevertheless, "My Sweet Lord" stands as Harrison's greatest achievement: a unique, instantly recognizable rock hymn whose masterly evocation of spiritual devotion addresses God and engages listeners with equal rapture.

The multitracked vocals, prominent percussion, and foregrounded brass section of "Wah-Wah" recall the Wall of Sound production techniques favored by Spector on the recordings he made with vocal groups such as the Crystals and the Ronettes in the early 1960s. But this is no innocent pop song. Harrison had written it, during the recording sessions of *Let It Be*, in response to John Lennon's apparent inability to acknowledge his contributions, and Paul McCartney's criticisms of his guitar-playing.[5] His simmering resentment at being overlooked by his colleagues boils to the surface. "You made me such a big star," he accuses, sarcastically. Yet they never take the time to notice his "crying" and "sighing." Tired of their condescending and patronizing attitude, he envisages a new future for himself in which he will, at last, be "free." Spector's powerful production may cloak Harrison's words behind the conventions of a hard rock song and conceal the ferocity of his attack, but its forceful rhythm also reflects the momentum of his anger. In future years, Harrison regularly included "Wah-Wah" in his live performances, not least for its sense of unbridled aggression.

The song is not an isolated or petulant outburst, but an indication of the way in which all of the songwriters within the Beatles were using their newfound solo status to settle old scores, right perceived wrongs, and question each other's integrity. McCartney's second album, *Ram*, released just a few months later, contained two songs that were direct attacks on Lennon ("Dear Boy" and "Too Many People"), and Lennon's blistering retort ("How Do You Sleep," on which Harrison played lead guitar) was included on *Imagine*. In passing, it is interesting to note that throughout this period of constant cross-sniping, none of the three launched any musical attacks against Ringo Starr. This may have been a consequence of his easygoing and cooperative personality[6] or a reflection of the fact that his position as a nonsongwriter nullified any professional rivalry with his former colleagues.

The combination of an insistent, almost oppressive, melodic narrative, culminating in an extended fadeout reminiscent of "Hey Jude," and its surprisingly complex lyrics make "Isn't It a Pity" one of the album's outstanding tracks. Starr's deliberately dark drumming and Spector's engagement of three personnel on pianos/keyboards (Gary Wright, Tony Ashton, and Billy Preston) create a somber musical background, against which

Harrison comments on the frequency with which a relationship will break down through personal selfishness: "We take each other's love without thinking." In this sense, the song is a personal observation about a failed love affair. However, at the same time, it is about the universal love for, and among, humankind, which Harrison had previously considered in "Within You Without You" and "While My Guitar Gently Weeps," and which would remain one of the prominent themes throughout much of his subsequent music. The absence of that love blights us all: despite the fact that they are "all the same," most people fail to see "the beauty that surrounds them." And, on an album whose title refers to the demise of the Beatles themselves, it is impossible to overlook the song's resigned conclusion about those events, too: the unhappy disintegration of the four young men from Liverpool, whose music had transformed and enchanted the world, but who now go out of their way to "cause each other pain." While these complementary themes compete for our attention, Harrison's guitar weaves elaborate patterns above the track's repetitive chord structure. Its effect is to counterbalance the underlying atmosphere of pessimism with shafts of beauty.

"What Is Life" was described by Harrison as a hastily composed pop song, originally written for Billy Preston.[7] While the title suggests a philosophical debate about the meaning of life, the song's actual words are commonplace: "What Is Life" becomes "what is my life . . . without your love." The addition of "my" reshapes it completely, reducing it to a simple love song whose only noteworthy feature is Harrison's somewhat confusing promise that if his love is rejected, he will still "try to make everything succeed." John Barham's effective arrangement and the impressive cast of backing instrumentalists, including the Derek and the Dominos lineup of Eric Clapton, Bobby Whitlock (piano), Carl Radle (bass), and Jim Gordon (drums)—plus West Coast session musicians Jim Price (trumpet) and Bobby Keys (saxophone)—give the track an undoubted excitement and energy, but there is little overall coherence between words and music.

That song is followed by a lovely version of Bob Dylan's "If Not for You," in which Harrison manages to make the song his own, before an equally tender and affectionate song written by Harrison in the summer of 1969 about Dylan himself. After his motorcycle accident near Woodstock in July 1966, Dylan had entered a period of retreat or, as he termed it, "amnesia,"[8] during which he had largely withdrawn from live performance. His "official recovery," marked by an appearance at the Isle of Wight festival in August 1969 in front of more than three hundred thousand expectant fans, was thus a hugely important and anxious occasion for him. "Behind That Locked Door" is a personal plea, from Harrison to Dylan, to pull out of his depression, to face the world again, and to look to the future.

A delicate pedal-steel guitar introduction by Pete Drake establishes a relaxed country mood that freely recalls Dylan's *Nashville Skyline*, released three months before the festival. "Why are you still crying?" asks Harrison. To the tempo of a country waltz, and against a gentle chord progression similar to "On Top of Old Smokey," he urges Dylan not to hide away, but reassures him that what he has is what "the world is waiting for." Throughout his career, Harrison would repeatedly affirm his enormous respect for Dylan,[9] and this song is no exception; while millions of others may look to the Beatles for guidance, he looks to Dylan, remembering again "the tales you have taught me." The song ends with a request for Dylan to help him, if the positions were ever to be reversed. In the middle of an album whose songs sweep across the grand themes of history, religion, love, sex, and death, it is a surprising and touching gesture of simple friendship from one man to another.

"Let It Down" is one of Harrison's most unashamedly erotic songs. Two lovers hide behind a veil of nonchalance, but both are equally aware of the other's intentions. "I can feel you here . . . your eyes are busy kissing mine," he declares. However, there is a constant threat throughout the song that their secret passion may reveal itself to others. He must endeavor to hide his feelings, "should someone be looking." The inclusion of this qualification makes it unlikely that the song is directed toward his wife Pattie Boyd; there is, after all, no reason why a married couple should need to conceal their emotions. It is far more likely—and this gives it an added impulse—that it describes an act, or acts, of infidelity. In fact, given Boyd's suspicions about his womanizing through the spring and summer of 1970 when Harrison was recording the album, it is tempting to see the song as a private commentary about a current affair.[10] As he envisages the sensual pleasure to come, the lyrical climax parallels the sexual climax: "Let your hair hang all around me . . . let your love flow and astound me." The switches between periods of pulsating rhythm and interludes of musical calm echo the ebb and flow of seduction itself. Like a painter who uses contrasting colors to create tension and movement, Harrison is, in this song, using the tools of the songwriter to create a dynamic and passionate depiction of lust and desire.

"Run of the Mill" is the final track on disc 1, and one of the album's overlooked songs. Its words examine the difficulties encountered in trying to maintain relationships—personal and professional—when the persons involved have different views and seek different outcomes. On the most obvious level, it appears to be directed toward McCartney and the internal disputes that had broken the Beatles and were threatening the future of Apple. Will you "send me down again?" Harrison asks, referring to the abuse and humiliation he had discussed in "Wah-Wah," before acknowledging that not only is their musical partnership over, but their friendship also seems to be at an end. He warns against trying to shift the blame; it may be easier to reproach someone else, but all of us (himself included) need to accept responsibility for our actions and decisions: "Everyone has choice . . . it's you that decides." On this occasion, Harrison chooses not to exacerbate the poisonous atmosphere that hangs over the group by merely adding to the endless stream of insults and counterinsults. More than anything, it is a statement of genuine regret. By choosing not to reprise the final verse, but to repeat instead the earlier observation "it's you that decides," the song becomes less of an accusation and more of a plea. Its rolling melody and warm vocals give it the texture of a love song, which, of course, it is: a love song to the Beatles. However, his despair at the hopelessness of their situation and his acceptance of its inevitable consequence are made explicit in the simple phrase "I may decide to get out."

Since his production of their single "Hare Krishna Mantra" in the summer of 1969, Harrison had maintained a continuing involvement with the members of the Radha Krishna Temple.[11] Their philosophical teachings about the absolute supremacy of spiritual concerns over material possessions underpin the themes of "Beware of Darkness." To an easy, undulating melody, the song warns, verse by verse, of the corrupting influences that lie in wait on the unenlightened traveler's journey through life. The "falling swingers" are those idols or personalities we may once have envied, but who have proven to be temporary diversions of no real substance. The caution against "thoughts that linger" tells us not to harbor negative emotions—jealousy, envy, hatred, revenge—since they bring only unhappiness. The "soft shoe shufflers" are confidence tricksters who take advantage of the weak and gullible, promising much but delivering little. And the warning against "greedy leaders" refers directly to the politicians who conspire, deceive, manipulate, and betray those who follow them. All of these temptations represent "*maya*," illusion, and lead us away from an understanding of the real purpose of life, which is "to grow," like trees that seek the light. Harrison's return to the kind of spiritual reflection that he first considered on Beatles tracks like "Within You Without You" and his use of an outstanding group of contemporary rock musicians (including Clapton, Starr, Wright, and Dave Mason) to provide its backing make this one of the weightier songs on the album.

Ever since Apple had moved into offices in Savile Row in the heart of London's West End in 1968, the area outside the building had become the regular gathering place for a group of devoted female fans who came there every day, whatever the weather, in the hope of seeing the Beatles.[12] They soon became a regular part of Apple's daily routines, established a membership structure, adopted the name "Apple Scruffs," and even published their own monthly magazine.[13] The song "Apple Scruffs" is a sweet and good-hearted personal acknowledgment of their dedication. Dylan's influence is again evident, not least in Harrison's decision to perform the song without any other musicians, accompanying himself on guitar and harmonica. He gratefully recognizes the extent of their loyalty and thanks them for their constant support "in the fog and in the rain, through the pleasure and the pain." He tells them not to worry about the negative comments or behavior of passersby; they simply don't understand the depth of the relationship between the group and these special fans.

In light of Lennon's murder in 1980 and the attempted murder of Harrison in 1999, there is a touching naïveté in the celebration of a unique and warm connection between the members of the Beatles and their public. Given today's relentless obsession with the cult of celebrity, it is more likely that such people would be regarded as stalkers than as companions, and they might expect to be the recipients of restraining orders rather than songs. Harrison's composition of "Apple Scruffs" is another example of the scale of the disruptions to the traditional relationship between stars and fans in the closing years of the twentieth century. Heard today, its sentiments evoke the last days of what novelist Edith Wharton had referred to, several decades earlier, as "the age of innocence."

Friar Park, near Henley-on-Thames in Oxfordshire, was bought by Harrison in March 1970. Surrounded by thirty-three acres of parkland, the seventy-room mansion had been substantially refurbished by a previous owner, Sir Frank Crisp, in the first two decades of the twentieth century. He had fashioned a startling combination of French Renaissance and Victorian Gothic styles to create one of the most eccentric country houses and gardens in the south of England.[14] Before Harrison's purchase, the house had, for nearly twenty years, been used by nuns of the Salesian Order as a convent and private school for girls and had been allowed to fall into a poor state of repair.

In the same way that the previous song was a tribute to characters in the present, "The Ballad of Sir Frankie Crisp (Let It Roll)" is Harrison's tribute to a character from the past. He takes the listener on a guided tour of the house and its grounds, pointing out features of particular interest: from "the fountain of perpetual mirth," past "the maze" and "caves," to "the long walks" and the "woode." His description of "fools illusions" refers to the many extraordinary features Crisp had installed: distorting mirrors, fantastic statues, bizarre gargoyles, illuminated caverns, underground rivers, and hidden stepping-stones. Friar Park was to be Harrison's home for the next thirty years; it became his passion, and the song is, as he admits, totally self-indulgent.[15] Its familiar, easy melody, reminiscent of Dylan and the Band's communal return to the roots of American country music on *The Basement Tapes*, possesses an undoubted attraction, but ultimately the song reveals far more about Harrison than it does about Crisp. Perhaps because of the deliberately idiosyncratic perspective, "The Ballad of Sir Frankie Crisp" is a pleasant but forgettable detour from the album's major preoccupations.

Without Harrison's words, "Awaiting on You All" could be mistaken for the instrumental track of a song by the Ronettes. Spector's uncompromising re-creation of the Wall of Sound and the urgency of Harrison's multitracked vocals recall "The Best Part of Breaking Up" or "You Came, You Saw, You Conquered." But with the words, the song reveals itself as a treatise on the benefits of meditation: salvation and freedom can be attained through "chanting the names of the Lord." However, as on "My Sweet Lord," Harrison is keen to emphasize the validity of all faiths, rather than to argue for the dominance of one, and here he accomplishes it by using "Lords" instead of "Lord." Whatever the name of our religion, the instruction is the same: "open up your heart." The fact that the song begins with a pointed criticism of John Lennon and Yoko Ono's recent publicity campaigns for peace—he mocks the politics of the "love-in" and the "bedpan"—suggests that it may have been written at a time when relationships between the former Beatles were at a particularly low ebb. At the same time, it is interesting to note that an equally barbed attack on the financial wealth of the Roman Catholic Church was deleted (presumably at EMI's insistence). The offending lyrics claim that "the Pope owns 51 per cent of General Motors, and the Stock Exchange is the only thing he's qualified to quote us."

"All Things Must Pass" is a recognition of the impermanence of human existence and all that it embodies—happiness, despair, love, hate, loss, and gain are all transitory. The lyrics oscillate between a sadness that what we cherish must inevitably vanish and an optimism that what causes us pain will gradually disappear. Ostensibly, the song is about the end of a love affair: "My love is up and has left you with no warning," regrets Harrison, but he has words of comfort, too: "It's not always going to be this grey." But it is equally valid as a statement of spiritual intent: this world itself is fleeting, temporary, illusory, and it, and our place in it, will cease. An unvaryingly steady piano and the rising and falling trajectories of pedal-steel guitar bring notes of light and dark that mirror the competing impressions of hope and melancholy throughout the song. Once again, the influence of the Band (and Robbie Robertson in particular) hangs over Harrison's performance. The modes, cadences, and suspensions of "The Weight" and "The Night They Drove Old Dixie Down" are never far away. The song contains some of Harrison's most insightful and pensive words. "Daylight is good at arriving at the right time" is a fine example of his maturity as a lyricist, and his ability to position the profound within the commonplace. And of course, the observation that "all things must pass" stands as a simple and poignant conclusion to the end of the Beatles themselves.

In contrast, "I Dig Love" is a throwaway track of little insight and no musical originality. Against a numbingly repetitive piano sequence that ascends and descends without any variation, the lyrics hammer home the simplistic slogan "I dig love." Harrison had recently cowritten a number of songs with Stephen Stills for Doris Troy's debut Apple album, and it may be that this instruction to enjoy love wherever and whenever it may occur—"small love, big love . . . left love, right love . . . bought love, short love"—is an attempt to mimic Stills's similar unbridled encouragement in "Love the One You're With," also released in 1970. But whereas that song is a celebratory endorsement of "free love," Harrison's is a gloomy and unconvincing contribution.

The swirling multi-instrumental introduction to "The Art of Dying" creates a momentum that continues to its conclusion. Harrison may have written a first draft of the song two or three years earlier,[16] but the version here displays all the features of his post-Beatles confidence. With additional energy provided by an expanded percussion section, the musical antecedents are less Indian than Middle Eastern. But the lyrical concerns are directed around the Hindu concept of rebirth and the belief that life is a long journey back to the creator: death is merely an interruption, before the person is ready to continue the journey in another body. The law of karma dictates that action and reaction (physical, mental, and spiritual) are equal and opposite. Thus, the first verse's opening statement that "there'll come a time when all of us must leave here" is balanced in the final verse by Harrison's declaration that "there'll come a time when most of us return here." The sole cause of death, he tells us, is birth itself. Reincarnation reflects the soul's desire for perfection, and the "art of dying" is not separate from, but an integral part of, the art of living. The deletion of the words "Nothing Mr. Epstein can do will keep me here with you; it will be the end of this short piece of nothing" from the original lyrics shows all too clearly the extent of Harrison's unhappiness with the Beatles at the time of its original composition.

Perhaps remembering the Beatles' decision to give the public two versions of "Revolution" in 1968 (a rock 'n' roll rendition on the B side of "Hey Jude" and a slower interpretation on *The Beatles*), Harrison returns to "Isn't It a Pity" and offers a solemn, even sluggish, version of the song. The lyrics are identical, and while it is interesting to compare the two, this second example contains nothing new. It is an apt reminder that while the practice of offering "variations on a theme" is well established in the worlds of art and classical music, it works less well in rock and popular music.

Harrison's final song, "Hear Me Lord," is, quite simply, a prayer. As he pleads for forgiveness, acknowledges his weaknesses, and promises his love, he presents a statement remarkably similar to the Lord's Prayer of conventional Christianity. On an album on which seven of the preceding seventeen tracks are about his quest for spiritual and religious understanding, it is entirely appropriate that it should conclude in this way. And yet there is, for the first time, a degree of self-chastisement that is almost flagellatory in his pleas for help to "love you with more feeling . . . rise a little higher . . . burn out this desire." He is confessing his unworthiness, and the impression is of a man cowed, rather than liberated, by his faith.

There is, too, an uneasy self-righteousness in the way in which he takes it upon himself to seek our forgiveness as well as his own. His supplication that the Lord should "forgive . . . those that feel they can't afford you" might well be intended as a genuine plea on behalf of all humankind. But by excluding himself from their number, it also suggests a recurrent "preachy quality" or "holier than thou" attitude toward the less enlightened[17] that seems slightly at odds with the advice of several years earlier to "think for yourself." The song's gospel-tinged backing matches the evangelical nature of its sentiments, but it is a slightly unsettling end to a collection of songs of great power and passion.

The album's third disc, collectively titled "Apple Jam," contains five examples of spontaneous studio jamming from various combinations of the participating musicians. The eleven-minute "Out of the Blue" is the most complete. Its powerful trajectory, driven by Eric Clapton's guitar and the keyboards of Billy Preston and Gary Wright, features an outstanding saxophone contribution from Bobby Keys. "It's Johnny's Birthday" (in celebration of Lennon's thirtieth birthday) is delivered in the style of a music hall sing-along, to the tune of Cliff Richard's 1968 hit single "Congratulations," written by Phil Coulter and Bill Martin. "Plug Me In" is a fast, guitar-dominated improvisation. Given the presence of Ginger Baker and Clapton, "I Remember Jeep" has all the hallmarks of a track by Cream—a musically sophisticated fusion of jazz/blues tempos within a contemporary rock format. "Thanks for the Pepperoni" converts the distinctive riffs and rhythms used by Chuck Berry in "Johnny B. Goode," "Little Queenie," and "Roll Over Beethoven" into a five-minute demonstration of guitar expertise. The five pieces are ostensibly credited to Harrison but, in truth, it is difficult to distinguish any real clues to authorship. They are exactly what they purport to be: improvised sessions that punctuated the months of recording.

Not only was the album bracketed with some of the year's outstanding releases by individual singer-songwriters, but the presence of Derek and the Dominos allowed it to bridge the gap between the concerns of the solo performer and the emerging genre of the "rock album," whose releases that year included Pink Floyd's *Atom Heart Mother*, the Who's *Live at Leeds*, Derek and the Dominos' *Layla*, Led Zeppelin's *Led Zeppelin 3*, Free's *Fire and Water*, Deep Purple's *Deep Purple in Rock*, and Traffic's *John Barleycorn Must Die*. The triple combination of Harrison's authentic personal statements, the music's dynamic instrumental power, and the lingering influence of the Beatles gave *All Things Must Pass* its sweeping musical impact and towering reputation. Four decades after its release, it is still regarded as his masterpiece.[18]

"BANGLA DESH"

British rule in India, which had lasted for 163 years, came to an end in 1947 with the partition of the country into two separate states: India, which contained the largely Hindu majority, and the Islamic state of Pakistan—comprising West Pakistan (Baluchistan, the North West frontier region, Punjab, and Sind) and East Pakistan (Bengal). The cultural, linguistic, and geographical distances between the two Pakistani regions led to long-running tensions, and in March 1971, the newly elected leader of East Pakistan, Sheikh Mujibur Rahman, declared unilateral independence and the creation of the independent state of Bangladesh. The response of the Pakistani army was swift and brutal; Rahman was imprisoned, tens of thousands of Bengali separatists were killed, and an estimated two million refugees fled across the border into India to escape the fighting, the devastating effects of a cyclone, and a rapidly spreading epidemic of cholera. The decision of Indian prime minister Indira Gandhi to seal the border between the two countries exacerbated the humanitarian crisis and led to an escalation of the military conflict.

In the midst of this increasing turmoil, Harrison was approached in Los Angeles by Ravi Shankar, who was hoping to stage a musical event to raise funds for his fellow Bengalis. He immediately agreed to help and organized the Concert for Bangla Desh, held in New York's Madison Square Garden on August 1, 1971. At the end of July, he released "Bangla Desh," the song he had composed to promote the cause and publicize the concert.

The song is prefaced by a gentle introductory passage in which Harrison explains that he was visited by a "friend with sadness in his eyes," before three verses in which he vents his anger and frustration at the situation that has been allowed to develop. The words are those of a politician beseeching his audience to take action: "So many people are dying fast . . . I've never known such distress . . . please don't turn away." The relentless rhythm and his own emotional delivery accentuate the song's sense of urgency. There is a clever pun in his appeal to "give some bread to get the starving fed," using "bread" to refer to both money and food. "Bangla Desh" serves as a model for the charity singles that would become commonplace in the decades ahead, although, in this instance, the power of Harrison's song lies not in its assembly of famous performers but in its literal and absolute commitment.

"Deep Blue"—a song written, but not recorded, during the making of *All Things Must Pass*—is on the B side of the single. Harrison's mother, Louise, had been diagnosed with cancer in 1969 and died in the summer of 1970. Constant visits to her in the hospital in Liverpool brought home to him his helplessness in the face of the illness, and it is this sense of despair that fills his words. The admission that the sunshine "is not enough to make me feel bright" paints a poignant contrast with the optimism it brings him in "Here Comes the Sun." Harrison's gently strummed guitar and easy, unpretentious melody draw their inspiration from the folk blues of performers like the Lovin' Spoonful and David Bromberg (with whom he cowrote "The Hold Up," a song that appeared on the singer's 1972 album, *David Bromberg*). The uncluttered production and economical backing (guitar, bass, drums) make this simple song an effective statement of grief that bears comparison to Lennon's declaration of love for his mother in "Julia" and McCartney's memories of his mother Mary in "Yesterday" and "Let It Be." Where they differ is that Harrison's song is about himself as much as it is about his mother; her death is a starting point for an exploration of the "suffering" and "darkness" that afflict us all. The raw imagery of "tired bodies full of sickness and pain" is also applicable to the situation in Bangla Desh, and the song's very specific personal and political relevance to a particular time explain why it was never to appear on any later albums. "Deep Blue" is unlike anything he had written or recorded at that time, and its relative obscurity is undeserved.

THE CONCERT FOR BANGLA DESH

For Harrison to mark his solo recording debut by releasing a triple album was an unprecedented decision. That he should now follow it up with another triple set was seen as utterly remarkable. Of course, *The Concert for Bangla Desh* was not his album alone, but the public perception of it as a Harrison project has increased over the years. His success in persuading fellow musicians such as Bob Dylan, Eric Clapton, Leon Russell, Jesse Ed Davis, Jim Horn, Ringo Starr, Klaus Voormann, Billy Preston, and Badfinger to donate their services overcame his temporary disappointment at McCartney's flat refusal and Lennon's insistence that Ono should also appear.[19] Delayed by legal and technological problems, the resultant live album (again coproduced by Harrison and Phil Spector) was released in January 1972.

After a lengthy opening set from Shankar, eight of Harrison's songs— the newly released single "Bangla Desh," plus three from his years with the Beatles, and four from *All Things Must Pass*—are included in the album's seventeen tracks, compiled from the concert's afternoon and evening performances.

Because of the short amount of time—less than a month—to prepare and rehearse for the concert, there are only a few significant variations between these live versions and the original studio tracks. "Wah-Wah" retains a full, multilayered arrangement, and benefits from the choir of soulful backing vocalists and Russell's flowing keyboard contributions. Harrison's voice wavers a little in parts, but a tangible mood of real excitement builds throughout the song. There is no uncertainty in his performance of "My Sweet Lord": Clapton's role on lead guitar allows Harrison to concentrate on his own vocal, which is clear and emphatic. It is followed by a spirited version of "Awaiting on You All," which is performed here in its entirety, including the previously omitted lines about the Pope.

The first significant variation comes during "Beware of Darkness," where, in the third verse, the lead vocal switches to Russell. There is a sudden, and immediate, contrast between Harrison's emotional delivery and the elongated, slightly drawling style adopted by Russell. His distinctive fusion of blues, country, and soul traditions had helped to make him one of the 1970s' most celebrated musicians, but on this track his voice lacks the personal sincerity demanded by the lyrics. Indeed, Harrison may well have recognized the extent of their musical differences; apart from contributing to some of the songs on *Extra Texture* in 1975, Russell was to play no further part in his recording and performing career.

The first of Harrison's Beatles songs is "While My Guitar Gently Weeps," in which the melancholic reflection of the original is replaced by a fierce and compulsive determination. It concludes with an intense guitar dialogue between Harrison and Clapton that demonstrably illustrates his technical proficiency. While Harrison may not have been counted among the elite guitar heroes of the late 1960s and early 1970s—such as Clapton, Jimi Hendrix, Jeff Beck, Alvin Lee, and Jimmy Page—he was clearly not embarrassed by such company, and his approach to guitar-playing was always founded on craftsmanship rather than histrionics.[20]

This is made abundantly clear on his next song: "Here Comes the Sun" is performed in a purely acoustic version and features a beautifully constructed and expressive instrumental duet with Badfinger guitarist Pete Ham. Harrison's voice is a little rough, and the gospel chorus unnecessarily loud, but the natural simplicity of the accompaniment—in contrast to the banks of brass, guitar, and vocal support brought in by coproducer Spector to reproduce his Wall of Sound—is striking. In fact, it is Spector's arrangement that dominates the performance of "Something," which follows. At times, Harrison's voice struggles to be heard and, perhaps in their eagerness to build toward a rousing finale, the musicians risk drowning the song's sensitive sentiments beneath an early example of stadium-rock extravagance.

The final song is "Bangla Desh" itself. Supported by a swirling fanfare of keyboards, percussion, voices, and guitars, Harrison's vocal captures the anger and impatience that had persuaded him to organize the concert. In doing so, it also emphasizes the validity of a phrase that was beginning to enter the intellectual and cultural vocabulary of the 1970s: "the personal is the political." The realization that personal circumstances and individual responses to them are not accidental or neutral, but are in fact shaped by political forces and have political consequences, is an insight with which Harrison had become increasingly familiar. The songs he wrote did not exist in a vacuum, isolated and protected from the world they described; they were part of that world. Music may not provide a solution, but it can criticize, stimulate, and inform.

But on this occasion, the music was less important than the humanitarian objectives it served. While the concert itself immediately yielded a quarter of a million dollars to the United Nations Relief Fund for the refugee children of Bangladesh, the eventual total (from album sales, CBS-TV coverage, and the 1972 movie directed by Saul Swimmer) was $15 million. Later all-star benefit concerts such as Live Aid (1985), Farm Aid (1985), Nelson Mandela's Seventieth Birthday Tribute Concert (1988), The Concert for New York City (2001), and Live 8 (2005) may have been larger, more spectacular, and more lucrative (through live global television transmission), but it was Harrison's hastily arranged event in Madison Square Garden that supplied the template and the example.

By mid-1972, Harrison, his music, and his humanitarian concerns were universally acclaimed. Not only had "My Sweet Lord" and *All Things Must Pass* topped the singles and albums charts in the United States and United Kingdom, but his efforts to draw attention to the tragedies in Bangladesh had propelled him to the position of popular music's first statesman. He had continued to engineer the fusion of Indian and Western musics, collaborated with an impressive array of the world's rock elite, and accomplished the transition from Beatle to ex-Beatle with apparent ease.

In the Material World

The euphoria surrounding *All Things Must Pass* and the energy he had put into the organization of the Concert for Bangla Desh had, for a time, effectively distanced Harrison from some of the more unpleasant realities of his everyday life. But as the impetus of those events receded, the relative peace of 1972 and 1973 forced him to confront them directly. When he did so, he discovered that there were to be no easy or quick solutions.

Far from being resolved, the legal and financial fallout from the disintegration of the Beatles continued, as attempts to settle the complex business relations among Apple, Allen Klein (who had acted as the group's financial advisor since 1969), and the four ex-Beatles became ever more bitter.[1] Although Klein's formal association with the group ended in March 1973, the contractual wrangling would drag on until October 1977, when Apple would eventually pay him $4.5 million. At the same time, the internal revenue services of the United Kingdom and United States were preventing the rapid transfer of funds to Bangladesh through their unyielding insistence on receiving immediate and complete taxation payments.[2] In July 1973, Harrison was forced to pay the British tax authorities £1 million, but it would take another ten years before the total sum raised from album sales and movie returns would find its way to its intended destination. In addition, Bright Tunes Music, the publishers of "He's So Fine," was aggressively pursuing a court action for the alleged plagiarism in "My Sweet Lord" that would not be resolved until February 1981.[3] Finally, the repercussions of the intermittent affair between Eric Clapton and Pattie Boyd, which had first begun in the spring of 1970, were imposing an intolerable strain on the Harrisons' marriage that could no longer be ignored; they eventually separated in July 1974 and divorced in June 1977.

In these circumstances, it was inevitable that the trio of albums George Harrison made between 1973 and 1975 contained some of his most cynical and frankly autobiographical songs, which mirrored the persistent disappointments and misfortunes he faced. The title of the first of those albums, released in May 1973, was an apt, if unintended, reflection of the difficulties that surrounded him, and a clear contrast to the spiritual enlightenment he had so joyfully celebrated on *All Things Must Pass*.

LIVING IN THE MATERIAL WORLD

This was the first of four consecutive albums to be produced solely by Harrison (apart from one track coproduced with Phil Spector) and included several of the musicians—minus Clapton—who had appeared on *All Things Must Pass*. Whereas John Lennon had used his second studio album, *Imagine*, to ask for "some truth" and to criticize "uptight, short-sighted, narrow-minded hypocrites" and "neurotic, psychotic, pig-headed politicians" (on "Gimme Some Truth"), Harrison used his opening track to ask for "love," "light," and "life." The contrast between what each wanted and expected from the world is laid bare: Lennon's brutal cynicism, against Harrison's gentle optimism.

"Give Me Love (Give Me Peace on Earth)" is one of his most beautiful songs; its uplifting melody is supported by Nicky Hopkins's rolling piano contribution and is marked by the supple and clear guitar-playing that distinguished "Here Comes the Sun." In its direct address to "My Lord" and its prayer for "peace on Earth," it seems to be continuing the religious dialogue Harrison had established in "My Sweet Lord." But the plea to "give me hope, help me cope with this heavy load" is, equally, an acknowledgment of the trials and tribulations he was facing in a more earthly setting. His faith is still intact, but it is, for the first time, tempered with an appreciation of the mundane obligations imposed by an unsympathetic and uncooperative reality—an unresolved conflict that is emphasized by the suggested syncopation that accompanies his singing of the title phrase. Harrison's hope that he may be kept "free from birth" reflects the fundamental Hindu concept that life is a long journey back to the creator: if, at the moment of death, a person has not lived wisely and compassionately, he will be reborn, or reincarnated, in another body to continue the journey again. Birth and death are therefore inextricably entwined, and the "freedom from birth" for which he longs would thus signal an exemplary life and the successful transition to a higher reality. Musically, the song illustrates his vocal ability to suspend one note over several bars, in the extended, and highly symbolic, delivery of the word "please." When released as a single, it topped the charts in the United States for one week.

Harrison's own cynicism is exposed on "Sue Me Sue You Blues," written in the midst of the Beatles' ongoing legal battles. However, by resisting the temptation to attack his former bandmates and choosing instead to comment on the absurdity of a situation that disadvantages them all, the song expresses frustration rather then hostility. It makes clear that amid the legal arguments, financial requirements, and technical language of "affidavits," "court receivers" and "joint escrow," there are four former friends who are powerless to control events. Had he chosen to use "I" instead of "we" when referring to the "lawyers' bills" and "bad times," his words might be seen as a personal complaint. Instead, they represent his hope for a shared and sensible outcome to an interminable struggle in which "all get screwed." The decision to mimic the style and tempo of a square dance reinforces the imagery of new partners, temporary alliances, interruptions, and realignments that characterize events on the dance floor and in the courtroom. His use of a bottleneck guitar introduces a mood of entertainment that is comic rather than tragic; there is a black humor in the ludicrous events that engulf them.

"The Light That Has Lighted the World" grew out of an attempt to write a song for Cilla Black, one of the many Liverpudlian performers who had found success during the period in 1963–1964 when the Mersey Beat was exported to the rest of the country. She too had left the city and, like the Beatles, had occasionally been accused of forgetting her roots. Harrison's elaboration of the song leads him to reflect on those people who regard any such movement or development as a bad thing, and whose insularity leads them to become "hateful of anyone that is happy or free." But, again, he resists the temptation to criticize them. Instead, they have his sympathy: "It's funny how people won't accept change," he muses, implicitly suggesting that they need to examine their own lives, to get out of the "hole" in which they hide. In addition, he expresses his gratitude to those who do understand the changes in his life—from Liverpool teenager to mop-top Beatle to humanitarian campaigner—without any malice or envy; their attitude helps to create an opportunity for him to come to know "the light that has lighted the world." But the source of this light is never made clear. Is it love? Is it spiritual enlightenment? Is it the Beatles themselves, who, after all, have illuminated the world for many millions of people? By leaving the question open, Harrison effectively encourages us all to pursue whatever path we may choose on our journey to happiness and freedom. The slow, almost stately, pace and lack of melodic variation add to the impression that it is as much a statement as a song.

After the songs of faith and the commentaries on the past or present Beatles that had taken up so much of his energies over the past three years, "Don't Let Me Wait Too Long" is a simple and unassuming pop song, whose message is in the title. It utilizes many of the stock motifs developed by the Brill Building's stable of songwriters in the late 1950s and early

1960s: a repetitive and attractive melody (based, in this case, around a descending sequence); a stereotypical choice of language ("how I love you . . . how I miss you"); the familiar topic of lost, or unrequited, love; even the conventional form of address from a man to a woman, in the persistent use of "baby." But through Harrison's careful production, it also possesses a fresh, contemporary quality, reminiscent of his future collaborator Jeff Lynne's work with the Idle Race and the Electric Light Orchestra.

As Lennon readily admitted on several occasions, "Please Please Me" was a conscious attempt to write a song in the big ballad style of Roy Orbison.[4] The same ambition lay behind Harrison's composition of "Who Can See It,"[5] and the positioning of the song immediately after "Don't Let Me Wait Too Long" completes a strange coincidence in that both Orbison and Lynne would be fellow members of the Traveling Wilburys twenty years later. The song returns to the theme of Harrison's past, when as a working-class boy in Liverpool (and as a Beatle) he was "held up," "run down," and forced to "toe the line." In other words, he has paid his dues. Now, he is his own man who has earned the right to say "my life belongs to me." A rather ponderous arrangement prevents the song from being an entertainment, but, like "The Light That Has Lighted the World," it is a unequivocal statement of who he is.

The title track of any album can provide clues not only to the current musical direction of the performers but also to their personal priorities. "Living in the Material World" is a perfect example of this. The position it occupies, as the final track on the first side, echoes George Martin's policy of always selecting a strong track to close each side of every Beatles album,[6] and illustrates Harrison's positive opinion of it. Furthermore, the song's comparison of the material and spiritual worlds indicates the internal dialogue in which he was engaging at the time: the difficulty of reconciling the physical and the astral planes of existence.

Against a powerful rock backing, he begins his account of the material world by referring to his body as a "car." The metaphor is well chosen, since it implies that we are not, in any absolute sense, our bodies; they are merely the vehicles that carry us on our journeys. In Harrison's case, his most significant physical journey has been that of a Beatle, and he explicitly refers to it and to his initial meeting with "John and Paul." In one of his cleverest puns, he tells how the group "started off quite poor" but "got 'Ritchie' on a tour." On one level, it refers to the financial success the group began to enjoy in 1963, with "Ritchie" being used as an assonant substitute for "richer." But at another level, it also refers to the sacking of drummer Pete Best and his replacement by Richard "Ritchie" Starkey, aka Ringo Starr. Many theories have been advanced to explain Best's sudden dismissal,[7] but Harrison's words suggest that Starr was simply a better drummer whose presence enriched the group.

The disappearance of the rock section and the appearance of a delicate tabla accompaniment signal the transition to his reflection on the spiritual world that has given him such "sweet memories." Returning—musically and lyrically—to the material world, he confesses that he has "a lot of work to do" if his journey is to be completed successfully. While there is no anger or conflict in the song, it succinctly presents a series of contrasts in Harrison's life: past and present, West and East, noise and calm, physical and spiritual.

After such an inventive set of lyrics, it is a disappointment to find that "The Lord Loves the One (That Loves the Lord)" returns to the same kind of turgid proselytizing that marked "Hear Me Lord." Whereas the Beatles' song "The End" had concisely summarized the essential nature of reciprocity in a simple phrase—"the love you take is equal to the love you make"—Harrison hammers home the same message relentlessly, with little charm, for more than four and a half minutes. The moody guitar introduction, which works to establish a sense of foreboding, is copied from Three Dog Night's 1970 hit version of Randy Newman's "Mama Told Me Not to Come." But on this occasion, the warning is not about a party that spirals out of control, but about the consequences of a life of selfishness and greed which finds no place for "the Lord." His rhetorical question "Who will stand and who will fall?" and his persistent message that "the Lord helps those that help themselves" sound like the imprecations of an evangelical preacher. Harrison's impressive guitar work helps to compensate for the absence of a clear melody, but the song is ultimately undermined by some of his least-effective lyrics; the description of political leaders as "big girls" is puerile and sexist.

"Be Here Now" is one of Harrison's most haunting and mysterious compositions, and its obvious similarity to "Long Long Long" is, in part, explained by their common subject matter: time. The title is taken from a book by Ram Dass. In the 1960s, Harvard psychologist Richard Alpert had, with colleagues including Timothy Leary and Ralph Metzner, abandoned the formal world of academia to concentrate on the study of elements of human consciousness and routes to spiritual growth. He became interested in psychedelic research and environmental action and, in 1968, traveled to India to learn the techniques of yoga and meditation and received the name Ram Dass or "Servant of God." His book *Remember: Be Here Now* was published in 1971 after his return to the United States. Harrison's advice that "the past was" and "now is" tells us to recognize who and what we are, "here" and "now": a mind that seeks to be somewhere else, or aspires to be something it cannot, is "unwise." The gentle, largely acoustic backing and Harrison's achingly beautiful vocal give the song a nebulous, yearning quality, almost as if something barely understood is slipping out of sight. In her performance monologue entitled "Time," (included on the 2008 compilation album *The Very Best of Joyce Grenfell*) the British actress, author, and songwriter concluded that "there is no such thing as time—only this very minute, and I am in it," and Harrison's sense of wonder and helplessness in the face of the spiritual, scientific, and metaphysical implications of time mirrors her individual response.

Two years after Ronnie Spector had recorded the song (along with the Harrison–Phil Spector composition "Tandoori Chicken") in an unsuccessful endeavor to reinvigorate her career,[8] Harrison's own version of "Try Some Buy Some" was included on *Living in the Material World*. It is a much weaker attempt than her earlier recording, and seems oddly out of place on the album. Acknowledged by Harrison as an awkward tune to compose and to play,[9] his wavering vocal and Phil Spector's unconvincing production merely emphasize that this is one of his least impressive performances. The words themselves are ambiguous. He describes himself as a man living a lonely and meaningless life who has seen and felt nothing until "I opened my eyes and I saw you." But the identification of "you" as another person or as a divine presence is never clarified. It may be a love song or a hymn of salvation but, unlike songs where this duality strengthens their impact (such as "Isn't It a Pity"), here it sits uneasily between the two. With a different arrangement, and offered to a performer like Shirley Bassey, whose distinctive vocals and melodramatic delivery had given her a hit single with "Something," the song might have been successful, but without that necessary emotional transformation, it remains curiously incomplete.

Harrison began to write "The Day the World Gets Round" after the Concert for Bangla Desh in New York, and it contains unmistakable elements of his anger at that time. He points to the world's "destructive" tendencies, its "foolishness," and the evil and stupidity of "killing each other." But while few would disagree with his sentiments, the song also contains elements of an increasingly familiar elitism in his apparent perception of himself. When he sings of "the pure of heart" and tells the Lord that "there are just a few who bow before you," the implied conclusion is that he counts himself among their number. Because of their friendship, their collaborations, and the politically inspired themes of many of their songs, comparisons were frequently made in the early 1970s between Harrison and Bob Dylan. But while there are obvious similarities, a key difference is that Dylan retains the ability to present himself as an outsider who is there to observe and comment, whereas Harrison appears as a campaigner who is there to convert. Dylan gives us *an* analysis; Harrison gives us *his* analysis. While the distinction may seem purely technical, the result is that, on occasion, Harrison's words carry with them, perhaps unwittingly, a suggestion of self-satisfaction.

There is an implied pun in the title. By hoping that the world gets "round" in the future, Harrison may be quietly suggesting that it is "square" at present—not square in the geometric sense, but in the sense of uncool, out of touch, and oppressive. While this might seem a fanciful interpretation, it corresponds with the song's overall pessimism, and also accords with his love of wordplay. Melodically, the most startling facet of the song is John Barham's ascending string arrangement, which is almost identical to that used on the Beatles' "Across the Universe" to introduce the "nothing's going to change my world" refrain. It reinforces Lennon's persistent and aggrieved claims that Harrison learned much of his song-writing style from himself and Paul McCartney.[10]

Fittingly, the album's final track begins with the words "That is all I want to say." "That Is All" is an adult-oriented love song in which Harrison reveals what it is that he wants to do for his lover ("to love you more") and what he hopes for in return ("a smile when I feel blue"). His complaint about "useless words getting in the way" is very similar to his comments several years earlier about "words that seem to slip away" on "I Want to Tell You." In both cases, he realizes, language is insufficient to express the depth of his emotion; "silence" can be more effective, more intimate, more *loving*. Musically, the song's romantic melody and lush production echo Martin's interpretation of "Good Night" and Spector's of "The Long and Winding Road." The last words on the album are "That is all."

Although the album was commercially successful, the mixed critical reaction left him deflated and bewildered.[11] While some commentators pointed to its altruistic sweep and impressive musicianship, others saw it as self-righteous, maudlin, and clumsy in its execution.[12] After a decade in which he had rarely known anything other than unadulterated praise and applause (both as a Beatle and a solo performer), the realization that his songs were no longer guaranteed unanimous admiration was a severe blow to his professional confidence. It coincided with a period of intense disarray and frequent infidelities in his personal life,[13] and the combination of these two sources of disappointment produced a mood of gloom and cynicism that would inevitably work its way into his next musical projects.

"MISS O'DELL"

When "Give Me Love (Give Me Peace on Earth)" was released as a single in May 1973, the B side was a track Harrison had recorded informally a few weeks earlier with Klaus Voormann and Jim Keltner. Chris O'Dell was a young woman from Tucson who had worked at Apple since 1968 and had become a close friend of the Harrisons. The song—"Miss O'Dell"— is a playful and lighthearted tribute to their relationship. While the rest of the world is beset by issues such as the war in Vietnam or the extent of pollution in California, and Harrison himself is surrounded by the everyday irritations of a broken record player and unwanted visitors at his door, he thinks affectionately of his friend: "Why don't you call me, Miss O'Dell?"

The impromptu nature of the performance—Harrison's vocal dissolves into laughter on three occasions—clearly owes much to the example of Dylan and the Band on *The Basement Tapes*. But, in fact, its musical roots go back to the mid-1950s, when the Lonnie Donegan Trio's brand of skiffle music was the original inspiration for Harrison to take up the guitar. The simple instrumental lineup (guitar, bass, mouth organ, and drums), the lack of any sophisticated production values, and the brisk tempo create a sense of spontaneous fun that is all too rare in his recordings. In contrast to the solemn and laborious nature of many of the songs on *Living in the Material World*, Harrison is enjoying himself.

DARK HORSE

Under Brian Epstein's tutelage, the Beatles had always been shrewd students of the popular music industry's commercial imperatives. One of the more obvious ways in which this was practiced was to time the release of their albums in order to benefit from the Christmas market. Harrison had continued this practice with *All Things Must Pass* (November 1970), and the release of *Dark Horse* and its accompanying single "Ding Dong, Ding Dong" in December 1974 was a clear example of his understanding of the strategies through which seasonal sales might be maximized.

The traditional function of an overture in operatic or stage musicals is to serve as an introduction to what is to follow; over time, it has also been recognized as a useful device that allows members of the audience to take their seats, settle down, and ready themselves. The opening track "Hari's on Tour (Express)" is Harrison's way of achieving the same objectives. The five-minute jazz-rock instrumental benefits from his recruitment of members of the L.A. Express (Tom Scott, John Guerin, Max Bennett, and Robben Ford) who had recently begun the first of several collaborations with Joni Mitchell, on her album *Court and Spark*. In particular, Tom Scott's open-ended saxophone solo produces an atmosphere of anticipation, in exactly the same way that a successful film or television theme aspires to do. Harrison's involvement with film would become increasingly important in his career, and the structure and form of "Hari's on Tour" indicate the extent to which he is able to effectively incorporate the conventions of the soundtrack within the codes of rock.

"Simply Shady" is Harrison's own personal account of some of the dangers lying in wait for the musician who succumbs to the temptations of "sex and drugs and rock 'n' roll" that are stereotypically linked with the mythology of rock.[14] His trembling, slightly nasal vocal is so similar to the style developed by his future partner in the Traveling Wilburys, Tom Petty, that it leads one to speculate about the degree to which Petty might have (perhaps unwittingly) attempted to imitate Harrison's voice. His straining guitar adds to the song's emotional plea, and while never directly asking to be forgiven for what he has done, there is a clear sense of remorse for the time he has wasted. Whatever the temporary pleasures provided by alcohol or promiscuity, he knows that "life won't be so easy anymore" and, in any case, "it's all been done before."

His continued thoughts on the relationship between actions and their consequences that he explored on "The Art of Dying" are in evidence throughout the song. "No sooner had I sown it, than I began to reap," he confesses in the second verse. In the third verse, he predicts that "the action that I've started sometime I'll have to face." This is significant, since it shows that, unlike some of the positions he adopted on *Living in the Material World*, here he is making no pretence of having moved on to a superior spiritual or moral plane. He regrets his behavior, but at the same time, he is realistic enough to admit that it will probably be repeated. The reference to "Sexy Sadie" at the song's conclusion has a triple function. She is not just a woman who offers him casual sex, but to those who are aware of the group's history, the name is also a pseudonym for the Maharishi Mahesh Yogi,[15] and thus provides a coded reference to the Beatles.

"So Sad" is Harrison's first song to explicitly address the collapse of his marriage. Switching between first-person and third-person narratives, its three verses make no mention of the causes of his imminent separation, but merely record his sadness. Images of the "sun," the "dawn," and the "light" are contrasted against references to "winter" and "a cold wind." He describes himself as "so alone, with no love of his own."

Harrison and Boyd had met in March 1964 and had been together through all the triumphs and tragedies of the years that followed: the scenes of global Beatlemania; the decision to stop touring; *Sgt. Pepper* and the Summer of Love; Brian Epstein's death; the creation of Apple; their discovery of, and devotion to, Indian spirituality; the dissolution of the Beatles; Harrison's spectacularly successful emergence as a solo singer-songwriter; the response to the crisis in Bangladesh; and much more. Having lost someone who was not just a wife but also his closest companion, Harrison's references to his "great despair" are perfectly convincing.

While the instrumental support—drums, bass, piano—is relatively simple, it is far from restrained and frequently threatens to overwhelm Harrison's double-tracked vocal and the indifferent melody. Given the intimate, and obviously sincere, nature of his lyrics, the song would be better suited to the kind of uncomplicated production that distinguished "Deep Blue." There is, however, no doubt about the poignancy of his words; when he sings that "it's too late to make a new start," the depth of his loss is made apparent.

Although authorship of the next track, "Bye Bye Love," is formally credited to Felice and Boudelaux Bryant, Harrison's reworking of the old Everly Brothers' hit alters it to the extent that it virtually becomes a different song. His motivation is difficult to comprehend. Positioned immediately after a song in which he tells of his profound melancholy at Boyd's departure, this is a sarcastic and bitter attack on her and her paramour Clapton. He refers dismissively to them as "our lady" and "you know who"; instead of mourning the end of his marriage, he now claims that she "did me a favor" and boasts that "I threw them both out"; and he states that she is the sort of woman to "plot and shove" and that she is now "out on a spree." Harrison's deliberate distortion of the original melody transforms it into an ugly and spiteful whine. For a man who devotes so much of his musical energy to calling for love and harmony, it is a distressing and petty example of malice.

"Maya Love" was originally composed as a tune for slide guitar, and the track bears the imprint of a song in which words and music have little authentic correspondence. The lyrics are disarmingly simple: love is compared to "the sea," "the day," "the wind," "the rain," and "a stream." But "maya" refers to illusion, and the song is an uneasy treatise about the illusory nature of love, which reflects the end of his relationship with Boyd. Unlike performers like Donovan and Marc Bolan, who were able to effectively integrate childlike and repetitive language into the rhythms of their music, Harrison's more thoughtful and complex vocabulary is not suited to this kind of apparently casual wordplay. Musically, "Maya Love" is a competent, and exciting, piece of contemporary rock in which Billy Preston's electric piano is prominent, but as an accompaniment to Harrison's reflections on the transient status of love, it appears to be wholly inappropriate.

As a group, the Beatles never recorded an official Christmas song (although their 1967 Fan Club record included the song "Christmas Time Is Here Again"). As individuals, however, they were willing to fall into line with traditional expectations. Lennon's "Happy Xmas (War Is Over)" was released in 1972, and McCartney's "Wonderful Christmastime" in 1979. Sandwiched between was Harrison's "Ding Dong, Ding Dong," a 1974 Christmas single and the opening track on side 2 of *Dark Horse*. Strictly speaking, its refrain of "ring out the old, ring in the new" is a New Year's message, but its female choir, prominent percussion, and imitative Wall of Sound production are drawn directly from Spector's *Christmas Album* (1963) and Wizzard's 1972 U.K. hit single "I Wish It Could Be Christmas Every Day." The melody is constructed around the familiar ascending and descending chimes of clock bells. Again, he ponders the passage of time, reproducing an inscription from the garden in Friar Park: "yesterday, today was tomorrow; tomorrow, today will be yesterday." However, it possesses neither the overt political message of Lennon's song nor the unashamed commercialism of McCartney's, and its somewhat halfhearted festive appeal seems strangely out of place on the album.

Given that Harrison chose to make "Dark Horse" the album's title track—and also used it as the name of the record label he was planning to establish—one might expect the song to be of considerable importance in his career. In fact, it is an unambiguous warning to people not to underestimate him, apparently directed at three separate targets, all of whom have, he believes, wronged him: Lennon and McCartney, who for so long regarded him as an inferior talent within the Beatles; Boyd, who deceived him and treated him badly; and the general public, which failed to recognize his importance. To each of them, the message is the same: while they thought they had him "all staked out" and in their "grip," he has proved "too slippery" and is now "breaking out" from their perceptions. What gives the lyrics an added edge is Harrison's claim that his new-found maturity and confidence are not recent acquisitions, but have always been there. It is "nothing new," he taunts them; he "warned" them long ago.

The phrase "dark horse" has a number of related meanings. It can refer to the outsider in a race, who defeats the fancied runners and wins against all expectations; to someone with a secret; or to a person about whom little is known, and who guards his or her privacy. In any case, Harrison's perception of himself is abundantly clear: for years, he has been dismissed as "the quiet one," but those who did this were merely "fooling" themselves.

Harrison's need to remind his alleged detractors of their mistakes may be an attempt to repair his damaged pride in the wake of the relatively poor reviews of *Living in the Material World* and Boyd's decision to leave him, but it is not entirely successful. The problems caused by the absence of a strong melody and the unnecessary addition of backing vocals and a flute section are compounded by Harrison's ragged vocal performance; his voice is simply too hoarse.

One of the principal inspirations for the song may have been the Capitols' 1966 hit single "Cool Jerk." Group member Don Storball's boastful lyrics tell of "those guys lookin' at me like I'm a fool, but deep down inside they know I'm cool"—sentiments exactly like those expressed in the words of "Dark Horse." Harrison's repeated use of the phrase "cool jerk" in the song's chorus is no coincidence, but a clear indication that, like Storball, he may regard himself as "the heaviest cat you ever did see."

Although the original tune to "Far East Man" came from Ronnie Wood (who had recently left the Faces to replace Mick Taylor in the Rolling Stones), Harrison's musical and lyrical embellishments transform it into a personal song about his friendship with Ravi Shankar. The Concert for Bangla Desh had taken place three years earlier, but the problems of that country were far from over, and his lyrics concede that in a world of sustained military conflict, where life is "hellish" and our time is "so short," creating and maintaining genuine friendships becomes ever more difficult. But this is one friendship he is determined to preserve: "I won't let him down, I won't let him drown," he promises.

However, while Shankar can be singled out as the individual of the title, the song is also about Harrison's commitment to the land, to the people, to the culture, and to all the things that India has given him. In this respect, there are similarities between this "far east man" and Dylan's "tambourine man." While it is tempting to think of Dylan's song as being about the influence and inspiration of his mentor Woody Guthrie, it is also about the ideas of freedom and salvation that his personal and professional experiences had led him to consider.[16] But "Far East Man" is a far less satisfying song than "Mr. Tambourine Man," and is symptomatic of the uneven tone of the entire album. His performance contains a lovely melodic passage (on the repeated phrase "I can't let him down"), but it is never fully developed elsewhere in the song. At times, Scott's smooth saxophone contributions are reminiscent of the soul stylings of King Curtis, Junior Walker, or Motown's Funk Brothers; indeed, the song would not be out of place on Marvin Gaye's 1971 album *What's Going On*.

The final track is "It Is He (Jai Sri Krishna)." During a visit to India with friends, Harrison had met, and been profoundly impressed by, Sripad Maharaj, a holy teacher in the town of Vrindavan. He had led them in a *bhajan* or devotional chant, which Harrison later adapted into this song. The word *jai* translates as "hail," and the title thus overtly confirms the song's devotional intent. But while it seeks to recapture elements of "My Sweet Lord" and the Radha Krishna Temple's "Hare Krishna Mantra," it is only partially successful and lacks their immediate ability to inspire a communal response. The awkward changes in tempo between the traditional Hindu mantra and the newly written passages restrict the momentum of the song. The gently floating Indian verses are somewhat undermined by the ponderous nature of the rock-oriented interludes, and the evangelical nature of the English words—"he who is complete"—finally discourage any attempts at participation.

To promote the album, Harrison spent the greater part of November and early December on a series of forty-five concerts across North America. The Dark Horse Tour opened with "Ravi Shankar, Family and Friends" playing a selection of traditional and contemporary Indian music. The second half presented "George Harrison and Friends," an ensemble featuring many of the musicians who had appeared on the album, including Scott, Preston, Keltner, and Jim Horn. In keeping with Harrison's comedic preferences, the band took the stage to the strains of John Philip Sousa's "Liberty Bell March"—better known to his audience as the theme tune to *Monty Python's Flying Circus*. While not missing the opportunity to introduce tracks from *Dark Horse*, Harrison also performed some of his earlier compositions, and even included one of Lennon's most personal songs. His nightly set-list was drawn from "Hari's on Tour," "The Lord Loves the One," "Who Can See It," "Something," "While My Guitar Gently Weeps," "In My Life," "Sue Me Sue You Blues," "For You Blue,"

"Give Me Love," "Maya Love," "Dark Horse," "What Is Life," and "My Sweet Lord."

Although it received some positive reviews, the majority of reaction to the tour was negative, focusing on the length, the structure, and the content.[17] In the early 1970s, concerts of two and a half hours' duration substantially infringed the conventions of the typical rock 'n' roll show; the presence of Shankar was seen as a bizarre anomaly by those who had come to see and hear the ex-Beatle; and Harrison offended many of the audience not only by his repeated sermonizing but also in the selection and treatment of some of his, and the Beatles', most popular songs. In particular, his lyrical reworkings were seen as gratuitously offensive: "something in the way she moves *it*," "in my life, I love *God* more," and "while my guitar gently *smiles*" were just some of his perplexing substitutions. The backlash so distressed him that he effectively retired from live performances for a second time (just as he had done with the Beatles in 1966) and did not tour again until the 1990s. The lack of critical acclaim for the album and the failure of "Ding Dong, Ding Dong" in the singles charts only served to deepen his despondency through the winter of 1974–1975.

"I Don't Care Anymore"

When "Ding Dong, Ding Dong" was taken from the *Dark Horse* album as a single, "I Don't Care Anymore" was placed on the record's B side. The track is another example of the synthesis of jug band, skiffle, and country traditions that Harrison had absorbed from recordings by Bob Dylan, the Band, Lonnie Donegan, David Bromberg, and the Lovin' Spoonful. But its spoken introduction reaches back even further into popular music's history, in its parody of the opening line of "Riders in the Sky," written and recorded by Stan Jones in 1948. "An old cowpoke went riding out one dark and windy day" becomes "An old cowpoke went riding out one cold December day." As the single was released in that month, his words give an indication of the last-minute nature of the recording. The introduction continues with Harrison announcing that he has "a B-side to make" and admitting "we haven't got much time now"— comments which seem to suggest an absence of any unreleased tracks that might be considered. Unfortunately, this sense of haste permeates the whole recording. Harrison performs alone, on guitar and Jew's harp, his call for "more juice on the [head]phones" is retained, and little attempt is made to disguise the rough shakiness of his voice. The lyrics tell of his determination to pursue a woman who already appears to be in a relationship, but they are surprisingly uneven. The wistfulness of words such as "There's a line I can draw that often leaves me wanting more" is undermined by an inelegant phrase like "It's our right to get back up them stairs." Again, this points to a song written in a hurry to meet a deadline.

Extra Texture

One of the few positive notes in Harrison's life through the winter of 1974–1975 was his burgeoning romance with Olivia Arias, whom he had met at the Los Angeles offices of A&M Records. His decision to record his next album there, in the summer of 1975, was not only an acknowledgment of her importance to him but also a pragmatic choice based on the proximity of many of the musicians with whom he wanted to work—a familiar cast including Jim Keltner, Leon Russell, Tom Scott, Jesse Ed Davis, Klaus Voormann, Carl Radle, Jim Horn, Jim Gordon, Nicky Hopkins, Gary Wright, and Billy Preston. Their near-constant presence on his records at this time seemed to provide an answer to the question posed on "Sue Me Sue You Blues," when he had concluded that "all that's left is to find yourself a new band." Effectively, this *was* his new band. Whether he believed that their greatest value to him lay in their musical abilities, their personal friendships, or a combination of the two is uncertain, but the regularity of their collaborations reflected Harrison's firm belief (from his years in the Beatles) that music is an organic activity that springs from mutual cooperation as much as individual inspiration.

The album opens with "You." Harrison had written the song some years earlier for Ronnie Spector, but she had never recorded it, and his reworked version is by far the strongest track on the album. It possesses three memorable features. First, its lyrical simplicity and its deliberate emphasis on personal pronouns—"I love you" and "you love me"—repeat the policy employed to great effect on many early Beatles' tracks such as "Love Me Do," "P.S. I Love You," "From Me to You," "I'll Get You," and "She Loves You," all of which aimed to include the listener within the songs' narrative. Second, the soaring, galloping melody (which McCartney would partially emulate the following year on "Silly Love Songs") encapsulates the joy of reciprocated love and the liberation of rock 'n' roll at its most exuberant. Third, the contribution of the backing musicians is outstanding; the insistent riffs of keyboards, bass, and drums never falter, and Horn's saxophone drives the song forward throughout. The contrast between the energy and excitement of "You" and the melancholy introspection of Harrison's more recent compositions could not be greater. Even the slight unease he has in striving to maintain some of the higher notes cannot detract from what is, quite simply, a near-perfect pop song.

The mood changes abruptly with "The Answer's at the End," a somber and contemplative composition in which life is described as an "enigma" and a "mystery," whose truth will only be revealed when it is over. Inspired by an inscription on the walls of Friar Park, the song also incorporates the sentiments (and title) of "Isn't It a Pity" in its bleak assessment of the human condition. Harrison is especially critical of our tendency to cause pain to those we love, and in exploring this, he borrows freely from the words of "You Always Hurt the One You Love," written in 1944 by Allan Roberts and Doris Fisher (a hit record for, among others, the Mills Brothers, Connie Francis, and Clarence "Frogman" Henry). The observation that the person you most often hurt is, ironically, "the one you shouldn't hurt at all" provides the underlying theme for Harrison's reluctant conclusion, perhaps based on his experiences with the Beatles and Boyd, that there is little hope of change. All we can do, he believes, is to "live on" until we reach the end. The lack of optimism in his words is matched by a largely inconspicuous melody and an inconsistent production in which alternate piano, strings, and guitar interludes fail to provide a coherent musical context.

On "This Guitar (Can't Keep from Crying)" Harrison appears to refer to his guitar as a sentient being in its own right, capable of independent thought. By singing about it in the third person, he seems to be indicating the distance between the instrument and himself, but in reality he is making an autobiographical statement. In the context of the song, he *is* the guitar. The attribution, or substitution, of emotions and actions to their instruments was already an established tradition in country, folk, and blues circles. Woody Guthrie's guitar had famously borne the phrase "This guitar kills fascists," a slogan copied by the young Bob Dylan. On the banjo played by Pete Seeger were painted the words "This machine surrounds hate and forces it to surrender." Donovan's guitar carried the inscription "This machine kills." Bo Diddley frequently referred to his guitar as "Arlene," and in 2005, Neil Young would complete the process of personification in his song "This Old Guitar," in which he described the instrument formerly owned and played by Hank Williams as a "messenger." And, of course, Harrison himself had adopted the same approach on "While My Guitar Gently Weeps."

Here, Harrison uses the song to launch a virulent personal attack on those who had criticized the Dark Horse Tour and his recent musical output. His guitar is made "sad" and "mad" by the unwarranted abuse that comes his way. He speaks of the "ignorance" displayed by those who "attack" him; the magazine *Rolling Stone* is singled out for the "offence" it has caused. His words reveal that he regards the latest round of criticism not as an isolated incident but as one more example of a musical press that has repeatedly failed to recognize his intentions, "just like before." The result is that his guitar, and therefore Harrison, "can't keep from crying."

The evident similarity of the melody to "While My Guitar Gently Weeps" only serves to highlight the gulf between the two compositions. While the first was a poignant and satisfying commentary that drew attention to his newfound maturity as a songwriter, this is a petulant and rather arrogant statement in which he appears to want to put himself above criticism. Although he claims to be "happier" than at any time in the past, the bitterness in his vocal performance tells a different story. Both words and music depict a sour and troubled performer, whose resentment is all too clear.

Harrison had long been a fervent admirer of Motown's songwriters and performers, and the label's enormous importance in the development of the Beatles' own musical style has been well documented.[18] Not only did the group's first two albums contain several cover versions of the label's songs ("Twist and Shout," "Please Mister Postman," "You Really Got a Hold on Me," "Money"), but both Lennon and McCartney consciously attempted to emulate them in many of their own compositions, including "There's a Place," "This Boy," "All I've Got to Do," "You Won't See Me," "Day Tripper," and "Got to Get You into My Life." In 1964, the Beatles had toured the United Kingdom with Mary Wells, but of all Motown's artists, Smokey Robinson (of the Miracles) was the one for whom they expressed the greatest respect, and the next song on *Extra Texture* is explicitly dedicated to him by Harrison.

"Ooh Baby (You Know That I Love You)" derives from, and is a tribute to, the Miracles' 1965 hit "Ooo Baby Baby," in which Robinson's sweet falsetto floats above the rest of the group's backing vocals. However, Harrison's performance shares none of that natural lightness of touch; instead, it is a rather awkward and limited attempt to create a "soulful" sound. The lyrics, too, suffer by comparison. Robinson efficiently condenses his story into a few, heartbreaking words: "My heart went out to play, but in the game I lost you . . . what a price to pay." In contrast, Harrison seeks to create emotion through mere repetition—"You're my baby, you know I love you"—with no attempt to construct a narrative. But the greatest flaw is in its wholly inappropriate choice of melody, which is unexpectedly mournful for a song that tells of the joy of love. Instead of creating a mood of happiness with what is, or excitement at what may be, the track produces an atmosphere of gloom and despondency that is quite removed from the positive emotions contained in the words. If the song is a comment on the promise of Harrison's new love for Arias, it may also betray a continuing, pessimistic reflection on recent events and circumstances in his life.

The album continues with "World of Stone," in which Harrison returns to his view of the world as a place of obstacles and trials in which there is little hope. He comments on the great distance we have to travel before we may reach "home." In this case, however, he refers not to the home of our friends and family, but home in the sense of spiritual understanding. His warning that we should not try to follow him may well be a rebuke to those who seek answers from the Beatles. Or it may be a frank confession that his own quasi-religious search for enlightenment has brought him little contentment. It may even be an instruction that we should all accept responsibility for our actions and endeavor to determine our own path through life. The variations in his vocal range fail to add variety or interest to what is, by now, a predictable and cheerless message, set to a leaden and monotonous score.

"A Bit More of You," which opens side 2, is exactly what its title indicates: a repeat of the forceful instrumental break from "You." The decision to reuse it suggests that Harrison was only too aware of the limitations of the other tracks at his disposal and had no other piece of music to which he could turn that might reengage the listener's attention. The contrast between the confidence of *All Things Must Pass* (with sufficient original music to fill three discs) and the desperation of *Extra Texture* (where one track must be used twice) could not be greater.

"Can't Stop Thinking about You" reprises the lyrical simplicity of "Ooh Baby (You Know That I Love You)." Day and night, Harrison's thoughts never stray from the lover who has left him, until he is forced to admit that "it's no good living without you." The repetitive nature of the words (the title phrase is sung, without any convincing emotional connection, no less than twenty-five times) is matched by an equally repetitive melody. While repetition can be an effective musical device, it must rely on a strong melody ("My Sweet Lord") or a powerful sense of movement ("Hey Jude") to carry it forward. Unfortunately, this contains neither, and what might have been intended as a pop anthem only manages to become an inconsequential album track.

Further evidence of Harrison's unhappy state of mind is provided on "Tired of Midnight Blue," a languid track whose jazz-based, stop/start structure ably conveys the setting it describes. Its theme is the world he visited in "Simply Shady": a world of decadence and dissatisfaction. It was inspired by a night spent in a Los Angeles club, which had degenerated into a tawdry round of sex and drugs that left him "chilled right to the bone." Reflecting on the emptiness of the previous evening, he now sits tearfully, wishing that he had "stayed home." Again, it presents a portrait of a profoundly unhappy man. Given the casualty rate from drugs among musicians in the early 1970s and the efforts of close friends like Clapton and Lennon to kick their habits, the fact that Harrison is involved—however peripherally—with what he clearly regards as a sordid lifestyle reveals much about his personal situation.

The pattern of melancholy introspection is continued on "Grey Cloudy Lies," in which the singer describes the sad state of his life as a "battlefield." It is one of his simplest and most poignant songs, in which a slowly descending melody parallels his personal descent into an aimless and isolated existence, where he even allows himself to contemplate the prospect of suicide. The dramatic introduction and top-heavy production (which anticipate the "power ballad" style of Celine Dion, Mariah Carey, and Whitney Houston) are somewhat out of place, tending to deflect attention away from what is, in effect, an intimate confession. Without the music, the words display the status and structure of a poem. His skillful use of language employs individual words such as "padlock," "fight," and "pistol" to immediately conjure images of imprisonment that convey the repressive nature of his life. The conclusion of each verse with a rhyming couplet conforms to the standard requirements of lyric poetry. Pain and regret are evident in his voice, and the final repeated contrast between "clear blue skies" and "grey cloudy lies" is particularly moving. Despite the inappropriate production, Harrison gives a memorable performance of a beautiful song, whose absolute honesty is reminiscent of the music of Leonard Cohen and Townes Van Zandt.

Of course, self-scrutiny can easily slip into self-indulgence, and nowhere is this more clearly illustrated than on the album's closing track, "His Name Is Legs (Ladies & Gentlemen)." Legs Larry Smith was a founding member of the Bonzo Dog Band, an eccentric group of musicians and performers whose career overlapped with the Beatles on several occasions: in 1967, they had appeared in the film *Magical Mystery Tour*; in 1968, McCartney had produced their single "I'm the Urban Spaceman"; in 1975, guitarist Neil Innes and Harrison performed a comedy number, "The Pirate Song," on Eric Idle's *Rutland Weekend TV* show; and in 1978, Innes would play the role of Ron Nasty in *All You Need Is Cash*, a spoof documentary written by Idle, in which the story of the Rutles parodied the story of the Beatles. Smith was a close friend of Harrison, and the song is peppered with oblique references and in-jokes about his idiosyncratic mannerisms and behavior.

There are undoubtedly some clever examples of wordplay in the song. *Comme ci comme ça* is rendered as "come Sikh come Czar," and "understands" is coupled with "over-sits." But Harrison lacks Lennon's formidable capacity to successfully distort common words and phrases that was evident in the books *In His Own Write* and *A Spaniard in the Works*, and much of the intended humor remains hidden. In much the same way, the music remains unformed; the chorus "ooh ooh ooh" seems to anticipate a natural melodic sequence that never comes. While the song is inoffensive and likable enough in itself, it has the character of a late-night sing-along or impromptu jam session, and its role on the album is difficult to understand.

Extra Texture presents, all too clearly, the work of a troubled and unhappy man. While his musicianship is as competent as ever, the songs—with the exception of "You" and "Grey Cloudy Skies"—are disappointing. It may be that Harrison allowed his personal frustrations to swamp his commercial ambitions, or that those difficulties rendered him temporarily unable to reproduce the sort of joyous and uplifting music he had created in previous years; or perhaps, in his desire to complete the terms of his contract with EMI/Capitol (who distributed Apple's recordings), he was prepared to release a substandard product. Whatever the explanation, the trilogy of albums released between 1973 and 1975 contain relatively little that matched the quality of his Beatles and immediate post-Beatles output, and *Extra Texture*, as Harrison himself admitted, was the least satisfactory of them all.[19]

WITH A LITTLE HELP FROM HIS FRIEND

Throughout this period, George Harrison's gratitude to the guest musicians who appeared on his albums was reciprocated by a continuing willingness to participate in their recordings. As a guitarist, he featured on tracks by Nicky Hopkins, Dave Mason, Alvin Lee, Ron Wood, Billy Preston, and Tom Scott, but his most prolific, and rewarding, collaborations were with Ringo Starr. During the years of the Beatles, when the songwriting achievements of John Lennon and Paul McCartney had been a predictable focus of public attention, Starr and Harrison had shared a close friendship that never wavered. Even his tentative affair with Starr's first wife, Maureen, had not weakened that friendship,[20] and in 1973 when the drummer recorded his third solo album, *Ringo* (his first since *Sentimental Journey* and *Beaucoups of Blues* in 1970), Harrison provided him with three new songs.

"Photograph" was the first, and only, song to be jointly credited to the composing team of Harrison and Starr. Like many of the most successful pop songs, its attraction lies in its simplicity: a tale of lost love and a single photograph that serves as a reminder of happier days. What is unusual here is the absence of any hope that love might be rekindled, and an acknowledgment that the relationship is over: "I realize you're not coming back any more," the singer admits. The "face" he sees is merely an image, and the only reality is a future that he is "not looking forward to." An easy melody that fits the limitations of Starr's vocal range, and an arrangement that includes not only Harrison on guitar and backing vocals but also many of his regular colleagues (Keltner, Hopkins, Voormann, Keys), helped to give Starr a chart-topping single in the United States.

If the musicians Harrison recruited for "Photograph" represent his immersion in contemporary rock, those he brought together for "Sunshine Life for Me (Sail Away Raymond)" demonstrate his parallel love of country, folk, and blues. Written while vacationing in Ireland with Donovan, it has four members of the Band—Robbie Robertson, Levon Helm, Rick Danko, and Garth Hudson—performing alongside Harrison, Starr, and David Bromberg (on banjo). The result is a convincing piece of good-time folk-rock that would have been at home on Fairport Convention's groundbreaking album *Liege & Lief*, which was itself hugely influenced by the spirit of the Band's *Music from Big Pink*. The lyrics tell of the "good life" to be had "in the country" or "at sea," and the instruction to "sail away" is perfectly apt, given the song's likeness to a traditional sea shanty. The one note of caution, in the singer's admission that he has a "cloud" hanging over him, does little to dispel the cheerfulness of the song, and the impression lingers that the track was as much fun to make as it is to hear.

"You And Me (Babe)" was cowritten by Harrison with Mal Evans, who had been with the Beatles as road manager and personal assistant since 1963. The song, which brings the album to an end in the manner of a stage performer closing the show, is imbued with a relaxed good humor. "I had a good time, singing and drinking some wine" conveys a clear sense of the enjoyment surrounding the recording sessions. The gently rolling tempo and the everyday language—"We all thought it was great," "Give us a smile"—strengthen what is already a warm and positive message. The strategy of speaking directly to the audience had been used before by the Beatles to announce the beginning or end of their albums (the title track on *Sgt. Pepper* and "Good Night" on *The Beatles*) and "You And Me (Babe)" repeats the pattern with great success.

Harrison played no part in Starr's next album, *Goodnight Vienna*, but did contribute a song to *Rotogravure*, released in September 1976, that had almost, but not quite, appeared on several previous occasions. Following her successful recording of "Something," Harrison had written "Whenever" for Shirley Bassey, who was well known for her dramatic performances of "Goldfinger" and "Diamonds Are Forever" from the James Bond films. Nothing came of the plans, though, and under a new title of "When Every Song Is Sung," recordings were attempted by Ronnie Spector, Cilla Black, Leon Russell, and Harrison himself. None of them was completed, and the song, now known by its third title, "I'll Still Love You," was eventually passed to Starr, who happily included it on *Rotogravure*.

Harrison is not present on the recording, but the track bears his clear signature. In structure and in theme, it closely resembles "Something"; its gradually descending melody, uplifting chorus, and promise of everlasting love are instantly recognizable. However, the guitar solo by Lon Van Eaton cannot re-create the haunting element of Harrison's distinctive style, and Arif Marden's overzealous production conceals any emotional connection between words and music. Although Starr's voice is a perfect vehicle for the midtempo country/pop songs he performed with the Beatles, it lacks the expressive quality required for a simple love song. Lyrically, it is remarkably uneven: delicate, poetic phrases imagining a future "when every wind has blown [and] every seed is sown" are interrupted by boisterous shouts of "yes, I will." It is surprising that Harrison never revisited the song; although incomplete in this version, it has the potential, lyrically and musically, to become one of his loveliest creations. As it stands, it is an unfinished masterpiece.

The lack of artifice and the explicit innocence of these songs contrast sharply with the cynicism, despair, and self-examination of those Harrison wrote at the same time for *Living in the Material World, Dark Horse,* and

Extra Texture. He often referred to this period—which coincided with Lennon's "lost weekend," when he separated from Yoko Ono for several months[21]—as his "naughty" years. Although the constant belief that his music should faithfully mirror the current circumstances, emotions, and discoveries of his own life made it difficult on occasions for him to perform well-crafted songs to entertain the public, it evidently did not prevent him from writing such material for others. Clearly, his songwriting skills remained intact. But while there was little doubt over the depth and integrity of his abilities as a singer-songwriter, the challenge he faced was to demonstrate, to himself and others, that he still possessed the ability to produce music that would repeat his earlier commercial and critical success.

A Dark Horse

Even though his own recording contract with EMI/Capitol would not expire until January 1976, George Harrison had established the Dark Horse label two years before that, intending it to be a creative outlet for musicians in the same way that the Beatles had hoped for with Apple. Only a few performers had been signed to the new label, and their poor sales had offered little encouragement to A&M, which distributed the records. The British duo Splinter enjoyed a minor hit single in the United Kingdom with "Costafine Town," which Harrison coproduced, but the label's other new artists—Attitudes, Stairsteps, Keni Burke, Jiva, and Henry McCullough— were unable to achieve any kind of success and were quickly dropped. A&M's unhappiness over these disappointments and its increasing frustration at Harrison's delay in completing his own album led it to sever its contractual connection with the label. In November 1976, a distribution deal was formally agreed upon between Dark Horse and Warner Bros., and Harrison's first album on his own label was released in the same month.

THIRTY-THREE & 1/3

The title of Harrison's first Dark Horse album is doubly significant. It refers not only to the number of revolutions per minute at which long-playing vinyl records revolve on the turntable but also to his age when recording of the album began in May 1976. The wordplay is not coincidental, but announces unequivocally that the man and his music are inseparable. That the album also signals a new beginning in his career is indicated by the absence of several of the West Coast session musicians who had been semi-permanent figures on his previous recordings.

Long before Jack Kerouac defined the world of the restless, rootless traveler through the adventures of Sal Paradise and Dean Moriarty,[1] the romantic tradition of a life "on the road" had been explored in the folk and blues traditions of such singer-songwriters as Woody Guthrie and Robert Johnson. "Woman Don't You Cry for Me" is Harrison's own version of the same tale, in which the singer leaves behind a woman who loves him in order to pursue his itinerant journeys. He hates the thought of settling down and fears the "complication" and "attachment" that inevitably result from extended relationships. Unsurprisingly, the setting for their farewell is one that figures in many songs, books, and films: the railway station. Like the protagonist in Bob Dylan's "Restless Farewell" or Tom Paxton's "Rambling Boy," the singer has no clear plan. As he boards the train, he knows he has a "long way to go," but there is "no one place" he has in mind. Harrison began to write the song during his 1969 European tour with Delaney and Bonnie, and their influence is unmistakable on this fine example of down-and-dirty Southern swamp-rock, whose use of bottleneck guitar is in keeping with the blues and country patterns on which it is based. One interesting, and slightly confusing, feature of the song is the way in which Harrison uses both "baby" and "woman" when addressing the other person: the use of one implies subordination, while the other suggests equality.[2] Nevertheless, his decision to use "woman" in the title does seem to indicate that the relationship has been a mature and adult affair, and that its end is not the result of a capricious whim but an honest (if rather selfish) choice.

"Dear One" is addressed to Paramhansa Yogananda, whose *Autobiography of a Yogi*, first published in 1946, is an engaging and highly revered account of the search for spiritual understanding. Harrison had encountered the book during his introduction to meditation in the 1960s, and it remained a formative influence in his life. It was not an entirely new theme for Harrison: "Be Here Now" and "It Is He" had both been inspired by specific teachers. This song's verses, in which he pays tribute to Yogananda (whose image appears on the cover of *Sgt. Pepper* just below that of Dylan) as a man of "simple Grace," who has been "reborn" and is "blessed" by God, have a hanging, droning quality reminiscent of the Incredible String Band. He wrote the song while holidaying on the Virgin Islands, and the influence of that location shows itself in the effervescent calypso chorus that recalls the sunniness of Donovan's "There Is a Mountain." "Dear one, I love you" Harrison affirms, with obvious delight. The song reveals the brighter side of his religious commitment and its musical expression. Others of his songs may have emphasized the personal difficulties and emotional tribulations of spiritual discovery, but "Dear One" shows the joy and energy that await the dedicated pilgrim.

The tune for "Beautiful Girl" had been composed in 1969, when Harrison was working on Doris Troy's debut album for Apple. Incomplete and without words, it had lain dormant until 1976, when the stimulus provided by Olivia Arias's entry into his life had prompted him to write a set of lyrics. His account of how she "quickly untied" him and got him "shaking inside" is a fitting description of the freedom and relaxation that had replaced the tension and constraints of his previous life. And his gratitude is evident: without her, his "soul" itself would have been threatened. The specific ways in which he refers to Arias provide clues to the personal and professional facets of his songwriting. His description of her as "A-1" rather than the expected "the one" is an example of his preference for an unconventional vocabulary, whereas the contention that she is "not the kind you go handing around" or "the kind that is lost or is found" may be a covert reference to his cynical view of Pattie Boyd's behavior. The confident melody, warm harmonies, and leaping guitar solos combine to produce the kind of uncomplicated and satisfying ballad that he (and Paul McCartney) had produced on *The Beatles* and *Abbey Road*. All in all, "Beautiful Girl" showcases a George Harrison rarely seen in the previous few years.

The ongoing legal dispute over Harrison's alleged plagiarism in "My Sweet Lord" had finally been concluded just before recording of *Thirty-Three & ¹/₃* began, as a result of which he had been ordered to pay damages of more than half a million dollars to the composer (Ronnie Mack) and publishers (Bright Tunes) of the Chiffons' "He's So Fine." "This Song" is his satirical comment on the whole experience, which had dragged on for six long years.

The track opens to the familiar riff of the Four Tops' "I Can't Control Myself," which is Harrison's way of announcing that the song is about the vexed topic of musical plagiarism, reinforced by Eric Idle's cameo vocal contribution in which he also compares the track to Fontella Bass's "Rescue Me," and by Harrison's own reference to his song "You." In fact, "This Song" does contain elements of all three songs, not just in its insistent melody but also in the momentum that drives it forward and in Tom Scott's saxophone solo, which has a much harder edge to it than those of Bobby Keys and Jim Horn. The following year, the spectacular success of *Saturday Night Fever* (dir. John Badham, 1977) and its accompanying soundtrack album and the glamorous notoriety of the newly opened Studio 54 would concentrate global attention on New York as the center of disco, but this tight dance track shows that Harrison was already well aware of the nascent East Coast club scene.

The lyrics mockingly repeat that there is nothing unusual about the song. It is not "tricky" or "bad" or "good" or "hip" or "square" or (in an allusion to the publishers of "He's So Fine") "bright"—it is merely a song, whose origins are quite innocent. But the most revealing insight into

Harrison's view of songwriting is in the final line. His admission that "without you, there's no point to this song" is an unexpected acknowledgment of the importance of the audience. While his songs may reflect and illuminate facets of his own life, they are ultimately performed for, and presented to, others. The relationships between the internal and the external, the creative and the commercial, lie at the heart of any artistic work. A song is simply a text and, like any other creative piece—a painting, a poem, a novel, or a play—only comes to life when it is received by an audience.[3] Harrison's perception of this is a sign of his sensitivity as a composer, as well as a response to the lukewarm public reception of many of his recent recordings.

The album continues with "See Yourself," a song Harrison began in 1967 and completed in 1976. It presents an acute reminder of the Beatles' world during the Summer of Love. It was originally inspired by the media furor in June 1967 over Paul McCartney's admission that he had taken LSD.[4] Harrison and John Lennon had been regular users for some time, and the song's opening observation that "it's easier to tell a lie than it is to tell the truth" refers to his mixed emotions over the wisdom of total honesty. But, while the dilemma about whether to reveal or conceal the truth to others is insuperable, the important thing is to be true to oneself: to "see yourself." In this sense, "to see" means "to know" and is compatible with the ideas he had expressed at the time in songs like "Within You Without You" and "It's All Too Much." Furthermore, Harrison's realization that "it's easier to say you won't, than it is to feel you can" is a restatement of Lennon's claim in "All You Need Is Love" that "there's nothing you can do that can't be done," showing that both were preoccupied with similar reflections about the politics of free will. The rather plain melody may explain why the track remained unfinished for so long, but its dedication on the album (with "Dear One") to Yogananda is a mark of Harrison's gratitude for the spiritual guidance that has allowed him to move toward a resolution of his private and public responsibilities.

In the years ahead, Harrison would become increasingly interested in the world of Formula One motor racing, but although "It's What You Value" contains references to motor car manufacturers Mercedes and Elf-Tyrrell, the song employs cars only as a symbol through which to explore the value we place on material possessions. Harrison's lyrics recognize that a person's car can be an item of "conspicuous consumption"[5]—a source of status and an object of envy. However, he refrains from any direct criticism of those who seek to own such expensive objects. Instead, he merely comments that it is up to all of us to organize our own priorities and, in doing so, to calculate "what you value" and "what it's cost you." It is a remarkably mellow and relaxed Harrison, compared to the cynical singer-songwriter who attacked greed and commodity fetishism on tracks like "Piggies," "I Me Mine," and "The Lord Loves the One." The recurrent tune, rapid tempo, and shuffling piano and horn sections reinforce the conventional imagery—and Harrison's own perception—of motoring as something which is exciting and pleasurable.

This is followed by Harrison's version of Cole Porter's "True Love," first performed by Bing Crosby and Grace Kelly in *High Society* (dir. Charles Walters, 1956). Porter's ability to combine lyrical dexterity and instantly attractive melodies produced some of the twentieth century's most memorable songs,[6] and Harrison's adaptation, featuring a double-tracked vocal and prominent slide guitar, is an effective interpretation of a popular standard.

After his disappointing attempt to emulate Smokey Robinson on "Ooh Baby (You Know That I Love You)," it is a little surprising to hear him do so again. However, "Pure Smokey," which takes its name from Robinson's 1974 album, is a superlative track that captures the smooth rhythms, seductive chord changes, and effortless singing style of the man supposedly described by Bob Dylan as America's greatest poet.[7] The song is Harrison's way of expressing his general thanks to all those "over so many years" who have influenced or inspired him, and Robinson is the specific example he chooses through which to illustrate his gratitude. The Beatles had included a powerful version of "You Really Got a Hold on Me" on *With the Beatles*, and the title is reprised here as part of Harrison's lyrics, which also praise Robinson for "always trying something new." It is a wonderful example of Harrison's obvious affection for sweet soul, both as a singer and a songwriter.

While it is sometimes difficult to nominate the standout track on an album, "Crackerbox Palace" leaps from this disc as one of Harrison's most perfect creations. He had been a fan of the eccentric comedy performer Lord Buckley for many years, and a chance meeting with his former manager George Greif inspired him to write this song, whose title comes from the name of Buckley's home in Los Angeles. From the sudden drum-roll introduction to the reluctant fadeout, this is a bright and lovingly optimistic celebration of life, in which "Crackerbox Palace" functions as a metaphor for the world. For Harrison, the world is clearly a place of wonder and exhilaration. "We welcome you . . . you bring such joy," he repeats, as each newcomer is greeted. Of course, there is no guarantee that our lives will be easy or straightforward, and there is much to learn, but the fact of life itself is something over which to rejoice, as his closing comment clarifies: "No matter where you roam, know our love is true." More evidence of Harrison's love of punning is in his double reassurance that "the Lord" (both God and Buckley) is with us. The repeated verse-chorus-verse structure and the marvelously sunny tune are reminders that Harrison is capable of writing simple but sublime pop songs. In addition, his voice shows no signs of the strain or fatigue present on earlier albums; it is a self-contained and blissful performance whose sense of well-being is almost tangible.

The album's final track is "Learning How to Love You," a song that encapsulates Harrison's ability to bring together various elements of his personal, professional, and musical history. He originally wrote it for Herb Alpert, but decided to record it himself. In 1962, Alpert and Jerry Moss had founded A&M Records, the company that had originally contracted to distribute the Dark Horse label. Although he was better known as a band-leader with the Tijuana Brass (which enjoyed a worldwide hit with "The Lonely Bull" in 1962), Alpert was also an accomplished vocalist, whose re-cording of Burt Bacharach and Hal David's "This Guy's in Love with You" was a #1 single in the United States in 1968.

The Beatles' inclusion of the Bacharach–David composition "Baby It's You" on their first album was just one example of their respect for the professional songwriting teams that worked out of New York's Brill Build-ing in the late 1950s and early 1960s.[8] Those teams—which also included Howard Greenfield and Neil Sedaka, Gerry Goffin and Carole King, Barry Mann and Cynthia Weil, Jeff Barry and Ellie Greenwich, Jerry Leiber and Mike Stoller, and Doc Pomus and Mort Shuman[9]—were responsible for hundreds of hit records that filled the artistic gap between the rock 'n' roll of the mid-1950s and the "British Invasion" of the mid-1960s. Harrison's wish to provide Alpert with a song in the style of "This Guy's in Love with You" was thus a reminder of his early musical influences, a declaration of their working relationship, and a mark of his confidence as a songwriter.

Although the track lacks the distinctive Latin rhythms of Bacharach's music[10] and the easy command of everyday language that marks David's lyrics, it is, nonetheless, a fine ballad. Harrison's vocals gently meander around a melody that is similar to "The Light That Has Lighted the World," and the cool, restrained keyboard and guitar contributions evoke the atmosphere of an intimate, sophisticated nightclub. Indeed, the song would not be out of place in the stage repertoire of Nat King Cole or Peggy Lee. While he is sometimes "unsure" of himself and conscious of the sadness of "teardrops," the singer is comfortable in the certainty of his emotions. "Left alone with my heart," he confides, "I'm learning how to love you."

Although *Thirty Three & ⅓* was recorded and released just one year af-ter *Extra Texture*, the two albums could not be more different. Pessimism has been replaced by optimism, suspicion by confidence, failure by success. More than anything else, the mood that washes over the album is one of relaxation. Musically and emotionally, Harrison appears as a man reborn. The cynicism and despair that threatened to overwhelm him are absent; the songs, and their words, are mellow, engaging, and full of gladness.

BEST OF GEORGE HARRISON

Although the creation of Dark Horse and its distribution deal with Warner Bros. were seen by Harrison as a platform from which he could exercise considerable artistic freedom, EMI/Capitol retained the rights to his earlier works. Anxious to exploit this back catalogue as effectively as possible and keen to benefit from any parallel publicity, the company issued its *Best of George Harrison* album the day after the release of *Thirty Three & ¹/₃*. Harrison had been aware of the planned compilation and had offered a track listing and alternative title. However, his suggestions were largely ignored, and his irritation turned to distress when he discovered that the seven songs on the first side of the album were taken not from his solo output, but from his recordings with the Beatles.[11] The six tracks on side 2 were "My Sweet Lord" and "What Is Life" (*All Things Must Pass*), "Give Me Love (Give Me Peace on Earth)" (*Living in the Material World*), "Dark Horse" (*Dark Horse*), "You" (*Extra Texture*), and "Bangla Desh"—a predictable, if rather cursory, selection from his solo years.

Compilation albums may serve a variety of functions: an introduction to a performer's work, a summary of his output, an example of his musical range, or a retrospective of his career. However, the implication that his individual recordings were of insufficient merit to justify a compilation in their own right was seen by Harrison as a direct insult. In addition, the fact that compilations in the previous year of material by John Lennon (*Shaved Fish*) and Ringo Starr (*Blast from Your Past*) were entirely comprised of their solo recordings only served to rub salt in the wound, adding to Harrison's sense of personal injustice and professional mistrust. Consequently, he refused to cooperate in any promotional activity and effectively disowned the release.

GEORGE HARRISON

There are various ways in which the history of popular music can be told. One approach is to see it as a distinct and unbroken line that can be either evolutionary or cyclical in nature.[12] Another is to locate it within a broad examination of social, political, and cultural sources and trends.[13] And yet another is to concentrate on key moments of change, in which an individual performer or event leads a rebellion against existing musical fashions and styles.[14] While the most plausible strategy may involve a combination of all three approaches, the significance of a small number of specific disruptions or innovations that have substantively altered the course of popular music history cannot be overlooked. Such moments would include the emergence of rock 'n' roll and the impact of Elvis Presley; the British Invasion, led by the Beatles; music video's emphasis on the visual element of popular music; hip-hop and its musical component, rap; and rave culture and the proliferation of forms of dance music.

The dramatic appearance of punk in the mid-1970s was an occasion of equal importance. Its vehement rejection of conventional assumptions about those attributes regarded as desirable (vocal ability, musical skills, attractive appearance), its contempt for the "show business" artifices of glam-rock and the pretensions of progressive rock, its do-it-yourself ethic, and its construction of a nihilistic style based on boredom and confrontation presented a challenge that many established performers found difficult to meet.[15] The Sex Pistols' infamous appearance on Thames Television's *Today* program in December 1976 (during which they swore repeatedly at presenter Bill Grundy) came just two weeks after the release of *Thirty Three & 1/3*, and the national outrage that followed was increased yet further in June of the following year when the group's second single, "God Save the Queen," topped the U.K. charts in the week of the queen's Silver Jubilee celebrations. A decade after the Summer of Love, "No future" replaced "All you need is love" as the year's iconic slogan.

No less significant were the profound changes in Harrison's personal life during the same period. In June 1977, eleven years after their marriage and three years after their separation, he and Pattie Boyd were granted a divorce on the grounds of irreconcilable differences. Harrison's father, Harold, who had spent increasing amounts of time with his son over the last few years, died in May 1978. And in August, Harrison and Arias's only child, Dhani, was born, and four weeks later the couple were married in Henley-on-Thames.

In such circumstances, Harrison was probably wise to delay his next recordings. *George Harrison*, his second album on his new Dark Horse label, was released in February 1979. In a move that again revealed his enduring affection for the songs of the Brill Building, he recruited Russ Titelman as coproducer. In the early 1960s, Titelman had worked as a session musician and occasional composer with Cynthia Weil, Gerry Goffin, Larry Kolber, and Phil Spector; he sang on the Paris Sisters' "I Love How You Love Me" and cowrote the Cinderellas' "Baby Baby I Still Love You." He had also collaborated with Jack Nitzsche and Brian Wilson, before going on to produce albums by Little Feat, James Taylor, Randy Newman, and Ry Cooder in the 1970s. His participation was thus a confirmation of Harrison's musical values and a shrewd affirmation of the benefits of having an additional presence in the studio.

The album picks up where *Thirty Three & 1/3* ended. "Love Comes to Everyone" is a mellow and deeply satisfying song whose message of optimism is underpinned by a warm and relaxed melody. Harrison reassures us that "it only takes time," even for those who see their position as hopeless, before "the door opens." As in many of his previous songs, the love to which he refers may be interpreted as romantic or spiritual, but the overall mood of sophisticated intimacy suggests that this is less Harrison-as-preacher and more Harrison-as-friend, reassuring the listener that love will dispel the blues. Eric Clapton's restrained guitar adds detail to the track, but the polished contributions of Steve Winwood on Moog synthesizer and backing vocals give the production an unusual depth. Winwood had first achieved fame as the prodigiously talented teenage vocalist with the Spencer Davis Group in the mid-1960s on hits like "Keep On Running," "Somebody Help Me," "Gimme Some Loving," and "I'm a Man," before joining supergroups Traffic and Blind Faith. This was his first collaboration with Harrison, and their joint performance is clearly, and instantly, effective.

"Not Guilty" was written in 1968 during the Beatles' visit to Rishikesh. A rough, unfinished demo from that time was eventually released on the group's *Anthology 3* album in 1996, but the version here was freshly recorded for *George Harrison*. The song contains references to many of the group's activities in the late 1960s: the financial arguments, the numerous requests from charity organizations, public bewilderment at the demise of the "Fab Four," his own associations with the Maharishi Mahesh Yogi and Ravi Shankar, and the creation of Apple. Now, reflecting on it all, he apologizes to those fans and friends who might have felt "misled," but denies any personal responsibility. "I'm really sorry," he repeats, insisting that he never promised anything more: "I only want what I can get."

Harrison was often cited as the most intensely private of the four Beatles, and the sentiments he expresses in this song aptly illustrate his reluctance to accept the responsibilities with which he was frequently burdened.[16] His soulful delivery and the jazz-inflected keyboard touches from Neil Larsen's electric piano create a cool and confident setting. Although the song was ten years old, the endings and beginnings in Harrison's own life at this time transform the themes contained within his lyrics into a valid, personal memoir. In contrast to the tortuous self-examination and introspection of some of the songs on Harrison's earlier solo albums, the inclusion of "Not Guilty" suggests that he had now reached a position in his life where he could comfortably respond, in an honest and dispassionate way, to the assessments and accusations made of him by others.

"Here Comes the Moon" was written during a lengthy holiday in Hawaii at the start of 1978. While it is not deliberately intended as a companion track to "Here Comes the Sun," the two cannot avoid comparison, although there are in fact considerable differences. The earlier song was less about the sun itself and more about the rebirth and optimism that the transition from winter to spring promises; the sun is a metaphor for a fresh hope. Here, the moon performs no metaphorical or symbolic function, but is the direct subject of the song. The sight of a full moon hanging low in the sky over the Pacific Ocean so inspired Harrison that, like a photographer compelled to record a memorable image, he was driven to preserve the experience. He suggests that some people may not appreciate the breathtaking beauty of the world around them and "act like they don't notice it." But he recognizes it as "God's gift," and his repeated call— "Here comes the moon"—not only celebrates its nightly appearance but also alerts others to what they are missing. The descending chorus and chiming guitar passages are the most attractive features of a pleasant, if bland, melody that lacks the crisp vitality of "Here Comes the Sun."

"Soft-Hearted Hana" is another illustration of Harrison's ability to infuse his musical sensibilities with personal elements. The ragtime song "Hard Hearted Hannah (The Vamp of Savannah)" had been recorded by many performers, including the Paul Whiteman Orchestra, Ella Fitzgerald, Sophie Tucker, Peggy Lee, and Ray Charles. Written in the 1920s by Jack Yellen, Bob Bigelow, Charles Bates, and Milton Ager, it warns men against falling for Hannah, "the meanest gal in town . . . colder than an arctic storm" who "loves to see men suffer . . . [and] pours water on a drowning man!" Fifty years later, the Harrisons had bought a vacation home in the village of Hana on the Hawaiian island of Maui (other celebrities with property there have included Kris Kristofferson, Dolly Parton, and Richard Pryor) and the pun in the title of "Soft-Hearted Hana" neatly brings the two together. Set against a background of party noise and conversation, with a good-time, sing-along accompaniment, the lyrics tell of a hallucinogenic trip Harrison experienced after ingesting "magic mushrooms" on the island. However, this is not the negative view of drug abuse that he had offered in "Simply Shady" and "Tired of Midnight Blue," but a lively and witty account of events. Among the Dylanesque characters conjured up are "Richard III," "seven naked native girls," and "lone-ranger smoking doobies," all of whom leave him "still smiling." Although the previous songs had emphasized the addictive dangers of hard drugs, his words indicate that he remains happy to endorse the occasional use of soft drugs for recreational purposes.

There is an abrupt shift in the final verse, where Harrison states, simply and affectionately, his fondness for his Hawaiian home. Even when he is far away, he can visualize it lying beneath the rainy slopes of Haleakala volcano. The feminine personification he employs in the phrase "she moves among the fruit and grain" is remarkably similar to the devices used by John Keats in his *Ode to Autumn*, in which he describes "fruit [filled] with ripeness to the core" and tells of Autumn "sitting careless on a granary floor." It suggests that comparisons between the Beatles and the young Romantic poets of the early nineteenth century (Percy Shelley, Lord Byron, and Keats, among others) may legitimately extend to their creative use of language, as well as their public fascination.

"Blow Away," which was the first song from the album to be released as a single, is a simple tune about the power of love. From the first few rising chords on slide guitar, it is apparent that this is one of Harrison's most tuneful and evocative creations. As it alternates between verse and chorus, the song joyously affirms that the daily irritations and annoyances which can cause us so much distress are mere products of the mind that can be easily banished. "All I got to do is to love you," the singer realizes, directly recalling the message, and words, of "All You Need Is Love."

While his promise that dark problems can be quickly replaced by "light," "warmth," "rainbows," and "breezes" might, in other circumstances, appear trite or fanciful, here it is perfectly in keeping with the bright and buoyant flow of the melody. In the same way that "Love Comes to Everyone" speaks of universal and personal love, so "Blow Away" is simultaneously effective as a general description of the human condition and an intimate statement of individual affection. In both cases, love brings happiness. His explicit reduction of philosophical, spiritual, and emotional confusions to the one simple equation shows the extent to which Harrison had succeeded in overcoming the turmoil of past years and achieving real contentment in his life.

In the late 1970s, the world's most successful band was the Electric Light Orchestra (ELO) led by Jeff Lynne. *A New World Record*, *Out of the Blue*, and *Discovery* topped album charts around the globe and produced a steady supply of hit singles. In addition, the group's spectacular live shows gave it a reputation for flamboyant musical performance that few could match. The initial musical impetus for ELO's formation in 1972 had been stimulated by the cello arrangements on the Beatles' "I Am the Walrus,"[17] and although the band had since developed a distinctive sound of its own, the legacy of the Beatles was still noticeable. In a neat example of the circularity of influences, Harrison's "Faster" is a convincing approximation of the ELO of 1978. Its repetitive staccato vocals, fast tempo, cascading string arrangement, and clear narrative structure could have come from the sessions that produced "Turn to Stone," "Mr. Blue Sky," and "Sweet Talkin' Woman."

The song is also Harrison's tribute to the stars of Formula One motor racing, a sport to which he had become increasingly attracted; the album's inner sleeve lists Jackie Stewart, Niki Lauda, Jody Scheckter, and Ronnie Peterson as the inspirations for the song. However, as he tells of how the unnamed driver entered a "circus," was regarded as one of the "special people," and fulfilled the fantasies of the "crowds pouring in," it quickly becomes apparent that the song is not just about those involved in Formula One, but applies to all those entertainers and celebrities in the public eye, including, of course, Harrison himself. In light of future events, his reference to "crazy people with love so frail" is a chilling insight into the dangers of obsessive fandom. In addition to his ownership of luxury Rolls-Royce and BMW saloons, Harrison also took great pleasure in driving a range of customized sports cars, whose brands included Ferrari, Porsche, and Lamborghini. More than anything else, "Faster" is a testament to that interest, which, as he readily admitted, provided a welcome alternative to the life of a rock star.[18]

"Dark Sweet Lady" is a love song from Harrison to Arias, and the first of three consecutive tracks on which he celebrates his newfound domestic bliss. The sensitive combination of his rippling guitar and plaintive voice makes this lilting ballad one of the album's key tracks. As well as stating his love, the song also expresses his thanks that she came to his rescue after he had "really fallen." Perhaps more than any other track in the collection, it measures out the gulf between the cynical, confused, and unhappy singer-songwriter of *Dark Horse* and *Extra Texture*, and today's relaxed performer. The Latin-tinged rhythms are a deliberate attempt to satisfy Arias's request for a Spanish type of song and, rather like the lyrics of "Something," the words evoke the details of an intimate conversation. When he confesses that he would "never have known what [he'd] done without [her]," the depth of his gratitude is all too apparent. By using the same adjective in the title (out of the hundreds potentially available to a songwriter), Harrison also makes it clear that his "sweet lady" is just as important to him as his "sweet lord."

This theme is continued in "Your Love Is Forever," Harrison's addition to the scores of pop songs that profess that true love will never end. It is a beautifully controlled track, on which the gently falling intonations of his voice contrast the "warm and lazy Summertime" against the "cold and dreary Wintertimes." Seasons may come and go, but the certainty of their mutual love is unbroken; Arias is "the only lover worth it all." The radiant melody carries with it some of the latent beauty of the Beatles' "Because," and the Hawaiian-style guitar helps to locate the song's origins. The importance of time and place in determining the style and subject of composition has been well recorded.[19] Just as the Beatles' visit to Rishikesh had led to a surge of songwriting activity ten years earlier, so Harrison's vacation on Maui seems to have uncovered a vein of sophisticated and delicate music that was previously hidden. Harrison was enormously proud of "Your Love Is Forever," naming it as one of two post-Beatles songs (the other was "Learning How to Love You") that he felt were as good as "Something."[20]

The mini-trilogy is completed by "Soft Touch." In colloquial English, this phrase is often used to refer to a person who is easily persuaded, but here the intention is to describe a caring and gentle nature. Much of the language reinforces the impression of physical and emotional tenderness: phrases like "eyes that shine," "treetops whisper," and "a new moon" help to create a mood of warm contentment, and references to the "ocean," "waves," and "sailing" imply an island setting. As on the previous two tracks, Harrison's marriage of words and music is effortless and entirely natural. While contemporary genres such as punk and heavy metal sometimes found it difficult to blend intimate, romantic messages with sympathetic musical accompaniments, Harrison seems to have achieved a near-seamless blend of the two. This is due in no small part to Titelman's polished production and the sophistication and professional expertise of backing musicians Winwood, Larsen, and bass guitarist Willie Weeks. The West Coast session players who regularly featured on his albums from

All Things Must Pass to *Extra Texture* possessed an extravagant showmanship whose attempts to outdo one another might have added to the force of the songs, but occasionally threatened to swamp the music. Beginning with *Thirty Three & 1/3*, and continuing on *George Harrison*, that tendency was replaced by a less aggressive, and more subtle, musical philosophy that saw music and words as complementary rather than competing ingredients. The delicate descending riff with which Winwood's synthesizer surrounds the phrase "like a snowflake falling" is a perfect illustration. An additional point of interest is revealed in the printed lyrics that accompany the album. "A warm sun rises" appears as "A warm son rises," a touching and personal reference by Harrison to the birth of his child.

The only musician to have appeared on all Harrison's studio albums up to this point was keyboardist Gary Wright. Born in New Jersey, he had traveled to the United Kingdom in 1967, where he had quickly been recruited into Spooky Tooth. Although never commercially successful, the group was one of the most highly regarded on the British underground scene, and Wright found himself in great demand as a guest musician. He was also an accomplished songwriter, composing many of the tracks on his solo albums, the first of which was *The Dream Weaver* in 1975. "If You Believe" was the first joint composition between Wright and Harrison. Harrison's distinctive chiming guitar introduces the midtempo track, whose message covers familiar ground: Nothing is impossible, but some decide to "give up" (and therefore fail), while others choose to "get up" (and therefore succeed). The secret is simply to have faith and to believe, in oneself and in others. However, the song lacks the innovative qualities of "Within You Without You," the melodic impact of "My Sweet Lord," and the lyrical complexity of "Living in the Material World." Next to the Beatles' iconic message that "the love you take is equal to the love you make," Harrison's assertion that "all your love's reflected back to you" seems rather redundant, in what is a perfectly pleasant but ultimately unremarkable track.

In form and content, the songs on *George Harrison* are distinguished by their musical sophistication and personal satisfaction. It was Harrison's last album of the 1970s. Whereas the 1960s had been a kaleidoscopic period of extraordinary and unbroken success, the 1970s had included much darker interludes of failure and frustration. This album was a confirmation, as he readily admitted, that he had been able to confront and overcome those problems and to restore balance and harmony into his life and his music.[21] It revealed him not just as a gifted composer of pop-rock songs but also as a craftsman of considerable depth and subtlety. At the end of a decade whose musical fashions had included heavy metal, punk rock, disco, new wave, progressive rock, West Coast, and reggae, Harrison appeared to have successfully steered a course through an increasingly complex terrain. Of course, the question "Will the Beatles ever re-form?" never went away, and there were occasions, such as the suggestion that they might reunite for a single concert sponsored by the United Nations in aid of the Vietnamese "boat people" in 1979, when it seemed to be a distinct possibility.[22] But, for the most part, the frenzied public interest and persistent media intrusion into every aspect of their lives had somewhat receded, and Harrison's pleasure in the state of his personal and musical activities was apparent.

SOMEWHERE IN ENGLAND

Following the release of *George Harrison* in early 1979, Harrison devoted much of the rest of that year and 1980 to the demands of fatherhood, his new hobby of gardening, and his increasing passion for motor racing. In May 1979, he, along with McCartney and Starr, attended the wedding of Eric Clapton and Pattie Boyd and were happily persuaded to join Clapton onstage for an impromptu jam. The film company Harrison had formed in 1978 with American businessman Denis O'Brien, Handmade Films, assumed a prominent public profile when it stepped in to provide financial backing for *Monty Python's Life of Brian* (dir. Terry Jones, 1979) after the original investors had withdrawn their support for the controversial comedy; it was the first of more than twenty movies the company would produce over the next ten years.[23] In August 1979, *I Me Mine*, an autobiographical account of his songwriting history, was completed and published in a limited edition. And in the autumn and winter of 1980, he returned to the studios at Friar Park (where *George Harrison* had been recorded) to begin recording tracks for *Somewhere in England*.

Then the murder of John Lennon outside his apartment in New York's Dakota Building on December 8 irrevocably shattered the contentment and peace of mind that Harrison had recently acquired.

The traumatic historical legacies of deaths in popular music are, sadly, all too familiar. The plane crash that killed Buddy Holly, the Big Bopper, and Ritchie Valens in 1959 was famously characterized by Don McLean, in "American Pie," as "the day the music died." The murder of Meredith Evans by Hell's Angels during the Rolling Stones concert at Altamont, California, in 1969 signaled for many the end of the counterculture.[24] Elvis Presley's death in 1977 shockingly undermined the glorious promise of the American dream that his life had seemed to exemplify.[25] The drug-related death of Sid Vicious in 1979, while awaiting trial for the murder of his former girlfriend Nancy Spungen, brutally exposed the dystopian heart of punk. The deaths of Keith Moon in 1978 and John Bonham in 1980 had emphasized the perennial dangers in the excesses of rock music, just as the death from AIDS of Freddie Mercury in 1991, the shotgun suicide of Kurt Cobain in 1994, and the sudden death of Michael Jackson in 2009 would lead to similar recriminations and accusations in the decades that lay ahead.

The tragedy of Lennon's death, however, surpassed all these in the sheer scale of the emotional drama it embodied.[26] As so many knew from the first time they heard their music in 1963 or 1964, and as the whole world later came to understand, the Beatles were far, far more than a pop group or rock band.[27] The extent of their achievements had been breathtaking. As the leader, Lennon's status was not just that of an entertainer: he had been perceived as spiritual guru, as political activist, as avant-garde artist, as religious messiah, as contemporary philosopher, as intellectual guide, and as a real and flawed human being.

As the repercussions of Lennon's death spread around the world, the three Beatles found themselves plunged into a luridly retrospective version of the earlier Beatlemania that Harrison, in particular, had found almost unbearable.[28] In the immediate aftermath, they reacted, at least publicly, in different ways. Starr declined to speak to the news media. McCartney's ill-chosen initial response—"It's a drag"—has haunted him ever since.[29] Harrison's brief press statement—"After all we went through together, I had, and still have, great love and respect for John"—was a vastly understated indication of his affection for the man who had been not only his fellow Beatle but also his mentor and idol for many years.[30] In the long term, they each increased the scale of their personal security; Harrison's retreat into a jealously guarded privacy was marked.[31]

Yet in the weeks of fear, bewilderment, and grief that followed Lennon's murder, the recording and rerecording of *Somewhere in England* continued. It was eventually released in June 1981, bearing a dedication to Lennon taken from the Bhagavad-Gita, one of the most important religious scriptures of Hinduism: "There was never a time when I did not exist, nor you. Nor will there be any future when we cease to be."

The album's opening track is **"Blood from a Clone."** It was prompted by Warner Bros.'s lukewarm response to the early tapes of *Somewhere in England* and is Harrison's attack on those record company executives who evaluate music in terms of its commercial potential rather than its creative qualities. There is, within the entertainment business generally and popular music specifically, a preferred strategy of "innovation within predictability." Put simply, this involves the replication of profitable formulas, in which each new output differs only very slightly from its successful antecedents. The sequels, prequels, and series favored by the movie industry (such as Bing Crosby and Bob Hope's *Road* films or the James Bond, Indiana Jones, and Rocky franchises) provide an ideal illustration of this in practice. So too do the relentless imitation of successful TV genres (the "reality" show, the celebrity show, and the domestic sitcom) and the invention or reinvention of popular paperback genres (such as the "medieval conspiracy" plots and the "young wizard" novels that were stimulated by the global sales of Dan Brown's *The Da Vinci Code* and J. K. Rowling's *Harry Potter* novels).

Harrison's use of the word "clone," with its connotations of synthetic or artificial creation, is therefore an appropriate way of describing the drive to replicate—as closely as possible—products that will satisfy the media's commercial imperative. In the course of his complaint, he reveals some interesting facets of his current musical tastes: he speaks up for the radical, if uncommercial, music of performers like Frank Zappa; he dismisses new wave as "crap"; and he declares that the sounds likely to be heard on the radio are "awful noises." There is also a resigned admission that the contribution made by the Beatles themselves may have been in vain; when he states "I thought we had freed us from the mundane," there is no doubt that he is referring to the Beatles (and their peers) in the 1960s.

However, the track is a clear example of the manner in which intent and meaning can be inferred not just by the words but also by the music. A bleak production, complete with sparse instrumentation and slow, aching vocals, would have made this song a bitter and pessimistic grumble of discontent. However, the ska tempo and jaunty backing, particularly from Herbie Flowers on bass, make it clear that this is no surrender to the power of the record company, but a defiant riposte to the bureaucrats and a justification of the music that follows.

Having nailed his musical philosophy to the mast, Harrison goes on to satirize one of the contemporary fashions in "Unconsciousness Rules," an indictment of the ubiquitous disco scene, which he saw as mindless and repetitive. Although brought to international prominence by *Saturday Night Fever* in 1977, New York's clubs had been promoting disco for more than a year by the time that film was released. In its wake, performers like Donna Summer, Kool and the Gang, Chic, KC and the Sunshine Band, and the Village People enjoyed enormous sales in the late 1970s. However, the biggest beneficiaries of the disco boom were the Bee Gees, who had been the main contributors to the movie soundtrack and whose career was resurrected by a run of eight #1 singles in the United States (from "Jive Talkin'" in 1975 to "Love You Inside Out" in 1979).

While not singling out individual artists for criticism, Harrison delivers a series of insults to those "half alive," "unsatisfied" people who invest so much time and energy on the dance floor. He not only attacks their physical appearance ("You look such a wreck") but also questions their mental stability ("You've lost a screw in your head"). Taken in conjunction with the previous track, it becomes apparent that his anger is fueled by disco's astonishing popularity, which made its incessant rhythms much more attractive to the executives and gatekeepers of Warner Bros. than the more mature, but less predictable, songs of contemporary singer-songwriters such as himself. The song's mock-disco arrangement reduces some of the outrage in his lyrics and imparts a touch of irony, but his frustration is clear: musically and personally, the dominant styles of 1980 are anathema to him. At a time when he was still actively grieving for Lennon and the broken musical promises of the 1960s, the ascendancy of disco's vacuous entertainment was an acute blow to his sensitivities.

"Life Itself" returns to the spiritual insights he had celebrated on *All Things Must Pass* and *Living in the Material World*. Assisted by a gorgeous melody of rising and falling phrases, the message is simple: there may be many religions, but there is one God, who is responsible for all that we "taste, touch and feel." The words tell of the numerous ways in which God can be characterized, but there is one quality to which Harrison constantly returns: love. He refers to god as "my love," "the love in life itself," and "the real love that I've got." In doing so, he rearticulates his belief that everything else is subservient to love. It is a beautifully crafted and gently sung track, which shows that although he may be beset by the irritations of record company politics and unwelcome musical styles, they are merely temporary distractions; his spiritual certainty is fixed, unchanging, and permanent.

It is followed by "All Those Years Ago," Harrison's overt reaction to Lennon's death and the most scrutinized track on the album. From Al Kooper's introductory keyboard riff onward, it is clear that this is not to be a sad lament but a robust and confident celebration. Harrison's announcement that he is "shouting," rather than singing or talking, also indicates his anger; he is in no mood for forgiveness, and he means to be heard. He argues that although Lennon's message of love and peace was unambiguous, very few were prepared to listen. The message of songs like "Imagine" and "All You Need Is Love" was spurned; he was "treated like a dog," "backed up to the wall," and seen as "weird." Not only his murderer but all those who turned away or tried to belittle him are guilty in Harrison's eyes. Whether unintended or deliberate, the similarities between the treatment of Lennon and Jesus Christ are compelling; even the repeated use of "the one" to describe Lennon has religious overtones.

The presence of McCartney (backing vocals) and Starr (drums) adds to the song's significance. By participating collectively, the three are effectively signing their names to a joint statement of unity and friendship that transcends their quarrels of the past. Furthermore, it speaks on behalf of many others; Lennon's ability to influence "our smiles and our tears" refers to us all. Many moving and eloquent songs were written about his killing, including Paul Simon's "The Late Great Johnny Ace," Elton John's "Empty Garden," and Mike Oldfield's "Moonlight Shadow," but "All Those Years Ago" and, in 1981, McCartney's "Here Today" have a special, and obvious, relevance. All three songwriters in the Beatles had composed tracks about the deaths of their mothers; that Harrison and McCartney now found themselves writing (in very different ways) about the death of their friend was a poignant addition to the group's remarkable story.

"Baltimore Oriole" is the first of two Hoagy Carmichael compositions on the album. Harrison sings the languid, jazz-oriented song in the melancholy fashion of its lyrics (written by Paul Francis Webster). Until eclipsed by "Yesterday," Carmichael's "Stardust" was the world's most recorded song, and "Baltimore Oriole" is a fine example of his reflective and personalized music.

The next track provides an example of Harrison's ability to consciously adapt his writing and singing styles in order to emulate the music of others. "Teardrops" is a convincing imitation of the up-tempo songs— "Crocodile Rock," "Philadelphia Freedom," "Don't Go Breaking My Heart," "Part Time Love," and others—that had provided Elton John with a string of hits through the 1970s. John and his regular lyricist Bernie Taupin rarely attempted to use their songs as vehicles of personal or auto-biographical communication. The creative division between words and music made this immensely difficult and the majority of their colla-borations were unashamed attempts to deliver hit records. Responding to Warner Bros.'s insistence on commercial priorities, "Teardrops" is Harrison's own attempt to write a hit song. Its similarity to John's catalogue derives in part from the presence of Ray Cooper as the album's coproducer. Initially a session percussionist, Cooper had contributed to several tracks on *George Harrison*, but was best known for his long-term association, on stage and in the studio, with John. The song is a perfectly plausible piece of middle-of-the-road pop, but lacks Harrison's signature. He sings, without great conviction, of a "lonely man" who needs a "friend and lover"—a situation completely at odds with the happy reality of his own personal life.

"That Which I Have Lost" offers a very different example of the dis-junction between words and music. On the one hand, Harrison's lyrics consider the profound demands of human existence in the face of the "darkness, limitation, falsehood and mortality" that surround us; we live in a "prison," confined to the "lower world." On the other hand, the jaunty, skiffle-tinged arrangement and exaggerated vocal seems better suited to a comedy number. The inclusion of Dave Mattacks on drums is a telling factor. A stalwart of the English folk scene, Mattacks was a longtime member of Fairport Convention, and his preference for folk-blues tradi-tions helps to propel the song. While Harrison may have seen "That Which I Have Lost" as a partial return to the jug band informality of "Apple Scruffs," "Miss O'Dell," and "I Don't Care Anymore," it is one of his more bizarre compositions, and its role on the album is difficult to understand.

In complete contrast, the next track illustrates what can be achieved when words and music are complementary. "Writing's on the Wall" is a soft and gentle reflection on human mortality and the requirement for each of us to take control of our lives while we can. The longer we live, the nearer we are to dying—and, in some cases, death comes quicker than we expect. When Harrison sings of "friends" who are "drunk away, or shot away, or die away from you" there is little doubt that Lennon's killing is uppermost in his mind. But the story of the Beatles is littered with premature deaths: Stuart Sutcliffe, Rory Storm, Brian Epstein, the group's lawyer David Jacobs, Badfinger's Pete Ham, and Mal Evans had all died in tragic circumstances by the time Harrison wrote this song.

Regrets for the passage of time have, of course, been considered by a number of singer-songwriters, most notably by Dylan in "Bob Dylan's Dream," where he recalls how "we thought we could sit forever in fun," and Harrison's comment that "all the time you thought it would last" appears to directly echo that sentiment. However, it is the focus on death itself that distinguishes his approach. Indeed, in structure and vocabulary, his words are more like those of the Argentinean writer Jorge Luis Borges, whose musings on the impermanence of life in the poem "Limits" prompted him to recognize that "death reduces me incessantly." Unlike Dylan Thomas's injunction, in "Do Not Go Gentle into That Good Night," to "rage, rage against the dying of the light," Harrison (and Borges) see the inevitability of death as something to be accepted; all we can do is to prepare for it. The poetic properties of his lyrics are seen here at their best, and although such thoughtful and evocative words may seem out of place and time alongside the noisy conventions of new wave and disco, they demonstrate his desire to continue to use language in expressive ways.

"Hong Kong Blues" is the second Hoagy Carmichael song to be covered on *Somewhere in England*. Given the nostalgic evocations of life and death that run throughout several of the album's songs, its inclusion is quite deliberate, as it was identified by Harrison as one of the first songs he could remember from his childhood.[32]

The final track is "Save the World," in which Harrison launches a wide-ranging attack against the forces and policies that threaten to destroy our planet. While the debate over environmental damage would become widespread and familiar in the 1990s, it was still relatively uncommon to find it in song in the early 1980s. It may, therefore, be possible to forgive Harrison for what is an undoubtedly well-intentioned but hopelessly vague indictment of the perils we are inflicting around the globe. Few targets escape his attention. The Soviet Union with its "bombs in outer space," the destruction of the rain forest, the threat to the survival of the whale, the dangers posed by stockpiles of plutonium, the extinction of wildlife, the uncertainty of nuclear energy, and the machinations of the international arms industry are all singled out for condemnation. The problem with such a general attack is that it lacks focus and, therefore, force. In addition, some of the lyrics are trite to the point of being risible: "Now you can make your own H-bomb, right in the kitchen with your Mom" is the most fanciful example. In addition, it displays the same lack of consistency between words and music that is evident on "That Which I Have Lost." Sung in a deceptively sweet voice to a march tempo and with sound effects that include a cash register, gunfire, bombs falling, the noises of a street protest, an explosion, and the crying of a baby, the track is a chaotic collection of images, ideas, and instructions that recalls the naïveté and confusion of the *Magical Mystery Tour* project.

The public interest attracted by the release of the hit single "All Those Years Ago" helped to make *Somewhere in England* the commercial success hoped for by Warner Bros. In itself, however, it is a disappointing and somewhat messy album, especially after the rich promise of *Thirty Three & ¹/₃* and *George Harrison*. It is as if Harrison had been temporarily distracted from his creative trajectory and had lost ownership of his own music. Ska, disco, and pop compete for space alongside skiffle and prewar standards, and his lyrics range from the sublime to the ridiculous; his music alternately inspires and embarrasses. Perhaps Lennon's death delivered a bigger blow than Harrison cared to acknowledge, perhaps the absence of key personnel (Eric Clapton, Gary Moore, Russ Titelman, Steve Winwood) was unsettling, perhaps Warner Bros.'s interference undermined his self-confidence, or perhaps Cooper was an unwise choice as coproducer. Whatever the explanation, *Somewhere in England*—even the title seems to suggest confusion about its precise origins—bears the imprint of an album that has been pulled together from a variety of sources, hastily recorded, and released to satisfy commercial deadlines.

PLAYING THE GAME

Harrison's disillusionment over the creation of *Somewhere in England* was tempered by an understandable reticence to publicly criticize Warner Bros. for its interference; after all, the company had stepped in at a crucial time to provide an outlet for his music when Dark Horse's contract with A&M Records had failed. His solution was to allow someone else to vent his frustration for him. It was a strategy that had been successfully employed by John Lennon some years before. In 1973, Lennon had known that the lyrics of "I'm the Greatest," in which he recalls his time "in the greatest show on earth," would lead inevitably to accusations of arrogance had he recorded it himself; consequently, he offered it to Ringo Starr, who included it on *Ringo*, where it attracted little or no adverse reaction. Harrison decided to do exactly the same, and his song "Wrack My Brain" appeared on Starr's album *Stop and Smell the Roses* in November 1981.

The Beatles' drummer had used a variety of producers—George Martin, Pete Drake, Richard Perry, Arif Marden, Vini Poncia—on his previous seven solo albums. Recent sales had been disappointing, however, and, for the new album, he recruited a stellar cast of musical celebrities to write and produce the ten tracks: George Harrison, Paul McCartney, Harry Nilsson, Ronnie Wood, and Stephen Stills. "Wrack My Brain" was Harrison's contribution, on which he also provided lead guitar and backing vocals.

The words of the song explicitly reveal Harrison's anger at the way Warner Bros. had treated him. "I try to do my best for you," he complains, but "what you want, I can't give." He admits to self-doubt and confesses that his music may be "out of touch" with current commercial trends. In despair, he wonders whether he is "all dried up" and sees little hope that the tensions may be resolved. It is, in effect, an open letter to the executives and "men in suits" who continue to exercise so much control over the creative ambitions of the musicians they employ.

This was a facet of his career that had always infuriated Harrison. An important component of Brian Epstein's strategy when he took over the management of the Beatles had been to persuade them to conform to the conventional demands of the popular music industry until they were in a position of strength and security; then, they could begin to engage in the sort of musical experimentations and challenges that they preferred.[33] Indeed, one of the stated aims of Apple was to free potential musicians, writers, and performers from the kind of paternalistic interference that the Beatles, and others, had been forced to accept at the start of their careers.[34] That Harrison should see himself again in a position in which he was forced to modify his musical ambitions—despite his achievements and his reputation—was something he found enormously disrespectful. His resigned conclusion, in which he reluctantly agrees to "play the game," is a sad but honest reflection of the realities of the corporate business world.

Although the intention behind the lyrics is unambiguous, the dance-shuffle tempo and Starr's typically cheerful sing-along delivery tend to mask its message on record. Furthermore, the melody carries no lasting imprint; it is a pleasant but bland piece of music, whose uninspired pop origins suggest that Harrison is indeed playing the game.

GONE TROPPO

Recording of the next album, *Gone Troppo*, began just a few months after the release of *Somewhere in England*. Jointly produced by Harrison, Ray Cooper, and Phil McDonald (who had been the engineer at many previous sessions), it was made without any of the familiar nucleus of globe-trotting musicians (Eric Clapton, Klaus Voormann, Nicky Hopkins, Gary Wright, Jim Gordon, Jim Horn) who had appeared on his earlier solo albums. In their place was a collection of distinctly British performers. Some (Dave Mattacks, Herbie Flowers, Mike Moran) had appeared on *Somewhere in England* and were invited back; others, including Henry Spinetti (former drummer with the Herd, and the son of actor Victor Spinetti, who had appeared in *A Hard Day's Night*, *Help!*, and *Magical Mystery Tour*), Deep Purple's keyboards player Jon Lord, and 1960s singer-songwriter Joe Brown were there for the first time.

"Wake Up My Love" is a continuation of the Elton John–derived "Teardrops" on *Somewhere in England*. The same urgent beat, insistent synthesizer riff, and forceful vocal are efficiently combined into a song that bears little of Harrison's own style, but all the hallmarks of 1980s power pop. For the most part, the lyrics are simple and predictable: "Won't you let me in?" he pleads, "I want your love." There is some reference to his own recent experiences, when he admits that his life has "been so many ways," but there is no inventiveness or ingenuity in his message. The one point of interest is his use of the word "Christ" as either an expletive or a religious reference, or both, in the lyric "Christ, I'm looking for some light." On the one hand, it functions as an irreverent invective that betrays his frustration; on the other hand, it can be read as an appeal to the Lord for guidance. The same dual use had been employed by John Lennon in "The Ballad of John and Yoko," released as a Beatles single in 1969. On that occasion, the line "Christ, you know it ain't easy" had caused some controversy, and the song had been banned by some American radio stations; on this occasion, it went unnoticed.

"That's the Way It Goes" is a lazy, lilting ballad in which a relaxed Harrison reflects on the state of the world around him. There is little anger in his account of contemporary greed and hypocrisy, but a resigned, if regretful, admission that things are unlikely to change. The financier who is preoccupied with the position of his shares in the stock market, the speculator who seeks to invest in land, the actor who replaces his real self with a series of roles—for each of them, Harrison expresses a kind of pity that this is all they know. In the final verse, he contrasts their discontent with his own spiritual salvation. "There's a fire that burns away the lies," he tells them, but rather than attempt to convert others to his point of view, as he had done on songs like "Awaiting on You All" and "The Day the World Gets Round," he now realizes that this is the way things are. Whatever he might do or say, he has to accept that they "won't understand the way I feel." The structure of the song repeats an AABBCC rhyming scheme over four verses. The precision of his slide guitar contributions complements the overall mood of wistfulness, and the delicate arrangement supports the deliberate restraint of both words and music.

As he had done on several of his previous albums, Harrison is again happy to include a cover version. Here, he reprises "I Really Love You," a minor U.S. hit for the doo-wop group the Stereos in 1961. It was written by their former vocalist Leroy Swearingen and, like many rhythm-and-blues songs that remained relatively obscure in the United Kingdom, it was a favorite live number of Liverpool groups in the early 1960s. Harrison's faithful revival is as much a nostalgic tribute to the Mersey Beat as it is to the Stereos.

That liking for occasional idiosyncrasies is further illustrated by his decision to follow a cover version with an instrumental. "Greece" is a light and sunny tune that conjures the sound of a Mediterranean beach holiday, especially through its recurrent use of a simple, descending melodic form played on Harrison's dobro. While the bass is somewhat intrusive, the track retains a refreshing appeal. Even the superfluous spoken references to Plato, Aristotle, and "Monty Pythagoras" fail to detract from its uncluttered charm. Harrison was, by this time, heavily involved in the routine management of Handmade Films, and it is no coincidence that "Greece" sounds convincingly like an extract from a movie soundtrack. Given the success years earlier of his score for *Wonderwall* and the easy imagery that this track conveys, the real surprise may be that he had not composed more instrumental pieces.

Three years earlier, Harrison had written and recorded "Soft-Hearted Hana" as a celebration of his vacation home in Hawaii. In 1982, the Harrisons purchased a second exotic property, on Hamilton Island, one of the Whitsunday Islands in the Coral Sea, off Australia's Queensland coast. "Gone Troppo" is his celebration of that home, and the laidback lifestyle it allowed him to enjoy. The phrase "gone troppo" is his variation of "gone tropical" or the more familiar "gone native": the idea that an individual will leave behind the rules and conventions of normal life and gradually adopt the conventions of the new surroundings in which he finds himself.

The melodic structure of the song is very similar to that of the Hollies' 1968 single "Jennifer Eccles," written by the group's regular songwriting trio of Alan Clarke, Tony Hicks, and Graham Nash. It has the same repetitive, almost childlike, verse-and-chorus form; this creates a sense of playfulness that is heightened by the pidgin-English lyrics, reminiscent of some of Donovan's calypso-style compositions. Much of the song's impact comes from the pairing of Harrison and Cooper on marimba, creating a mellow backdrop that evokes the natural rhythms of sun, sea, and wind in the South Pacific. In straightforward fashion, the song describes the life Harrison is able to lead in his secluded tropical paradise far away from the cares and worries of his everyday existence in England. Instead of "shovelling snowfall," he sits "mucho in a sunshine," where he is able to enjoy the delights of "eata the papaya" and "drinking on me bottle."

Harrison was forced to sell the property in 1987, after Hamilton Island became a tourist destination for hundreds of curious day-trippers, but the pleasures of the idyllic life he enjoyed there for a while are clearly presented. Furthermore, his announcement that "it's time you know I've gone troppo" is an unequivocal and defiant message to those who have interfered with or criticized his musical output: he intends not only to live the life he chooses but also to make the music he wants.

"I've heard how some people have said that I've changed" announced Harrison in 1973, on "The Light That Has Lighted the World." A decade later, "Mystical One" opens with the same affirmation of independence from the pressures of the material world. "They say I'm not what I used to be," he admits, before going on to list some of the simple pleasures that bring meaning to his life. The image of a man "sitting by a stream," dreaming of "humming birds," and gazing into "raincloud eyes" is the image of Harrison himself: he *is* the "mystical one" of the title, who may have been temporarily lost, but has now reappeared. The relaxed tempo mirrors his own contentment, and the gentle, mandolin-inspired melody has none of the dramatic shifts and climaxes of some of his earlier songs, but retains a natural and obvious continuity. With "That's the Way It Goes" and "Gone Troppo," the song provides a clear insight into his frame of mind. Here is a man who has lived through the extravagances of the 1960s, received global acclaim for the humanitarian and spiritual facets of his music, experienced the darker side of popular music's excesses, seen the murder of one of his closest friends, and has now settled on a life away from the constant spotlight of public scrutiny. He is no longer Beatle George, nor is he the earnest teacher with a spiritual message for others; he is, at last, himself. Echoing the dictum of seventeenth-century French philosopher René Descartes—"I think, therefore I am"—Harrison arrives at a similar conclusion about the nature of his existence: "I am, yes I am. I know what I feel."

Of course, one of the events that prompted Harrison to restore a balance to his life was the birth of his son in 1978, and "Unknown Delight" is about the joy that the four-year-old Dhani has brought to him. The child is an "angel" and a "treasure," whose beauty, sweetness, and freedom gladden the hearts of all who see him. While the melody lacks the anthemic quality of Bob Dylan's "Forever Young" (written for his son Jakob in 1973), the immediate impact of Stevie Wonder's "Isn't She Lovely" (composed to celebrate the birth of his daughter Aisha in 1976), or the haunting beauty of Lennon's "Beautiful Boy" (written for his son Sean in 1980), Harrison's voice is confident and his sincerity is evident. His choice of the word "unknown" has two implications. The first is that the delights brought to Harrison by his son surpass anything that has happened before; such pleasures were hitherto unknown to him. The second, equally important, implication is that, as a father, he has much to look forward to that cannot be predicted; their future is, by definition, unknown. The creation of songs inspired by, and dedicated to, their children has gradually become a relatively common practice among contemporary singer-songwriters. Kate Bush's song to her son, "Bertie," and Paul Simon's "Father and Daughter" (written for daughter Lulu) are among the more recent examples of a genre that obliges performers to reveal their most intimate hopes and fears, in ways that would once have been considered maudlin and self-indulgent.

Harrison's ability to compose sensitive or uplifting love songs is without question, but "Baby Don't Run Away" is neither of those. Hampered by a depressing melody and a plodding rhythm, it falls midway between a celebration of mutual affection and a yearning regret for lost or unrequited love. Indeed, the emotions behind the words are difficult to discern. Although the singer repeatedly begs his lover not to go, there is no clue in the lyrics that she may be about to leave him. The alternation of "lady" and "baby" recalls the dual use of "woman" and "baby" on "Woman Don't You Cry for Me" and is symptomatic of the uncertainty running through the track. References to the "ocean," the "sea," the "stars," and the "moon" suggest a Hawaiian or Australian setting, but the overheavy arrangement does nothing to encourage such speculations. As a bright, up-tempo track, the song might have been more effective; as it stands, it is a tedious and charmless piece that even the unexpected presence of Billy Preston on backing vocals cannot improve.

Time Bandits (dir. Terry Gilliam, 1981) was one of the most celebrated and successful movies produced by Handmade Films. Made on a production budget of around $5 million, within ten weeks of its release, it had taken more than $35 million at the U.S. box office alone. The project was especially attractive to Harrison; not only did it reunite members of the Monty Python troupe (Gilliam, Michael Palin, and John Cleese), but his regular collaborator Mike Moran composed the score. Harrison wrote and recorded an additional song, "Dream Away," played at the end of the movie, which is included here on *Gone Troppo*.

Two quite separate musical elements are brought together in a repeated verse-and-chorus structure. The verses expand the Beatles' desire on "Hello Goodbye" to contrast opposing states or conditions: yes/no, stop/go, high/low, goodbye/hello. Here, Harrison offers a similar list of binary opposites—in/out, hot/cold, up/down, young/old—but amplifies them with a selection of surreal or oxymoronic fantasies: "midnight sunshine," "silent thunder," "waking sleeping." His intention is to mirror the illogicality and disruption of time travel for those characters in the film who go "tumbling through a thousand centuries." The chorus is a convincing imitation of a Gaelic or Celtic refrain—"Oh ry in eye ay, key ooh lay"—that works to create a mood in which the myths and legends of past history might come to life. In the context of the album, it is an eccentric and surprising track, but in the context of the film, it is an evocative and perfectly matched piece of music that complements Gilliam's imaginative and random meanderings through time.

The final track is "Circles," a song originally written in 1968, which, in form and content, displays a direct connection with the unspoken psychedelia that underpinned compositions like "Blue Jay Way" and "Long Long Long." A melancholy drowsiness hangs over the track, as Harrison intones a series of observations around the notion that "he who knows does not speak, he who speaks does not know." The quotation is from Lao-Tse, whose *Tao Te Ching* (written in the fifth century BC) was also the source for "The Inner Light." The lyrics proclaim that we constantly recycle the past in order to reinvent the present: our enemies become our companions, affection turns into hatred, "loss and gain" are indistinguishable. Reincarnation—the moment of rebirth, which enables the transition between death and life to take place—is the epitome of the circular nature of human existence. Whether Harrison simply retrieved a previously discarded song to use as a filler on *Gone Troppo* or was subtly announcing that his own musical journey had followed a circular route is unclear. However, the decision to use "Circles" to bring the album to a close suggests that he was, at least partially, conscious of the message it contained.

Of all Harrison's albums, *Gone Troppo* is perhaps the most difficult to evaluate. Commercially, it was an unquestionable failure, an outcome not helped by Harrison's refusal to promote it; artistically, it contains no outstanding songs and seems to be the work of a man who no longer cares about public or critical reaction. As on *Somewhere in England*, there is no consistency in the album's musical personnel. Instead, the tracks feature an assortment of friends and musicians who seem to have been invited to take part on the basis of their proximity rather than their suitability.

Rather like a sportsman whose competitive days are behind him and who no longer feels the need to exercise and train as he once did, Harrison appears disinclined to engage in challenging or innovative musical activity. This not an album by a performer who has tried, but failed, to make a memorable record, nor is it an album by someone who has been forced by managerial or organizational demands to produce a record that will suit the public taste. It is an album by someone who, in his quest for personal respite from professional obligations, has not bothered to try at all.

REEL MUSIC

Deflated by the lack of enthusiasm generated by the release of *Gone Troppo*, Harrison would not record another album for five years. He readily admitted to a profound disillusionment with the state of popular music in the mid-1980s, and the widespread perception of him as a recluse during this period was a natural consequence of his failure to engage in any of the activities expected of the contemporary rock star.[35] Even the Live Aid concerts at London's Wembley Stadium and Philadelphia's John F. Kennedy Stadium in the summer of 1985 failed to entice him out of what some feared might be a permanent retirement.[36] The presence of some of Harrison's closest friends and popular music's biggest stars (including Bob Dylan, the Who, Robert Plant and Jimmy Page, Paul McCartney, Mick Jagger, David Bowie, Eric Clapton, U2, Elton John, Tom Petty, Neil Young, and the Beach Boys) and the debt owed by the Live Aid organizers to the model provided by the Concert for Bangla Desh in 1971 made his absence all the more regrettable.

But while he took full advantage of his extended sabbatical to escape from the routine pressures of celebrity status, Harrison maintained an intermittent involvement in songwriting and recording, much of which centered around film and television commitments. The Handmade Films production *Water* (dir. Dick Clement, 1985) was a comedy starring

Michael Caine as a British diplomat in the West Indies, whose work becomes increasingly difficult after large deposits of natural mineral water are discovered on the island. In addition to briefly appearing in the film as a member of the Singing Rebels band—with Ringo Starr, Eric Clapton, Jon Lord, Ray Cooper, and Mike Moran—Harrison also cowrote, with Moran, two songs that were featured in the soundtrack. Although he neither plays nor sings on either track (the vocals are performed by American singer Jimmy Helms), the pursuit of freedom ("Celebration") and the problems of fame ("Focus of Attention") are indicative of the sort of themes with which Harrison was, once again, preoccupied.

The high school movie *Porky's Revenge* (dir. James Komack, 1985) was not a Handmade Films project, but Harrison was persuaded to contribute a song to the soundtrack by Dave Edmunds, who wrote the original music for the movie. The country-flavored "I Don't Want to Do It" is a Dylan composition that Harrison had considered recording for *All Things Must Pass*. Lyrically and musically, it has much in common with John Lennon's unfinished "Real Love," which would be completed by the remaining three Beatles in 1994.

His friendship with Edmunds also led to Harrison agreeing to appear live on stage for the first time in more than a decade. *Blue Suede Shoes: A Rockabilly Session with Carl Perkins and Friends* brought together Edmunds, Harrison, Clapton, and Starr before a live audience in London's Limehouse Studios in October 1985 to record an hour-long concert with Perkins. Televised on the Cinemax cable network in the United States and on Channel 4 in the United Kingdom, the show allowed Harrison to trade lead vocals with Perkins, and lead guitar with Clapton, on songs like "Everybody's Trying to Be My Baby," "Your True Love," "Gone Gone Gone," and "Blue Suede Shoes," all of which had been regularly covered by the Beatles in the early 1960s. His enjoyment was evident throughout, and the pleasure he derived from performing with friends was to be an important factor in shaping his musical activities over the next few years.

In the mid-1980s, the success of the action-adventure-comedy-romance movie typified by *Raiders of the Lost Ark* (dir. Steven Spielberg, 1981) and its sequel, *Indiana Jones and the Temple of Doom* (dir. Steven Spielberg, 1984), had led to a resurgence of a genre whose roots can be traced back to the 1930s and 1940s. Obvious imitations of Spielberg's films, such as *High Road to China* (dir. Brian G. Hutton, 1983) and *Romancing the Stone* (dir. Robert Zemeckis, 1984) had done well at the box office, and it was unsurprising that Handmade Films should also try to capitalize on their popularity. As it turned out, *Shanghai Surprise* (dir. Jim Goddard, 1986) was a resounding flop. Based on Tony Kenrick's 1985 novel *Faraday's Flowers*, it starred Madonna and Sean Penn as two adventurers searching for a stash of missing opium who become caught up in an exotic tale of intrigue and danger in 1930s China. Unfortunately, it suffered from a weak script, a troubled production schedule, and abysmal acting. However, *Shanghai Surprise* gave Harrison the opportunity to make his most sustained musical contribution to a film since *Wonderwall*. As well as jointly composing the score with Michael Kamen, he also provided five new songs that were featured in the movie: "Someplace Else," "Breath Away from Heaven," and "Zig Zag," all of which were held over until the following year, when they were released as part of the *Cloud Nine* project; "Hottest Gong in Town," which did not appear until 1992, when it was one of four tracks on the limited-edition *Songs by George Harrison 2* EP; and the title track, "Shanghai Surprise."

"Shanghai Surprise" is notable, among other things, for featuring a perfectly matched duet between Harrison and Vicki Brown. A member of the 1960s Liverpool trio the Vernons Girls, who had minor hits in the United Kingdom with "Lover Please" and "You Know What I Mean," Vicki Haseman had married Joe Brown, and through the 1960s and 1970s, she became one of the country's top session singers. She had provided backing vocals on "Gone Troppo," and her participation here indicates again Harrison's desire to work, wherever possible, with friends. The track (which features drummer Bruce Gary and bassist Prescott Niles from the Knack) opens with the crashing of a gong, and the Oriental flavor is maintained throughout by a reliance on the pentatonic scale and prominent percussive elements of traditional Chinese musical forms. Lyrically, the repeated declarations of cautious affection made by Harrison and Brown broadly parallel the relationship between principal characters Glendon Wasey (Penn) and Gloria Tatlock (Madonna), and the insertion of persistent rhyming schemes (liner/China/Asia Minor; surprise/eyes/fries/unwise) helps to create a momentum that drives the song forward.

Had the movie been made a few years later, it is probable that the track would have been released as a single to tie in with the film's promotion. The development of a commercial synergy between music and film—in which each mutually benefits from the success of the other—provided some of the biggest chart and box-office hits of the 1990s, including Bryan Adams's "(Everything I Do) I Do It for You" from *Robin Hood: Prince of Thieves* (dir. Kevin Reynolds, 1991), Wet Wet Wet's "Love Is All Around" from *Four Weddings and a Funeral* (dir. Mike Newell, 1994), and Celine Dion's "My Heart Will Go On" from *Titanic* (dir. James Cameron, 1997).[37] While the movie may not stand comparison with those titles, Harrison's song certainly does; it is another example of those occasions on which his personal commitment to a project and a lack of outside interference allowed him to compose songs that are both distinctive and attractive. Given its instant commercial potential, it is astonishing that it was not formally made available until 2004, when it was included on the remastered version of *Cloud Nine*.

5

Fellow Travelers

At the beginning of 1987, George Harrison was a very different person from the nervous young man who, barely out of his teens, had made his U.S. television debut on *The Ed Sullivan Show*, twenty-four years earlier. Approaching middle age, a father, and several years into his second marriage, he had been a Quarry Man (and then a Beatle) from 1958, a distinguished solo singer-songwriter since 1970, and one of the major players in the British film industry for more than a decade. And it had been five years since he had released a new album or single.

It was entirely appropriate therefore that his return to recording and performance should be prompted by the friendships with fellow musicians that had always been so important to him and that had kept him in touch—albeit from a distance—with the professional routines of a rock star. In March 1986, for example, Harrison had appeared briefly on stage at the National Exhibition Centre in Birmingham, England, with some of that city's best-known musicians, including Robert Plant and Denny Laine, during the finale of Heartbeat '86, a fundraising concert for Birmingham Children's Hospital, in which he contributed to an all-star performance of Chuck Berry's "Johnny B. Goode."

A year later, he agreed to participate in the Prince's Trust Concert at Wembley Arena.[1] Helped by Eric Clapton, Ringo Starr, Jeff Lynne, Elton John, and Phil Collins, Harrison performed "While My Guitar Gently Weeps" and "Here Comes the Sun." Apart from Harrison's immediate satisfaction with the performance itself, the event was to prove highly significant in a more permanent way. With thoughts of returning to the recording studio reawakened, Harrison invited Lynne to produce the sessions, a proposal that was quickly accepted.

Lynne had been a pivotal member of Birmingham groups Idle Race and the Move, before forming the Electric Light Orchestra with Roy Wood in 1971. When Wood left to form Wizzard in 1972, it was Lynne who assumed leadership and creative responsibility within the restructured group, which quickly became one of the most successful international acts through the 1970s and early 1980s. His career had long been guided by the example of the Beatles. One of ELO's first singles was "Roll Over Beethoven," which had, of course, been featured by Harrison on *With the Beatles.* In addition, he had contributed cover versions of "With a Little Help from My Friends" and "Nowhere Man" to the soundtrack of *All This and World War II* (dir. Susan Winslow, 1976), a documentary movie that juxtaposed the songs of John Lennon and Paul McCartney with newsreel footage of the war. Furthermore, the distinctive cello arrangements on "Strawberry Fields Forever" and "I Am the Walrus" have regularly been cited as the inspiration behind ELO's entire musical trajectory.[2]

Given the persistence of these associations, it was perhaps inevitable that Lynne and Harrison would, at some time, work together. With a nucleus of Clapton (who had recently separated from Pattie Boyd), Starr, John, and Ray Cooper, and bolstered by the reintroduction of Jim Keltner and Jim Horn, they went into the studios at Friar Park to record *Cloud Nine,* his first album since 1982.

CLOUD NINE

The blues tempo of the album's opening track, "Cloud 9," belies its subject matter, which is a declaration of altruistic love and a promise of a blissful future. Harrison invites the listener to take advantage of all that he can offer—his "love," his "time," his "smile," his "heart," his "hope"—on their journey to happiness. But he seeks nothing in return; the listener is free to "bail out" or "quit" at any time. The unselfish nature of Harrison's proposal is made clear in his acknowledgment that he is ready to step aside to allow the listener to continue independently: "You may make it all your own . . . the pieces you don't need are mine." It is a pragmatic message from a mature man, enhanced by the texture of his voice, which is noticeably deeper and rougher than on previous albums. The guitar duet between Harrison and Clapton and Horn's repeated saxophone riff flesh out a beautifully controlled and concentrated track. To his credit, coproducer Lynne resisted the temptation to embellish the production with the extravagant string and voice overdubs associated with ELO. Although the album shares its title with the Temptations' *Cloud Nine,* Harrison chose to use the numeral 9 rather than the word to differentiate between his song and that written by Norman Whitfield and Barrett Strong for the Motown group in 1969.

The immediate pop impact of "That's What It Takes" reflects very clearly the input of Lynne and Gary Wright as the song's cowriters. From Lynne's cascading introduction, through a chorus that recalls the familiar spiraling chords of Elton John, to an exquisite guitar solo played by Clapton over a background of chanting voices, this is an exemplary and cleverly constructed piece of composite pop music. As on the previous track, Harrison is contemplating a personal journey; the difference here is that this is a journey that can only be made "together." In the face of the decisions that have to be made, he urges his companion(s) to be "strong" and not to shy away from the challenges and opportunities that lie behind the waiting "open door." It is a song about the perennial need for change, and about the way in which true friendship can supply the confidence and cooperation needed to negotiate that change.

The imagery of "Fish on the Sand" presents a picture of someone lost, floundering, gasping for breath, and struggling to hold onto life. This is Harrison's vision of life without any spiritual guidance and, although he is aware of God's presence all around him, he is calling for reassurance. "You know I love you, you know I need you," he restates, in a near word-for-word duplication of his lyrics from "Long Long Long"; but at the same time, he confesses, "You know I feel a pain." However, the track has none of the solemnity suggested by its lyrics; it is an energetic, up-tempo performance that uses many of the devices favored by the Beatles of *Help!* and *Rubber Soul*: the twelve-string Rickenbacker heard on "If I Needed Someone," overlapping backing vocals, direct mode of address, and an intentionally soulful delivery. Only the falsetto voices are missing from a Beatles pastiche that is strengthened by typically direct drumming from Starr, and Lynne's re-creation of McCartney's forceful bass line.

As if to emphasize Harrison's continuing emotional connections with the Beatles, the words and melody of "Just for Today" are defined by the musical example of John Lennon. Wright's stark piano and Harrison's bleak vocal bring together the yearning quality of "Imagine" and the desperation of "Mother" to fashion a heartbreakingly honest song, in which the singer longs for a respite from the difficulties that constantly surround him, yet from which there is no escape. He dwells on the "sad and lonely" nature of his existence and movingly describes himself as "my own life's problem." While he prays for freedom, even for "one night," from the torments and doubts that plague him, it is clear (to him and to us) that there can be no reprieve. This is an insight into the human condition that recurs throughout English literature: in *Leviathan*, the seventeenth-century philosopher Thomas Hobbes characterized human life as "solitary, poor, nasty, brutish, and short"; two hundred years later, in his poem "Dover Beach," Matthew Arnold pointed to "the eternal note of sadness . . . [and] the turbid ebb and flow of human misery"; and novelist Thomas Hardy concluded *The Mayor of Casterbridge* with the desolate observation that "happiness was but the occasional episode in a general drama of pain." The song's inclusion of an evocative melodic phrase from "Unchained Melody," written by Alex North and Hy Zaret in 1955 (and also borrowed by Lennon for his version of Ben E. King's "Stand by Me") increases the sense of recognition. As a result, "Just for Today" sounds less like a new composition and more like a familiar, well-loved piece of music. Like Lennon and Dylan, Harrison is unflinching in his commitment to authenticity, however painful that might be, and his willingness to lay bare the most private recesses of his personality is never better exemplified than it is here.

In complete contrast, the Harrison–Lynne composition "This Is Love" presents four minutes of glorious and effervescent popular music that illustrates the range of his commercial sensibilities. The chorus—"This is love, this is lo-lo-lo-lo-love"—is one of the most effective hooks in his entire output, distilling the energy and optimism of the song into a single phrase. While the song is manifestly a celebration of love, it combines two recurrent and related themes in Harrison's work: awareness of our responsibility to others, and, at the same time, taking responsibility for our own actions. Taken together, they form the framework within which much of his approach to music (and life) is grounded. Love, he reminds us, is "what we are here for" and has the "power [to] overcome our problems."

Lynne's production includes a descending eight-note arpeggio and a series of ethereal guitar interventions that allow Harrison to display a finesse that is often overlooked, especially when compared to the powerful contributions of Clapton, who does not appear on this track. The upward emphasis given by Harrison to the line "out of the blue" is, of course, a deliberate reference to ELO's multimillion-selling double album *Out of the Blue*, which produced a string of hit singles in the late 1970s. And *Out of the Blue* itself shares its title with one of the tracks from the "Apple Jam" sessions that appeared on *All Things Must Pass*.

Although Harrison's songs revisited the life and times of the Beatles on many occasions, "When We Was Fab" is perhaps the most explicit in its intention. Even the title is not innocent: the use of "was," rather than the grammatically correct "were," not only recalls the conventional preference for the singular form in working-class and juvenile language (thus recapturing the Liverpudlian environment of the early Beatles) but also signals the identification of the "Fab Four" as a singular unit. The song does not seek to provide a coherent insight into the group, but rather, in keeping with the decade it depicts, presents a patchwork of apparently random images and events from the 1960s. References to some of his own songs, including "Taxman" and "Within You Without You," compete for space with musical quotations from "Magical Mystery Tour" and "I Am the Walrus." Lyrical acknowledgments to Bob Dylan ("It's All Over Now, Baby Blue") and Smokey Robinson ("You Really Got a Hold on Me") jostle alongside personal memories of drug arrests, excessive media intrusion, and unexpected tragedies that punctuated their lives. And, most tellingly, Harrison's message to Lennon—"You saw it all"—contained in "All Those Years Ago" is transformed here into the more inclusive "We did it all." The montage-like impression is reinforced by cowriter Lynne's production, which swoops and jumps from one example of the Beatles' music to another, but always returns to the psychedelic era of 1967. Charles Dickens's description (in *A Tale of Two Cities*) of another turbulent period in history as "the best of times . . . the worst of times" is mirrored in Harrison's half-remembered, half-forgotten memories of the Beatles as they were "a long time ago, when we was fab."

Harrison uses "Devil's Radio" to launch a barbed attack on the styles of talk radio and celebrity journalism that had angered him throughout his career. The song opens, and is sustained by, a repeated chorus of "Gossip, gossip." The crucial point about gossip is that its accuracy is beside the point,[3] and it is this disregard for truth that Harrison criticizes in his condemnation of the "thoughtless words" spoken by the kind of broadcaster who is "talking about what he don't know." In a series of powerful metaphors, he refers to media personnel as "vultures" who generate the "industrial waste" and "pollution" of untruth that "spreads like a weed." Against their relentless barrage of intrusion, Harrison admits that he has to "hide behind shades." "You wonder why I don't go out much?" he asks, with the same cynical rhetoric that Dylan had employed on "Desolation Row": "You asked how I was doing . . . was that some kind of joke?" In light of his gradual return to recording and performance after five years of semiretirement, it is a revealing glimpse into the mind of someone who has lived for three decades in the media spotlight.

Just as "Strawberry Fields Forever" and "I Am the Walrus" provided a blueprint for much of Lynne's subsequent career, "Devil's Radio" can be seen as an early model for the musical urgency and lyrical wit that would typify the songs on Tom Petty's *Full Moon Fever* (1989) and *Into the Great Wide Open* (1991), both produced by Lynne. With its banks of keyboards and backing vocals, powerful drumming and intense guitar, and an impassioned lead vocal, "Devil's Radio" is a fiery dose of contemporary rock 'n' roll at its most compelling.

"Someplace Else" was one of the songs written for the soundtrack of *Shanghai Surprise* and retrieved for inclusion on *Cloud Nine*. That it was composed as a contribution to an external project, rather than as a personal statement, is evident in its subject matter—a predictable lament for a love affair that seems destined to end. Saddened at the prospect of saying goodbye to his lover, and reentering the "crazy" and "untidy" life from which she has temporarily rescued him, the singer wishes that he could jettison the "loneliness" and "empty faces" to which he fears he must now return. Despite Lynne's attempts to polish the track by adding an unnecessarily lush backing, it fails to produce any tangible sense of loss or regret. In addition, the sudden bursts of percussion that are clearly intended to emphasize the singer's emotional turmoil actually have the opposite effect, interfering with the creation of a sympathetic mood. Harrison's vocal is suitably warm, and his guitar solo closely resembles the elegant sophistication of Clapton, but the song is little more than a pleasant ballad. There is a note of optimism at the end of the song, when the singer reflects once more on the problems that await him. Having sung throughout that "I wish I could leave them all in someplace else," he finally decides "I'm think I'm gonna leave them all in someplace else."

Written in 1839, Henry Wadsworth Longfellow's poem "The Wreck of the Hesperus" told the tale of a schooner that breaks up on a reef off the Massachusetts coast, leaving no survivors. Harrison uses the same title to pointedly, but good-humoredly, reject claims that he—like the ship—may also be too old, too decrepit, to survive in the tumultuous waters of rock 'n' roll. He admits that he is "no spring chicken," but chooses to compare himself with a string of iconic landmarks that remain as robust as ever—the Great Wall of China, the Eiffel Tower, and the Rock of Gibraltar. While the lyrics of "Wreck of the Hesperus" are much less abrasive toward the media than the sentiments expressed in "Devil's Radio," Harrison takes the opportunity to remind us of the "poison penmen who make up lies" and the "brainless writers [who] gossip nonsenses." And he is not alone; his defiant "I tell you I got some company" is a reference not only to the members of his current backing band but also to all the other performers from the 1960s who remain active. In addition, by mentioning Big Bill Broonzy, he implicitly focuses attention on the cohort of twentieth-century blues musicians whose histories are even longer than his own, such as Muddy Waters, Willie Dixon, Howlin' Wolf, and John Lee Hooker. The driving rock tempo and occasional blues riffs match the confident message: Harrison may have withdrawn from "the line of fire" for a while, but now he's back and, as his final words confirm, "it's alright." "Wreck of the Hesperus" tells all who care to listen not to write him off just yet—he still has work to do. Reports of his obsolescence are, as Mark Twain might have said, "greatly exaggerated."

The stately, deliberate pace and halting, fragmented interludes of "Breath Away from Heaven," the second song from *Shanghai Surprise*, may succeed in replicating the somber cadences of Chinese music within the film, but the track itself is sadly out of place on the album. In one sense, this is a great pity, since the lyrics contain some of Harrison's most beautiful words, which—consciously or unconsciously—suggest the poetry of Yoko Ono. His descriptions of "an iridescent cloud being blown by a westerly wind" and "an opalescent moon all alone in the sky of a foreign land" not only recall her fixation with clouds and sky but also mimic the rhythms of language and vocabulary that are apparent in many of the poems, or "pieces," she produced in the early 1960s.[4] The lover whose beauty is so arresting that she takes a person's breath away is a familiar theme in popular music, and the fact that Harrison manages to interpret it in a fresh way is a testament to his often overlooked skill as a lyricist. On this occasion, however, the music is too disjointed to provide a plausible setting for his words. As on "Someplace Else," the only supporting musicians are Lynne and Ray Cooper, and the absence of the other collaborators serves to emphasize the tracks' peripheral status on the album.

Cloud Nine closes with Harrison's cover version of "Got My Mind Set on You." The song had been written by Rudy Clark and recorded by James Ray in 1962; the previous year, Ray had enjoyed a hit record in the United States with another Clark composition, "If You Gotta Make a Fool of Somebody," a song that became widely known in the United Kingdom when recorded by Freddie and the Dreamers in 1963. Perhaps inspired by his memories of *Blue Suede Shoes: A Rockabilly Session with Carl Perkins and Friends*, Harrison attacks the song with an exuberance that captures the pure excitement of rock 'n' roll. Unlike songs written to create precise impressions for the scenes of a movie, this represents a different kind of setting. It conveys all the abandon, disorder, and urgent activity of a fairground at night: its neon illuminations and harsh bulbs; the heavy odor of machine oil mingled with the smells of hot dogs, fried onions, and cotton candy; the screams of those on the rides, and the shouts and laughter from the sideshows; the unmistakable undercurrent of adolescent sexuality; and the constant volume of rock 'n' roll, amplified and distorted, that envelops the whole scene. Its position as the final track on the album gives it the same kind of dramatic musical impact that made "Twist and Shout" (on *Please Please Me*) and "Money" (on *With the Beatles*) such memorable performances. His fortuitous discovery of the song not only gave Harrison a U.S. #1 single but also allowed him to reconnect with his musical roots in a very direct and effective way.

Cloud Nine is often regarded as Harrison's "comeback" album. In truth, he had never been away, but the five-year hiatus since the relative failures of *Somewhere in England* and *Gone Troppo* had certainly removed him from the familiar public position he had occupied in the 1960s and 1970s. Its immediate success and positive critical reaction did much to reestablish his damaged reputation, and there is little doubt that the rediscovery of his musical energies was prompted by Jeff Lynne. On previous albums on which Harrison had been coproducer (with Phil Spector, Russ Titelman, Ray Cooper, and Phil McDonald), his name had preceded theirs. Significantly, the credits for *Cloud Nine* reversed that policy; the album was, quite clearly, produced by Lynne and Harrison.

SINGLED OUT

With no other new songs available, Harrison was obliged to search his back catalogue to find a B side for "Got My Mind Set on You." From four unreleased tracks left over from the *Somewhere in England* sessions, "Lay His Head" was chosen to fill the gap. A simple song about friendship, it makes the point that "a true friend's shoulder to lean on" is not always easy to find. Although sung from Harrison's own point of view—he confesses that he may appear "strange" at times—the meandering lyrics make it clear that all of us have the same needs for companionship, reassurance, and understanding. "What can I tell you that you don't know already?" he asks. The pretty, country-influenced melody and his quietly double-tracked vocal are enhanced by some delicate guitar work, but this remains a routine, and rather restrained, piece of music with none of the insights of which Harrison is capable. The obvious similarity between its words and those of "Blow Away" suggest that the two may have been written in tandem or have stemmed from the same early draft.

The success of "Got My Mind Set on You" created the need for a follow-up single, and the track chosen to provide the B side of "When We Was Fab" was another song from the soundtrack of *Shanghai Surprise*. "Zig Zag" is an effective pastiche of Cab Calloway–inspired jive, designed to evoke the period setting. Set to a steady, unbroken tempo, it is led by authentic solo passages from trumpet and saxophone, supported by brief piano and (Harrison's) banjo flourishes. The recurrent sung chorus of "zig-zag, oh zig-zag" mimics exactly the style of 1930s dance-hall jazz orchestras, whose members were expected to add to the excitement by regular vocal encouragements. In the movie, it is little more than incidental background music performed by the film's Gaslight Orchestra, but on record, it is a surprisingly convincing, and obviously enjoyable, performance that confirms Harrison's familiarity with prewar styles. Nevertheless, the decisions to retrieve "Zig Zag" and "Lay His Head" from his back catalogue suggest that the songs on *Cloud Nine* had exhausted his supply of new compositions. Ironically, however, that situation was to provide the impetus that would lead to an unexpected, and celebrated, burst of collaborative creativity.

TRAVELING WILBURYS (VOLUMES 1 AND 3)

While the critical reception and commercial success of *Cloud Nine* did not immediately tempt Harrison to go back on the road, they did confirm his own belief that his return to musical activity had been well judged, and encouraged him to seek out further opportunities to make new music with some of his old friends.[5] The chance came in the summer of 1988, when Warner Bros.'s initial request for a B side to accompany the release of a third single from the album, "This Is Love," coincided with Harrison's presence in Los Angeles. Jeff Lynne was there at the same time, working with Roy Orbison to produce the Texas-born singer's first studio album (*Mystery Girl*) in ten years. Accepting Bob Dylan's offer to use his Santa

Monica studio to rehearse possible material and then taking advantage of a chance encounter with Tom Petty, the five came up with "Handle with Care." Warner Bros.'s reaction to the tape was so positive that its status was immediately elevated from a possible B side to the inspiration for a whole set of songs. In less than two weeks, Harrison, Dylan, Petty, Lynne, and Orbison wrote, recorded, and produced ten songs, calling themselves the Traveling Wilburys.

The concept of a "supergroup" was first introduced in the late 1960s, when the desire by popular musicians to move away from traditional forms of membership and association toward the kind of flexible, temporary liaisons common in jazz began to take shape.[6] The union between 1966 and 1968 of Eric Clapton (from John Mayall's Bluesbreakers), Ginger Baker (from Graham Bond's Organization), and Jack Bruce (from Manfred Mann) was perhaps the earliest example of supergroup formation and presentation. For a few years, the practice became commonplace among rock's elite performers. In 1968, Stephen Stills, Mike Bloomfield, and Al Kooper combined to record their *Super Sessions* album. In 1969, Clapton and Baker invited Steve Winwood (Traffic) and Ric Grech (Family) to form Blind Faith. In the same year, Humble Pie brought together Peter Frampton (the Herd), Steve Marriott (Small Faces), Greg Ridley (Spooky Tooth), and Jerry Shirley (Little Women). The practice reached its apogee in the early 1970s when two supergroups of contrasting styles and sounds mapped out alternate directions for rock music's future: the West Coast harmonies of Crosby, Stills, Nash, and Young, and the progressive aesthetics of Emerson, Lake, and Palmer.

The formation of the Traveling Wilburys not only revived a practice that had gradually become less frequent during the 1980s—it also convinced many that its five members constituted the ultimate supergroup. For Harrison, the motivation was simple: he had long relied on a semipermanent set of familiar musicians to support his recordings, and the Traveling Wilburys was merely a more formal extension of his preferred way of working. To consolidate the fiction of a group identity, they adopted fresh names: Otis Wilbury (Lynne), Nelson Wilbury (Harrison), Charlie T. Jnr Wilbury (Petty), Lefty Wilbury (Orbison), and Lucky Wilbury (Dylan). In addition, the group's first album, released in November 1988, did not distinguish individual songwriting credits but, in keeping with the spirit of musical camaraderie that had brought them together, listed all songs as group compositions. However, it is apparent that each song bears the immediate imprint of its significant contributor(s), and three of the ten tracks on *Traveling Wilburys, Volume 1*, jointly produced by "Otis and Nelson Wilbury," carry Harrison's distinctive musical and vocal signature.

The completed version of "Handle with Care" that opens the album is a glorious example of the way in which a synthesis of contrasting talents can produce music that is effortless and natural. Orbison's brief, twice-repeated chorus, in which he laments his "lonely" condition, reproduces both the form (a powerful, soaring vocal) and content (a melancholy introspection) that distinguished so many of the memorable hit singles he wrote and performed thirty years earlier, including "Only the Lonely," "Running Scared," "In Dreams," and "It's Over." And the plea in Dylan's short bridge to "put your body next to mine" echoes the straightforward sexuality he displayed in a clutch of songs from the late 1960s, such as "You Ain't Going Nowhere," "I'll Be Your Baby Tonight," "Lay Lady Lay," and "Tonight I'll Be Staying Here with You." These two interludes alone make the song noteworthy, but it is Harrison's ongoing and frank assessment of the circumstances that have dogged his career that finally makes it such a compelling, and rewarding, track.

Against a continuously descending guitar line and an unrelenting drumbeat, Harrison recalls a life in which he has been "beat up, battered round, sent up, shot down." Some of his descriptions ("stuck in airports, sent to meetings") indicate the routine pressures faced by any popular musician; others ("fobbed off, ridiculed, over-exposed, commercialized") refer rather more pointedly to specific events in his own life, with and after the Beatles. During the period of recording, Harrison was beginning a ten-year court battle against Denis O'Brien, his business partner in Handmade Films, over allegations of embezzlement and fiscal mismanagement. A Los Angeles court would eventually find in favor of Harrison and award him a financial judgment of more than $11 million, but the deliberate references to being "robbed" and "fooled" suggest not only anger but also personal disappointment at finding himself once again in a legal arena of claims and counterclaims with former friends. However, his resolution to "clean it up myself" and the ironic exclamation "Oh, the sweet smell of success!" show that his idiosyncratic brand of optimistic, if slightly resigned, cynicism is still intact.

The song's confident melody is matched by the strength of Harrison's voice, and it is apparent that the enjoyment he experienced while recording *Cloud Nine* remains undiluted. The track was a hit single in the United States and Britain, but its real significance rests less on that fact than on its symbolic fusion of three revolutionary moments in the history of rock 'n' roll that had their beginnings in Sam Phillips's Sun Studio in Memphis, in the clubs and bars of Liverpool and Hamburg, and in the folk venues of New York's Greenwich Village.

On "Heading for the Light," Harrison delivers his most joyous account to date of the spiritual journey that had saved him from despair. Taken by themselves, his words seem to indicate a bleak, forlorn assessment of his former self: he admits to being "lost in the night," remembers how "blue and lonely" he has been, "close to the edge" on occasions. The reference to "jokers and fools on either side" may have been suggested by Gerry Rafferty's "Stuck in the Middle with You," recorded by Stealers Wheel in

1972, in which Rafferty complains of "clowns to the left of me, jokers to the right." But Harrison's surging melody (a more mature reinterpretation of "I Want to Tell You") and Lynne's ebullient production transform "Heading for the Light" into an exhilarating track that celebrates his current life instead of regretting his past. Indeed, there is a clear sense of personal triumph in the recognition that his "dreams are coming true" and "there's nothing in the way" to prevent him from reaching his goal. As he nears the end of the journey, the song gathers momentum, and a false ending allows Jim Horn to contribute a galloping saxophone solo that confirms its positive intent. Like "Handle with Care," the song is suffused with an unadorned enjoyment that is perfectly distilled in Harrison's bright, supple vocal.

Harrison's third major contribution, and the album's closing track, is the country-influenced "End of the Line." Although the lead vocals are shared among Harrison, Lynne, and Orbison, it is Harrison's musical approach that defines the track. Lyrically, he returns to the kind of personal and professional observations he offered in "Wreck of the Hesperus." His words are the reflections of a man who—like his fellow Wilburys—has paid his dues and now feels able to relax, take his time, and live the life he chooses. The theme is a familiar one among rock's elite (and Harrison's closest friends): Dylan's intention to "sit here so contentedly and watch the river flow" (in "Watching the River Flow") and Lennon's description of a life "just sitting here watching the wheels go round" (in "Watching the Wheels") are the musical antecedents of the satisfaction Harrison now gains from simply "riding around in the breeze."

Unlike many of his previous songs, the track shows no malice or hostility toward those who have disappointed him; instead, his hope is to "live and let live" and to "forgive" those who have wronged him. And it is a statement about his future aspirations, too: even when he is "old and gray," he believes that "everything will work out fine." Petty's chorus adds to the overall mood of contentment, and the frequent assertions that "it's alright" aptly summarize Harrison's state of mind. It is a song whose country roots and laidback sentiments might have made it an ideal vehicle for another contemporary supergroup, the Highwaymen, whose members (Johnny Cash, Waylon Jennings, Kris Kristofferson, and Willie Nelson) used their occasional liaisons in recordings and performance to display exactly the same kind of musical and mutual affection that had brought the Wilburys together.

Within a few weeks of its release, the worldwide success of *Traveling Wilburys, Volume 1* was tempered by the sudden death of Orbison, who suffered a massive heart attack in December 1988. Amid the speculation about future recordings was a persistent rumor that Orbison's replacement would be a fellow singer-songwriter from the early 1960s, Del Shannon. In 1963, Shannon's version of "From Me to You" had made him the first

U.S. artist to cover a Beatles song. Petty had produced Shannon's 1982 album, *Drop Down and Get Me*, and Lynne his 1989 album, *Rock On*, on which Petty and the Heartbreakers also featured as supporting musicians. In addition, Shannon and Harrison had contributed backing vocals to Lynne's first solo album, *Armchair Theatre*, released in 1990. Their involvement suggested a natural continuation of the relationship within the Traveling Wilburys, but in February 1990, Shannon's suicide abruptly ended any further conjecture.

When *Traveling Wilburys, Volume 3* was released in October 1990 (there was no volume 2), the album was dedicated to Lefty Wilbury, and the four remaining members had adopted new personas: Spike Wilbury (Harrison), Muddy Wilbury (Petty), Clayton Wilbury (Lynne), and Boo Wilbury (Dylan). The songs were again credited to all members equally, but, as before, their individual origins are apparent, and three tracks are distinguished by significant contributions from Harrison.

"Inside Out" provided an opportunity for Dylan and Petty to continue a private, and somewhat tuneless, joke by exchanging nonsense lyrics about the "yellow" state of the world. Harrison's ascending chorus introduces, all too briefly, a much-needed note of originality. Not only does its musical transition interrupt a sluggish series of repetitive sequences, but its words carry an undefined sense of menace: stressing the need to be watchful, he warns that "something's happening out there." Unfortunately, the climax toward which it seems to be leading evaporates in favor of more inconsequential wordplay from the two lead vocalists, but for a moment, Harrison's lyrics provide an alternative, and slightly mysterious, direction.

The shared vocals of "New Blue Moon" exemplify, and fully justify, the musical partnership between Harrison and Lynne. Their elongated harmonies and ringing guitars synthesize elements of the Beatles in the 1960s and ELO in the 1970s to produce a warm and mellow soundscape. Waiting and hoping for love to be reciprocated is hardly a new theme, and the words are among the simplest ever written by Harrison, yet the lyrical comparison to "looking for a new blue moon" matches perfectly the gentle and unforced beauty of the song. Dylan's overenthusiastic chorus detracts from the unhurried mood, but the song is one of the Wilburys' most memorable. An instrumental version of the song was used as the B side of the Traveling Wilburys' single "Wilbury Twist."

"You Took My Breath Away" reworks some of the ideas and imagery of "Breath Away from Heaven." Musically and lyrically, the song presents a repetitive series of observations in which Harrison expands the basic theme of the title. In the first verse, he merely complains of his position now that his lover has left him: "Look at the mess I'm in," he accuses. The second verse uses the metaphor of music to describe his confusion: the "words don't fit," the lyrics are "hard to rhyme," and the melody is "impossible to play." The juxtaposition of song and emotion is a powerful and effective strategy, as Cole Porter's "how strange the change from major to minor" showed so movingly on "Ev'ry Time We Say Goodbye," and Harrison's words contain some of the same originality and sensitivity. It is all the more puzzling that in the third and final verse, he misses the opportunity to develop the comparison further and chooses instead the rather clumsy image of a broken-down car to complete the description. "You knocked my headlights out" and "I've lost a wheel" sound like phrases written in haste by a man whose concentration is waning. Lynne's production provides a dramatic backing that is too ponderous for the song's sentiments, and the track calls out for the range and purity of Orbison's voice to transform it into the powerful ballad it was clearly intended to be.

Musically, *Traveling Wilburys, Volume 3* is dominated by Petty, and Harrison's contribution to the album is primarily as coproducer. In contrast to the spontaneity of their previous album, several of the tracks appear rather trite and predictable. Whereas *Volume 1* contained several outstanding songs ("Handle with Care," "Heading for the Light," Orbison's "Not Alone Any More," and Dylan's "Tweeter and the Monkey Man"), only "New Blue Moon" is genuinely impressive, and some ("Inside Out," "7 Deadly Sins," and "Wilbury Twist") are little more than self-indulgent pranks.

In retrospect, the Traveling Wilburys project was an incidental, rather than integral, part of Harrison's career. Clearly hugely enjoyable at the time, its importance resides less in its musical output than in the fact that it gave Harrison the opportunity to collaborate formally with some of the major influences in his professional life. His adamant belief that John Lennon would also have been an automatic and enthusiastic member of the group[7] has led to speculation about who else might have been involved (Elvis Presley? Buddy Holly?) had the course of popular music history been different. However, for Harrison, the fulfillment and enjoyment the project gave him was sufficient in itself.[8]

BEST OF DARK HORSE, 1976–1989

Although his membership (and de facto leadership) of the Traveling Wilburys was the most visible of his activities from 1988 to 1990, Harrison was also able to devote time to completing a number of additional projects during that period. The first of these was to cooperate in the release of *Best of Dark Horse, 1976–1989*, a compilation album to which he was contractually committed and to which—given his lingering resentment over the release of his only previous compilation album, *Best of George Harrison*, in 1976—he had readily agreed to provide three new songs. With Lynne, ELO pianist Richard Tandy, and Deep Purple drummer Ian Paice, he recorded the tracks at the studio in Friar Park in July 1989.

"Poor Little Girl" sees Harrison integrate various musical components to create a pastiche of "perfect pop." Vocally, he returns to the derivative brand of Elton John–inspired urgency that marked "Teardrops" and "Wake Up My Love." Musically, the song's forceful tempo and much of its melody are driven by the same plucked guitar riff used on ELO's "Livin' Thing." Lyrically, he revisits the familiar theme of frustrated teen-age love. The result is a knowingly assembled, but surprisingly efficient, track that shows once again that he can be a master of pop music in its purest form. In addition, the fact that "Poor Little Girl" bears an instant and obvious resemblance to many of Del Shannon's hit singles in the early 1960s, including "Keep Searchin'," "Little Town Flirt," and the similarly titled "Hey Little Girl" adds further weight to the rumors that Shannon was very much in Harrison's mind as a potential replacement for Orbison in the Traveling Wilburys.

However, what makes the song his own is his use of verse and chorus to contrast the confusions of adolescent desire against his own preoccupation with universal love. Thus, one strand describes the "horny boy [with] one thing on his mind" and the "poor little girl with her head in the air" (a kissing cousin of Shannon's "little town flirt with that look in her eye"). The other explores Harrison's "need and desire to express what's inside" and "the endless amount of joy" that he knows is there for all of us. Love is thus simultaneously exposed as a personal pursuit and a spiritual quest, and the added confidence with which he sings of the latter signals the relative importance he attaches to them.

"Cockamamie Business" is another in an increasingly long list of Harrison's songs in which he reviews his own career. As on "Sue Me Sue You Blues," "This Guitar (Can't Keep from Crying)," "When We Was Fab," and "Handle with Care," he looks back with cynicism rather than nostalgia over the events of his life. A detailed inventory of places and events in the Beatles' story, including the BBC (which gave the group its first regular radio show, *Pop Go the Beatles*, in 1963), the Marquee (the club at the heart of the "swinging London" scene in the mid-1960s), the *New Musical Express* (sung in its abbreviated form, so that *NME* sounds suspiciously like "enemy"), and Ed Sullivan (whose TV show introduced the Beatles to North America in early 1964) is presented, alongside some more personal recollections: "lost the missus" is his blunt assessment of the failure of his first marriage. Interspersed with these is a rerun of his concern with environmental damage that featured on "Save the World": he refers to the disappearance of the "ozone ring" and blames McDonald's and Burger King for the destruction of the rain forest. However, its upbeat delivery, distinctive guitar riff (a variation of a motif from "Hong Kong Blues"), and evocative bass line (borrowed from Johnny Kidd and the Pirates' "Shakin' All Over") save the song from being a catalogue of despair and turn it into a satisfying example of contemporary rock that reaffirms his spirit of resistance. Echoing Dylan's intention in "Tangled Up in Blue" to "keep on keepin' on," Harrison issues a similar message: "You do what you can, you can't do much more" is his perennial advice. And his closing confession that he "didn't want to be a star, wanted just to play guitar" tells us how he would prefer to see himself—not as a Beatle, a former Beatle, or a Traveling Wilbury, but, quite simply, as a musician.

The trilogy of new songs is completed by "Cheer Down," which also featured on the soundtrack of *Lethal Weapon 2* (dir. Richard Donner, 1989). Cowritten with Petty, it is another exemplary piece of commercial rock, which allows Harrison to demonstrate his considerable virtuosity on slide guitar. In this instance, the whimsical words are largely irrelevant; they tell the listener not to worry, whatever may happen—"when your teeth drop out" (a repeat of the warning given to Clapton in the lyrics of "Savoy Truffle") or "if your dog should be dead"—because his love will always be there. Paice's drumming drives the whole track forward and provides the foundation upon which Harrison is able to build a number of powerful guitar contributions that dominate, and ultimately define, the track.

Faced with a formal obligation to compose and record three new songs, and limited time in which to do so, it might have been expected that Harrison would come up with nothing more than "fillers" of adequate, rather than outstanding, quality. That he delivered three solid, well-crafted tracks illustrates the resurgence of confidence and enthusiasm that his participation in the Traveling Wilburys had prompted. It also, beyond doubt, demonstrated his flexibility. Whether working within the chameleon strains of Dylan's folk-country-rock, Orbison's rock 'n' roll roots, or Paice's contemporary heavy metal rhythms, Harrison seems able to adjust his musical ambitions with consummate ease. Of course, after three decades of superstardom, he was in a position to pick and choose his musical peers, but the music he was producing in the late 1980s and early 1990s is among the most sustained and satisfying of his career.

Songs by George Harrison

Although uncommon in the United States, the EP (Extended Play) record was a familiar format in the United Kingdom and Europe during the 1960s. Originally intended to bridge the gap (in price and length) between singles and albums, the seven-inch vinyl EP typically contained four songs (two per side) and was played, like a single, at 45 rpm. EP sales were included in the U.K. singles charts, and the Beatles enjoyed several successful releases in this format: in 1963, *Twist and Shout*, containing four songs from their *Please Please Me* album, became the first EP to enter the U.K. Top Ten and eventually sold 800,000 copies; *The Beatles' Hits*, *The Beatles No. 1*, and *All My Loving* repeated the practice of compiling single and/or album tracks; in July 1964, *Long Tall Sally* was their first EP to contain previously unreleased songs ("Long Tall Sally," "I Call Your Name," "Slow Down," "Matchbox"); and in December 1967, the soundtrack of *Magical Mystery Tour* was released in the United Kingdom as a double EP and reached #2 (behind the group's "Hello Goodbye") in the singles charts. Other British performers, including the Rolling Stones (*The Rolling Stones, 5 x 5, Got Live If You Want It*) and the Searchers (*Ain't Gonna Kiss Ya*) were among those quick to copy the Beatles' strategy.

Harrison's decision to return to the format in 1988 was therefore not altogether surprising. The four tracks on *Songs by George Harrison* brought together a live version of "For You Blue" from the 1974 Dark Horse tour, "Lay His Head" (the recently released B side of "Got My Mind Set on You"), and two additional tracks left over from the *Somewhere in England* sessions: "Sat Singing" and "Flying Hour." What was surprising was the form the release took: instead of being available to all, the EP was sold as a limited-edition, high-cost package that remained unheard, unseen, and unavailable to the vast majority of international audiences.

The twelve-bar blues origins of "For You Blue" are emphasized in this rather ragged live rendition, which fails to capture the spontaneous appeal of the version that appeared on *Let It Be*. Harrison's enthusiasm is evident, but his voice is clearly suffering after several weeks on the road, and much of the performance is given over to instrumental solos by Emil Richards (percussion), Robben Ford (guitar), and Willie Weeks (bass).

"Sat Singing" marries a sublime melody with an intimate account of the spiritual joys of meditation. Warm, rippling rhythms, led by Harrison's rising and falling guitar progressions, establish an unbroken sense of serenity and calm that is matched by the mellow tone of his voice. From the "noonday sun" until "the sun has sunken low," he sits in absolute contentment. Oblivious to the passage of time, and forgetting the cares and concerns of everyday life, he experiences intense bliss, as the "glow" and "golden flow" through which he passes enable him to become one with God. Harrison's regular commitment to meditation—sometimes for hours at a time—had provided a spiritual refuge from the material world since the late 1960s, and the song's final promise that he would "gladly kiss it all goodbye" to prolong the mystical encounter with the Lord leaves little doubt about his willingness to "surrender" to God's will. The use of "sat" in the title carries a double significance. On one level, it refers directly to Harrison's situation as he sits, as if in a dream, under the "clear blue sky" of a summer afternoon. But, in addition, *sat* is a Hindu word for "existence" or "truth," and the song thus presents a direct connection to his search for understanding and self-realization.[9]

"Flying Hour" returns to the theme—our place in time—that had exercised Harrison in "Be Here Now." While some people are nostalgic for what they fondly imagine to be the "good old days," and others live in perpetual hope that they might "see better days" ahead, he reminds us that the present is all that matters. However tempting they might appear, the past is "gone" and the future "may not be." But, while "Be Here Now" presented the same observations by musically evoking the mystery and profundity of time, here Harrison chooses to deliver his reflections in a much more relaxed manner. Unfortunately—or perhaps deliberately—the serious intent of his lyrics is lost within a competent, but routine, mid-tempo pop production.

A second limited-edition EP, *Songs by George Harrison 2*, was released in 1992. On this occasion, the four tracks were his original demo version of "Life Itself," a live version of "Hari's on Tour (Express)" from the 1974 Dark Horse tour, "Hottest Gong in Town" from the soundtrack of *Shanghai Surprise*, and "Tears of the World," the final unused track from the *Somewhere in England* sessions.

Harrison's delicate performance of "Life Itself," on which he supplies all vocal and guitar tracks, is a reminder that, in their formative stages, songs can possess a natural simplicity that is sometimes lost in later versions. Although the transitions from vocal to instrumental passages are a little tentative, and his voice rather hesitant, it is nonetheless a charming example of Harrison's gentle and persuasive style. In complete contrast, "Hari's on Tour (Express)" is a multilayered, boisterous performance that announced the start of each of Harrison's North American concerts, just as it had opened the *Dark Horse* album.

"Hottest Gong in Town" is a period pastiche that again sees Harrison imitating the 1930s scat style of Cab Calloway. Calloway's best-known song was "Minnie the Moocher," but among his other recordings was a version of "Kicking the Gong Around," written by Harold Arlen and Ted Koehler. "Kicking the gong" was prewar slang for smoking opium, and Harrison's choice of title is a reference to the movie's plot and to Calloway himself. While the lyrics urge the audience to get down to the Chinatown club owned by "Si-Fu Yow," it is uncertain whether its attractions are based around the entertainment it offers or the availability of drugs; either way, "once you've been down there, you're never gonna go back home." Harrison clearly enjoys the opportunity to try out an unfamiliar singing style and to demonstrate his prowess on the banjo, and it is an enjoyable, if minor, example of his diverse musical interests. The song was included in the movie during an early restaurant scene where it is performed by the club's resident band, the Gaslight Orchestra (as opposed to the Electric Light Orchestra), and Harrison's fleeting appearance as its featured vocalist continued the Hitchcockian liking for cameo screen roles that he had previously revealed in *Monty Python's Life of Brian* and *Water*.

"Tears of the World" is a companion piece to "Save the World." Not only does it present a near-identical critique of the political and industrial agencies that are endangering the planet, but it does so with the same lack of precision and, therefore, impact. He accuses "war mongers," "leaders," and "big business" of conducting policies without any regard for their consequences. Their "unrighteous actions" and "bad jazz" have created problems that need to be urgently resolved, but there seems to be no immediate desire to do so. His reference to "saviours" who have warned of the dire consequences that lie ahead makes it unclear if he regards himself as being among them, and rather confusingly, his lyrical shifts between "our" and "my" in his catalogue of fears suggest that he sees himself simultaneously as part of a community *and* as a lone voice.

Toward the end of the track, his question "Where's your love been sleeping?" draws directly from the lyrics of "While My Guitar Gently Weeps" but, despite an attempt to emulate its iconic guitar solo, there is no comparison between the haunting beauty of that earlier song and the rather cumbersome, uneven music here. Observations about the general effectiveness of popular music's political functions range from an optimistic belief that it can play a decisive role in changing the political and cultural environment of which it is a part[10] to the cynical assertion that it can provide little more than a superficial and trivial commentary,[11] but whatever the truth, there is little that is memorable in "Tears of the World," either in its music or its message.

Loose Ends

In the two decades since he had organized the Concert for Bangla Desh to provide financial help for that country's refugees, Harrison had tended to distance himself—at least, publicly—from many of the fund-raising events designed to raise awareness of specific humanitarian and charitable causes. However, when the fall of Romania's Communist government in December 1989 revealed the appalling circumstances in which tens of thousands of abandoned children (many of whom were suffering from tuberculosis, hepatitis-B, or syphilis or were HIV-positive) had been forced to live under Nicolae Ceausescu's dictatorship, there was an immediate worldwide response. Among those who became involved in the Romanian Angel Appeal was Olivia Harrison; she quickly recruited the other Beatles' wives, Linda McCartney, Barbara Bach, and Yoko Ono, and they persuaded Harrison to put together a compilation album, featuring tracks by some of the world's leading performers, to raise additional money for the Romanian orphans or, as they became known, "Ceausescu's children." As a result, *Nobody's Child* was released in April 1990. The musicians donating songs for inclusion included Van Morrison, Elton John, the Bee Gees, Stevie Wonder, Guns N' Roses, and Ringo Starr. Harrison appeared on three of the fifteen tracks.

The first is the title track, "Nobody's Child," performed by the Traveling Wilburys. Although it was popularized by Hank Snow in the United States and Lonnie Donegan in the United Kingdom, the song possessed an additional relevance for Harrison, as it was one of the numbers the Beatles had recorded with Tony Sheridan in Hamburg thirty years earlier. The version here is, unsurprisingly, an uncomplicated and straightforward treatment of the song. In the second verse, Harrison replaces the original words with an alternative set of lyrics that more accurately, and poignantly, reflects the conditions in Romania faced by infants who have "long since stopped crying, as no one ever hears."

The acoustic duet between Harrison and Paul Simon of "Homeward Bound" (originally recorded by Simon and Garfunkel in 1966) was excavated from an edition of NBC-TV's *Saturday Night Live*, broadcast in 1976. Harrison's voice lacks the purity of Art Garfunkel's, and although the opportunity to hear two iconic singer-songwriters together on a record is a welcome one, the track is more of an interesting curio than an overlooked masterpiece. Harrison and Simon were obviously close friends in the mid-1970s; Simon had also appeared (as himself) in the spoof TV documentary *All You Need Is Cash*, which followed the rise and fall of the Rutles as the "prefab four" conquered the world, and it is surprising that the friendship led to no more musical liaisons.

The third track on which Harrison appears is Eric Clapton's version of "That Kind of Woman," which extends the sequence of robust, blues-influenced rock begun on *Cloud Nine* and continued by the three additional tracks on *Best of Dark Horse, 1976–1989*. Composed but never recorded by Harrison, his participation here is limited to guitar and backing vocal. In keeping with the traditional ethos of rock 'n' roll—which is, after all, a euphemism for making love—the words are lustful, rather than loving. The singer is looking for a woman who is "kind of crazy" and who has "the wickedest smile that I've ever seen." The unrelenting rhythm adds to the air of overt sexuality, and the "promises" in the woman's eyes leave little room for doubt about what is on offer: "I think I know what I'm looking for," he concludes. Another version (again featuring Harrison on guitar and vocals) was released in the same year by former Thin Lizzy guitarist Gary Moore on his solo album, *Still Got the Blues*. While the song may appear an odd choice to be included on a charity album devoted to sick and starving children, both recordings emphasize the enormous range of Harrison's musical styles—from commercial pop and gentle ballads to spiritual anthems and no-nonsense rock 'n' roll.

Perhaps the most bizarre project in which Harrison chose to become involved in this period was to contribute to the soundtrack of a made-for-television children's cartoon series about the adventures of a group of cricket-playing rabbits. In 1986, cricket enthusiast David English had formed the Bunbury Cricket Club, a celebrity fund-raising team that has so far donated more than £10 million to charitable causes in the United Kingdom. An offshoot of the project was a collection of cartoon story books, written by English and illustrated by Jan Brychta. In 1992, these stories were used as the basis for an animated television series, and the musical soundtrack from the series, which included songs by the Bee Gees, Elton John, Eric Clapton, Level 42, and Dave Dee, Dozy, Beaky, Mick and Tich, was released in October 1992 under the title *Bunbury Tails*.

Harrison's contribution was a song he had recorded some years earlier with his son, Dhani, and Ravi Shankar. "Ride Rajbun" opens with a delicate sitar solo from Shankar, before father and son share a nursery-rhyme-like chorus, in which Rajbun is urged to leave his home in Delhi and ride away on his cycle—"across the mountains, through the valleys, across the desert, through the forest"—in search of his destiny. Like many characters in nursery rhymes and fairy tales who must leave the security of their home in order to discover themselves (Dick Whittington's trip to London, Jack's adventures in the land at the top of the beanstalk, Pinocchio's flight from Geppetto, and Dorothy's journey to Oz, to name a few), Rajbun has a "quest" that awaits him, which he must confront without "fears" or "tears." But the message is overwhelmingly positive: "Bunbury stands for freedom, being young, and having fun."

Perhaps Harrison's eagerness to take part in this project was prompted by fond memories of the childhood affection that his generation held for a host of familiar cartoon characters during the television-free era of the 1940s and early 1950s in which the Beatles grew up. In the late 1980s, Starr had been the narrator of the *Thomas the Tank Engine* television cartoon series, adapted from the postwar stories of the Reverend W. V. Awdry, and Paul McCartney had scripted and produced the animated film *Rupert and the Frog Song* (dir. Geoff Dunbar, 1985) derived from the original Rupert Bear stories, created by Mary Tourtel and Alfred Bestall in the 1920s and 1930s. At the pinnacle of their success, and in the midst of their psychedelic years, several Beatles songs—"Yellow Submarine," "All Together Now," "Cry Baby Cry"—had continued to show their fascination with the conventions of the children's nursery rhyme. They had even (reluctantly) agreed to endorse a U.S. television cartoon series in which they were the leading characters[12] and had, of course, appeared briefly in the closing scenes of the animated film *Yellow Submarine*. Even so, the eccentric combination of cricket and rabbits makes *Bunbury Tails* a surprising outlet for Harrison's first piece of wholly Indian music since "The Inner Light," and it is probable that his participation was prompted by the involvement of close friends such as John and Clapton.

Finally, one remaining loose strand in Harrison's musical output was partially resolved in 1994. In 1977, he had written and recorded "Mo," a fiftieth-birthday tribute to Mo Ostin, the chairman of Warner Bros. Records, which was then distributing Harrison's Dark Horse releases. Ostin had been persuaded by Frank Sinatra to leave Verve Records in 1963, to take charge of his Reprise label after it had been sold to Warner Bros. Ostin stayed there for more than thirty years, and under his guidance, Warner-Reprise shaped the careers of such performers as Joni Mitchell, Neil Young, the Grateful Dead, Van Morrison, James Taylor, Fleetwood Mac, Ry Cooder, and Paul Simon. The song had never been publicly available, but in 1994, when Ostin left the company, it was included on a commemorative six-box CD set (*Mo's Blues*) given exclusively to the six hundred invited guests who attended his retirement party.

Its descending guitar chimes and soaring melody recall the musical elements that had previously made "You" and "Crackerbox Palace" outstanding examples of Harrison's commercial songwriting style. It is not, as might be expected, a casual or spontaneous improvisation (as "It's Johnny's Birthday" had been), but rather a carefully crafted and fully formed track that would sit comfortably on any of his albums. Vocally and instrumentally, Harrison is at his most engaging, and his obvious pleasure in creating the song is immediately evident. In addition to addressing Ostin as Mo, he also uses the word as a variation of "more," as he wishes him "mo' love," "mo' smiles," and "mo' hits." His assurance that "a smile that you give out comes back always to you" is again reminiscent of the Beatles' insight that "the love you take is equal to the love you make," and the track possesses much of the joyous quality that permeated their music. However, the sentiments of friendship and good will were soon tested. Less than a year after Harrison presented him with the song, Ostin rejected several of the planned tracks on *Somewhere in England*; angry and frustrated, Harrison's response was to write "Blood from a Clone."

LIVE IN JAPAN

Harrison had not toured since his ill-received concert dates in North America to promote *Dark Horse* in 1974, after which he had angrily insisted that his touring days were behind him.[13] The success of the two Traveling Wilburys albums had encouraged him, and other group members, to take part in several impromptu gigs in and around Los Angeles with performers like Taj Mahal and John Fogerty, but he had (unlike McCartney and Starr) declined to appear at Liverpool's Tribute to John Lennon concert in October 1990, and it was widely assumed that any future live appearances would be restricted to the occasional, unannounced guest spot. His decision to embark on a three-week tour of Japan in December 1991 was therefore a huge surprise. Harrison's own explanation listed three reasons: a sentimental curiosity to take part in one last tour; the advantages of performing away from the media glare of the United States or United Kingdom; and the encouragement of Eric Clapton, who had generously invited Harrison to accompany his band, which included percussionist Ray Cooper, bassist Nathan East, organist Greg Phillinganes, and backing vocalists Andy Fairweather-Low, Katie Kissoon, and Tessa Niles.[14]

The series of concerts opened at the Yokohama Arena on December 1, and ended at Tokyo's Dome Stadium on December 17. The subsequent album, *Live in Japan*, was released in July 1992 and contained the nineteen songs performed nightly on stage by Harrison; it was credited to "George Harrison with Eric Clapton and his Band" and produced by "Spike and Nelson Wilbury." The four songs performed by Clapton ("Pretending," "Old Love," "Badge" and "Wonderful Tonight") were not included on the album.

It is significant that Harrison chose to open the set with a trio of Beatles tracks before performing any selections from his solo career. The opening riff of "I Want to Tell You" reproduces exactly the guitar introduction he used for its recording on *Revolver*. Although this live version lacks the sharpness of the studio track, it does have the added interest of some extended guitar solos (a rather tentative attempt from Harrison, and a much more confident contribution from Clapton) that extend the song to twice its original length. The backing singers' replication of Lennon and McCartney's harmonies are surprisingly able, and Harrison's vocal makes few changes to the original.

"Old Brown Shoe" again faithfully reprises the Beatles' treatment, although there are stronger piano and organ parts, and another guitar solo by Clapton, to propel the track. His vocal emphasis on the "zoo" from which he wishes to be rescued may be an indication of his continuing dissatisfaction with the plight of performers who are regarded as specimens to be displayed for the public's entertainment. While he was generally positive about the behavior of Japanese audiences, his underlying cynicism about the demands of the popular music industry had clearly not diminished.

"Taxman" is the first song to show any significant changes: Two new verses were inserted to take account of the political and financial changes in the United Kingdom since Harrison had written the song in 1966. The names of politicians Edward Heath and Harold Wilson are replaced by contemporary leaders John Major, Boris Yeltsin, and George Bush, and there is a reference to the VAT (value added tax), introduced in Britain in 1973. In addition, Harrison singles out other items that might attract the attention of the avaricious taxman: "your hat," "your cat," and "your fat."

Although the reports about Harrison's preoccupation with money and investments may be exaggerated, there are enough examples to suggest that he was certainly happy to lend his name to projects whose primary motivation seems to have been financial, particularly in a series of limited-edition records and books. In 1980, the original publication of his musical memoirs, *I Me Mine*, was restricted to two thousand deluxe, leather-bound copies, priced at £148. The painstakingly illustrated, lavishly packaged, and personally signed copies of *Songs by George Harrison* (1988) and *Songs by George Harrison 2* (1992)—which were essentially four-track compilations of discarded songs and/or alternative versions of previously released material—both retailed for more than £200; only 2,500 copies of each were offered for sale. And in 1993, 3,500 autographed copies of the 274-page *Live in Japan*, Harrison's own written and photographic account of the Japanese tour (with the added bonus of exclusive memorabilia) were published at a price of £275. As the constantly spiraling prices in the world of fine art testify, the value, or rather the price, of any item accrues from its rarity, and through his participation in these ventures, he was knowingly depriving many ordinary fans of the opportunity to purchase his songs and consciously contributing to the creation of a market of relatively wealthy collectors, whose interest may not have been solely musical. There is, therefore, a certain irony in the words of "Taxman," which persistently complain about a society that penalizes the superrich.

"Give Me Love (Give Me Peace on Earth)" is the first post-Beatles song on the album. It is, for the most part, a straight copy of the version that appeared on *Living in the Material World*, but there are two notable variations. One is Harrison's impassioned delivery, especially in the chorus; he is not merely singing about love, but pleading for it. The second is the impressive interplay between him and the backing singers, particularly in the syncopated sections toward the end of the song, when the accent shifts between lead and supporting vocals.

He returns to the Beatles' catalogue for "If I Needed Someone." His own vocal contribution, particularly in the verses, is much more prominent than on the 1965 version; without the familiar three-part Beatle harmonies, it becomes a more personal statement. His adoption of a Dylanesque tone threatens to rob the song of much of its brightness, but the track is transformed by Clapton's looping guitar solos. The musical advantages of having one of the world's greatest rock guitarists in a backing band have to be judged against the potential disadvantage of being overwhelmed by his virtuosity, but on this track, the balance is perfectly achieved. He complements rather than undermines Harrison's performance, and the result is a glorious reworking of George Martin's original production.

The inclusion of "Something" is probably inevitable, given its status as one of Harrison's (and the world's) finest love songs. However, its place here carries with it an extra poignancy, in that the woman for whom it was written had been married to, and divorced from, Harrison and Clapton in turn. During the Dark Horse tour seventeen years previously, audiences had been offended by the way Harrison had crudely altered some of the lyrics, but here it is sung as it was written. Given the events through which he had passed in the twenty years since he had composed the song, there is an unsurprising anguish, almost a desperation, in his voice that contrasts sharply with the simple stillness of the original. The guitar dialogue between Clapton and Harrison deliberately avoids any unnecessary elaboration and its emotional overtones are achieved through restraint rather than exertion. It is not a new interpretation of the song, but it does suggest a new perspective, in which words and music are used by two close friends to reflect on the lives they have led.

"What Is Life" is clearly a song that Harrison likes to perform on stage. It was the closing song on the Dark Horse tour, and here it is one of the few tracks to be performed without the addition of a Clapton guitar solo. The only change to the original is that the phrase "who are you" is rendered as "wooo are you," a small but significant variation that looks back to the earliest Beatles songs, in which the calls of "hey-hey," "wooo-wooo," and "yeah, yeah" were used to generate excitement and liberation.

The next two tracks are surprising choices, in that neither of them are songs commonly regarded as among Harrison's strongest or most popular. "Dark Horse," introduced in a mock-Scottish accent, departs very little from the 1974 album track, and although there are brief moments when it appears that he might be prepared to extend his vocal pitch, it remains a routine presentation. "Piggies" contains a new verse, in which he plays with a pun about "piggy banks." Harrison's vocal delivery is slightly less mannered than it is on *The Beatles*, but there is no attempt to rework the track and little obvious energy in its performance. The inclusion of both songs might be attributed to Harrison's obstinate promise—expressed in the lyrics of songs such as "Blood from a Clone," "Unconsciousness Rules," and "Wrack My Brain"—that his musical preferences will not be dictated by passing trends or commercial considerations but will remain, stubbornly, his own.

Both *Cloud Nine* and its single, "Got My Mind Set on You," had been relatively minor hits in Japan. Although there remained a massive, almost fanatical obsession with the Beatles, the country's audiences had shown less interest in their subsequent solo careers. "Got My Mind Set on You" is therefore another unexpected selection, and the band's performance is competent rather than inspired. Many musicians have commented on the way a positive interplay between singer and audience can galvanize a live performance,[15] and on this occasion, the lack of audience familiarity with the song does seem to restrict Harrison's onstage energy.

Much the same can be said of "Cloud 9." The call-and-response interplay with the backing vocalists gives it a more soulful feel than on the album version, and the twin guitars of Harrison and Clapton add an "extra texture" to the song. Unlike many contemporary guitarists, Harrison was never intimidated by Clapton's prowess; he regarded him as a friend and peer, rather than as a role model or guitar hero. Indeed, Clapton's trepidation when invited to play on the Beatles' "While My Guitar Gently Weeps" suggests that, if anything, he was in awe of them.[16] Nonetheless, their long association, based on mutual respect rather than rivalry, produced many notable moments, and Clapton's presence alongside him on occasions like this gave Harrison the opportunity to relax and enjoy his music in a way that would otherwise have been impossible.

"Here Comes the Sun" is one of Harrison's prettiest compositions, and although his voice here is a little less distinct than the recording on *Abbey Road*, it is a faithful re-creation of the song. It is followed by an equally accurate, and uplifting, version of "My Sweet Lord," in which an expanded mantra of gurus, teachers, and religious leaders (including Jesus Christ and Buddha) includes several of those explicitly denied by Lennon in his song, "God." Long regarded as the two "intellectual" members of the Beatles,[17] Lennon and Harrison eventually arrived at very divergent solutions to the questions that had initially led them both to the Maharishi Mahesh Yogi in the late 1960s. Lennon was the auto-didact, who resolved to plot his own course and value only his own experiences; Harrison was the disciple, ready to listen to the prophesies and prayers of others. In every performance, including this one, the underlying message of "My Sweet Lord" is one of gratitude for the combined wisdom of all faiths that embark on the search for grace.

Fittingly, the next song is "All Those Years Ago," Harrison's tribute to Lennon. Its inclusion has more than passing significance, since the Beatles had played several dates in Tokyo in July 1966, only a few weeks before their last official concert. Furthermore, Clapton, who contributes a fiery guitar solo to the track, had performed and/or recorded with Lennon on a number of occasions, including their collaboration (with Mitch Mitchell and Keith Richards) in the Rolling Stones *Rock 'n' Roll Circus* in December 1968, and the Plastic Ono Band's appearance at the Toronto Rock 'n' Roll Festival in September 1969. In fact, Clapton is one of only a handful of musicians (the others include Elton John, Billy Preston, and Klaus Voormann) to have appeared on stage with all four ex-Beatles at some point in their solo careers.

"Cheer Down" is the most recent song to be featured on the album. After he has jokingly introduced it as a song from *South Pacific*, Harrison's solid performance retains the structure and rhythms of the studio version. "Devil's Radio" is similarly true to the original, and has an additional piece of advice: "Don't be a broadcaster," he calls to the audience after the final notes.

The final three tracks are drawn from three of Harrison's most memorable periods. "Isn't It a Pity" is the album's outstanding song; not only does it recall the period in the early 1970s when Harrison was emerging as rock's spiritual statesman, but the dramatic fusion of his intense vocal, twin guitars, and ethereal supporting voices eclipses the version on *All Things Must Pass* in its emotion. The sense of despair for a world that fails to value human relationships is all too evident, and while Harrison may have achieved a balance in his own life, his sorrow at the continued intolerance and selfishness around him is as profound as ever.

"While My Guitar Gently Weeps" revisits the Beatles of the late 1960s. Having made the decision to stop live appearances in 1966, the group had been freed from the pressure to produce two- or three-minute pop songs, and the mature collection of songs they had written during their visit to Rishikesh in early 1968 included some of Harrison's most thoughtful lyrics. To some extent, those lyrics are overshadowed here by the strength of the lead guitars, but as with the previous track, the depth of his sadness for "the love that's sleeping" is evident in his broken vocal.

Finally, "Roll Over Beethoven" returns to the Beatles of 1963. The song had featured in their repertoire since 1957 and, when it was released on *With the Beatles*, perfectly captured the exuberance of their early recordings. Unfortunately, the version here lacks the brash simplicity of the group's lead, bass, and rhythm guitar template and attempts to replace it with a contemporary arrangement that is fundamentally unsuited to Chuck Berry's iconic riffs. Missing, too, are the falsetto cries and double-tracked vocal that added to the song's excitement, and the result is a rather top-heavy arrangement in which Harrison's voice struggles to make any impact.

Of the nineteen songs featured on *Live in Japan*, nine come from the eight-year period in which the Beatles were recording as a group and ten from Harrison's twenty-one years as a solo performer; in fact, there are only four songs written and recorded since 1974. The set list was clearly influenced by Harrison's perceptions of audience expectations, but it does show that his claims to have put the Beatles behind him are rather misleading. For the fans who came to see him, the chance to listen to some of the Beatles' most memorable songs, a quarter of a century after they were first heard, was an opportunity not to be spurned, and the tour sold out within days of the tickets becoming available. To the disappointment of many, there were never any suggestions of additional dates in the West, and when the album was released, it was given very little promotion. Harrison had clearly achieved the goal he had set himself—to tour one last time—and that was sufficient in itself. In relying so heavily on his back catalogue, and choosing to depart very little from precise re-creations of the original versions, he had opted for a relatively safe approach in which professional competence replaced the personal controversies of the Dark Horse tour.

WITH THE BEATLES . . . AGAIN

Over the next few years, Harrison retreated again to his mansion at Friar Park. His temporary flirtation with the fringe politics of the Natural Law Party attracted passing media interest,[18] but otherwise he was content to relax in the grounds of his estate, where he and his wife, Olivia, devoted more and more time to designing and maintaining the gardens.[19] He was happy to participate in occasional musical liaisons, most notably the Bob Dylan 30th Anniversary Concert in New York's Madison Square Garden, in October 1992, where he performed "If Not for You" and "Absolutely

Sweet Marie" (backed by Booker T. and the MGs), introduced Dylan to the audience as "Lucky," and joined Neil Young, Roger McGuinn, Eric Clapton, Tom Petty, and Dylan for a storming version of "My Back Pages."

Throughout 1994, Apple was in cooperation with the BBC to release a double album of songs performed by the Beatles during their radio appearances in the 1960s, many of which had been bootlegged over the years. *The Beatles Live at the BBC* brought together fifty-six of these tracks. There were no new compositions, but the collection contained several cover versions of rock 'n' roll standards that had formed the nucleus of their live performances in Liverpool and Hamburg but had not been officially released. Among those on which Harrison took the lead vocal were the Crickets' "Don't Ever Change," Carl Perkins's "Glad All Over," the Everly Brothers' "So How Come (No One Loves Me)," the Coasters' "Young Blood," and Elvis Presley's "I Forgot to Remember to Forget." The album reached #3 in the U.S. charts in December 1994.

Encouraged by the success of *The Beatles Live at the BBC*, the first steps were also being taken on a process that would eventually lead to a temporary reunion of the three surviving Beatles, the release of two "new" singles and three triple albums/double CDs of previously unheard Beatles music, a six-part television series chronicling the history of the group, and the publication of a 350-page coffee-table book in which the Beatles offered their own account of the story that had fascinated the world for nearly four decades. *Anthology* was a project largely instigated by the Beatles themselves, and although many of the 150-plus tracks that appeared on the albums were outtakes, demos, or live versions of studio tracks, the compilations did include Harrison's unreleased "You Know What to Do" and the jointly credited group instrumentals "12-Bar Original" and "Los Paranoias."

However, the most significant pieces of music to emerge from the *Anthology* project were the attempts to fashion two entirely "new" Beatles' songs from home recordings of unfinished compositions made by John Lennon in the late 1970s. Under Jeff Lynne's supervision, Paul McCartney, George Harrison, and Ringo Starr entered McCartney's studio in Sussex to add instrumental and vocal passages to the tapes created by Lennon fifteen years earlier in his New York apartment. It was not an entirely new idea. In 1991, studio technology had been used to splice Natalie Cole's contemporary vocal performance of "Unforgettable" with the track originally recorded in 1954 by her father, Nat "King" Cole—a hugely successful project for which she received several Grammy Awards.

The first of the Beatles' songs, "Free As a Bird," was released as a single in December 1995. The track opens and closes with Harrison's yearning slide guitar, setting the mood for Lennon's (original) and McCartney's (additional) lyrics that expose their nostalgia for a fondly remembered past.

In "A Shropshire Lad," poet A. E. Housman movingly recalled the "blue remembered hills" and "land of lost content" of his childhood; in its poignant depiction of the homing bird that enjoys the freedom of the skies and the safety of a home, "Free As a Bird" captures the same elusive spirit of romantic innocence. And there is a postscript to the song, in the form of a short ukulele solo by Harrison, which further increases the sense of nostalgia.

"Real Love" contains no new lyrics, and the Beatles' contribution is to add harmony vocals, guitar, and percussion in order to augment Lennon's basic track. Again, Harrison's lead guitar guides the song, both through his solo break and intermittent flourishes. Lennon's lyrical conclusion that "all we really were doing was waiting for love" is very much in keeping with Harrison's own insights, and the song undoubtedly benefits from the decision to leave its original structure untouched.

A third Lennon song, "Now and Then," was deemed to be unsuitable, and plans to transform it into a Beatles track were abandoned.

Each of the three *Anthology* albums topped the U.S. charts on its release (in November 1995, March 1996, and October 1996), selling in total more than twenty million copies in 1996 alone. The broadcast in ninety-four countries of the *Anthology* television documentary series in November 1995 and the expanded video release of the series in September 1996 concentrated public attention on the Beatles in a way that had not been seen for thirty years. Reports that Harrison, McCartney, and Starr were recording together—and filming the sessions—were largely unfounded,[20] but Harrison was certainly in a mood to renew musical collaborations with old friends again, contributing to new albums by Alvin Lee (*I Hear You Rockin'*), Gary Wright (*First Signs of Life*), Carl Perkins (*Go Cat Go*), Ravi Shankar (*Chants of India*), and Ringo Starr (*Vertical Man*). With the wisdom of maturity, he could enjoy this second wave of Beatlemania with a degree of relaxation that was missing during the chaotic years of the 1960s.

6

And in the End

In the summer of 1997, Harrison noticed a small lump in his neck; when it was confirmed as cancerous, an operation was performed to remove several enlarged lymph nodes. During the medical investigation, early signs of lung cancer were also detected, and a second operation removed part of his lung. In 1998, a recurrence of the original cancerous growth was found to have spread to his throat, and he began an extensive course of radiation therapy.

Publicly, Harrison denied that the condition was serious and issued a press statement, in which he thanked his fans for their concern and declared that he was making a full recovery.[1] Privately, he was well aware of the dangerous legacy that a lifetime of heavy smoking had left inside his body. The death of his mother from cancer in 1970 and his father from emphysema in 1978 had failed to persuade him to quit smoking, but the cancer-related deaths of three close friends during the period of his own treatment left him in no doubt about the seriousness of his condition. In September 1997, Derek Taylor, Apple's press officer and one of the Beatles' oldest and most trusted companions, died from throat cancer; four months later, Carl Perkins also died after a long battle against throat cancer; and in April 1998, Linda McCartney died from breast cancer. Harrison attended the funerals or memorial services for all three.

Through 1999, Harrison attempted to resume as normal a life as possible, despite his ongoing medical treatment. He continued to indulge his passion for motor racing by attending several Formula One races on the Grand Prix calendar (Melbourne, Long Beach, Silverstone) and also began to rehearse and record demo versions of old and new songs, assisted by his son, Dhani, and Jeff Lynne. Whether the act of making music is viewed as a therapy, an addiction, a distraction, or a divine inspiration, his decision to immerse himself in it during a troubled and uncertain period of his life suggests, as Harrison himself admitted, that a primary motivation may have been to use it as an act of catharsis.[2]

On December 23, 1999, the Harrisons' home in Hawaii was burgled by a homeless woman who spent several hours there before police were alerted and arrested her; her claim to have a psychic connection with Harrison was an unwelcome reminder of the bizarre and unsettling relationships between popular musicians and their fans with which the Beatles were all too familiar, and about which there is a growing academic literature.[3] Harrison had been the recipient of death threats since the mid-1960s,[4] and although he steadfastly refused to engage any additional security personnel—even after John Lennon's murder—the threat of real and potential intrusions into his personal life was a constant anxiety.

One week later, in the early hours of December 30, Friar Park was broken into by a former heroin addict and paranoid schizophrenic from Liverpool. The thirty-four-year-old man had been receiving treatment for his mental illness since 1990 and had developed an obsession with the music of the Beatles, repeatedly describing Harrison as a sorcerer and a witch. Awakened by the sound of breaking glass, Harrison confronted the intruder in the hallway and, in the struggle that ensued, received several knife wounds, one of which narrowly missed his heart and pierced his lung. When Olivia Harrison rushed to help, the two managed to overcome the attacker and knock him unconscious. Harrison was taken to the Royal Berkshire Hospital in Reading, from where he was quickly transferred to the specialist chest unit at Harefield Hospital in London. Within a few days, he was discharged and allowed to continue his recovery at home.

The cumulative impact of his attempted murder and his ongoing battle against a progressively aggressive cancer restricted Harrison's musical activity, and although there were occasional suggestions that the tracks he had been working on with Dhani and Lynne might find their way onto a new album, there was little enthusiasm to complete them. His illness advanced relentlessly, and the last few months of his life were spent in attempts to postpone what was, by now, an inevitable outcome.

In April 2001, Harrison underwent surgery at the Mayo Clinic in Rochester, Minnesota, to remove a cancerous growth from one of his lungs. When it was discovered that the cancer had spread to his brain, he traveled to Switzerland for a course of intensive radiotherapy at the Oncology Institute of San Giovanni Hospital in Bellinzona. In October, he was admitted to the Staten Island University Hospital in New York for a program of fractionated stereotactic radiosurgery, a procedure in which radiation is directed at brain tumors with unusual precision; while there, he was visited by Paul McCartney and Ringo Starr. In mid-November, he flew to the UCLA Medical Center in Los Angeles, where he was visited by Ravi Shankar. On November 29, 2001, George Harrison died. His body was cremated, and within days his ashes were taken to India, to be scattered in the Ganges River, by his wife and son.

"Horse to the Water"

Incredibly, just six weeks before his death, Harrison had agreed to record a vocal track for a forthcoming compilation project. The album *Small World Big Band* was credited to Jools Holland and His Rhythm and Blues Orchestra, although in reality their role was to provide instrumental and vocal backing to individual tracks performed by an impressive collection of star musicians, including Van Morrison, Steve Winwood, Eric Clapton, John Cale, and Paul Weller. Many chose songs written by other composers, but Harrison offered a new song of his own. Holland visited him in Switzerland at the beginning of October, the recording was concluded in one day, and the album was released in the week before his death.

"Horse to the Water" has the same soulful impetus that defines so many of the tracks Harrison had completed in the previous few years. Holland's keyboard, a substantial brass section, and urgent backup singers (led by Joe Brown's daughter, Sam Brown) provide a convincing contemporary framework, although the guitar solo that seeks to replicate Harrison's distinctive style is less successful. But it is his vocal contribution that demands attention. Although the big-band accompaniment partially disguises it, there is no mistaking the effort in his voice as he strains, and sometimes fails, to deliver the words and notes. At several points, he abruptly, and audibly, struggles to catch his breath. And yet it remains a compelling performance, made all the more pertinent by the honesty of the lyrics.

The old adage that "you can lead a horse to water, but you can't make him drink" refers to the difficulty in persuading people to do what is right for them—even when a person knows what he ought to do, he may not do it.[5] In this case, Harrison's words refer all too clearly to the factors in his own history that have created his current circumstances. From the first diagnosis of cancer in 1997, he had accepted that his heavy smoking and his refusal to act on the health warnings about the links between cigarettes and lung cancer were responsible for his illness. The words of "Horse to the Water" describe "a friend in so much misery" who rejects the "wisdom" offered to him; all the information is "laid out" for him, but still he refuses to "think." The bluntest reference comes when Harrison uses the analogy of the alcoholic to illustrate the folly of the man who refuses to listen: when told of the risks of continued drinking, he insists, "'Everything's OK', as he downed another bottle of whiskey."

BRAINWASHED

In the spring of 2002, Jeff Lynne and Dhani Harrison (assisted by drummer Jim Keltner) resolved to complete the production of the tracks Harrison had begun to record in 1999. Some were little more than snippets of unfinished music, but the majority were fully developed songs with Harrison's own suggestions or instructions for their final shape. The album was released in November 2002, one year after his death.

"Any Road" is a rockabilly number in which Harrison looks back over the road he has traveled. His sumptuous slide guitar and confident vocal give the song an authority that is somewhat at odds with the nature of the questions he still seeks to answer. Although his life has taken him to so many places, he knows that much is random and unpredictable: "a spin of a wheel and a roll of the dice" can determine the paths along which we journey. Like the traveler who must choose between two divergent roads in Robert Frost's poem, "The Road Not Taken," Harrison is aware that none of us is in complete control of our destiny, and that all we can do is "bow to God."

In a similarly contemplative mood (in the lyrics of "Truckin'"), the Grateful Dead recall "what a long, strange trip it's been"; Harrison's career was longer and stranger than most, and the words of "Any Road" show that he is still unable to explain or understand it. Of one thing, however, he is certain: his observation that "there was no beginning, there is no end" confirms the sentiments in the quotation from the Bhagavad-Gita that he had used after Lennon's death, which is reprinted in the sleeve notes to *Brainwashed*: "There never was a time when you or I did not exist. Nor will there be any future when we shall cease to be."

The attack that Harrison had launched against the greed and hypocrisy of the Roman Catholic Church in the original lyrics of "Awaiting on You All" is repeated in his next song, but in a less confrontational way that reflects the mellowing effect of thirty years. Melodically, "P2 Vatican Blues (Last Saturday Night)" has some of the ragtime feel of Scott Joplin's music that was used in *The Sting* (dir. George Roy Hill, 1973); it also recalls the infectious, sing-along rhythms of "Last Night" from *Traveling Wilburys, Volume 1*. Harrison's mother was Catholic, but her hopes that any of her four children might become regular churchgoers had been dashed by Harrison from an early age.[6] However, with its considerable Irish population, Liverpool (particularly the postwar Liverpool in which Harrison grew up) had one of the largest Catholic populations of any British city, and the church's influence among working-class communities was hard to ignore. In view of the increasing number of allegations (and subsequent convictions) relating to the improper behavior of Catholic priests that began to circulate in the 1990s, Harrison's guarded reference to "the things they do at night" is especially significant; it is, as he says, "quite suspicious." The contrast between the small, secretive world of the local priest and the opulent grandeur of the Vatican in Rome (which he dismisses as a "show") may be gently mocked, but there is an underlying sense of resentment in his words that cannot be concealed by the jaunty, good-natured music and its shuffling beat.

"Pisces Fish" is one of Harrison's most arresting and moving compositions, whose beautifully lilting melody is matched by equally emotive words. His search for spiritual illumination was far too profound to attach any significance to astrology, and the song's title is used metaphorically, to describe the way in which he swims in the waters of life, rather than as an indication of any personal belief in star signs. From the opening line, in which he points out "rowers gliding on the river," to the closing statement that "the river runs through my soul," there is a constant emphasis on the imagery of water: it cleanses us, carries us, surrounds us, and sustains us. Many of the images he provides—people walking their dogs along the towpath, farmers in the fields watching over their sheep, routine activity at the local brewery—come from places around the River Thames in Henley, but unspoken impressions of the Mersey (where he was born) and the Ganges (where he was laid to rest) complete the circle of birth, life, and death that his lyrics evoke.

The admission in the song that his life "seems like fiction" is another acknowledgment of the astonishing story of the Beatles. Although—especially toward the end of his career—he often angrily dismissed those years as a relatively trivial part of his life, such outbursts were fueled by frustration rather than genuine hostility, and he retained a real pride in all that the group had accomplished.[7] Indeed, the description he offers of himself as the embodiment of "all life's contradictions" typifies not only the contrast between the material and the spiritual but also the vast difference between the young, uneducated, working-class boy of forty years ago and the mature, wealthy figure he had become. The melody recalls some of the patterns in "Crackerbox Palace" (and also the Eagles' "Lyin' Eyes"), but its simple, acoustic-based production with minimal additional instrumentation and soft, warm vocal track make this a startlingly intimate exploration of his past, present, and future self. This is Harrison at his most serious.

In "Looking for My Life," Harrison relates the traumatic effects of the attempt on his life in 1999. He tells of how "things exploded" and he was suddenly faced with "a state of emergency" that threatened to shake his faith. There is a double meaning in the reference to the "birds and bees" with which he has spent his time. The first is a traditional euphemism for the "facts of life," and in this sense, the phrase suggests Harrison is looking back to the naïveté and innocence of his adolescent years and his youthful pursuit of sex and romance. The second refers to the insect and bird life in the gardens at Friar Park, which had occupied so much of his recent energy. Both are equally pertinent, and either way, the portrait is of a simple man, unprepared for his confrontation with a potential killer and frightened by its implications. After staring death in the face and having been, quite literally, "down upon [his] knees," only now can he begin to overcome his desolation and seek to rebuild his trust in God. After thirty years of religious exploration, during which his songs had often commented on the transitory nature of life and the permanence of the soul, his fear and distress recall Jesus's words during his crucifixion: "Lord, why hast thou forsaken me?" Of course, another reading might point to a man whose faith has been tested and is now stronger than ever as a result, but there is a degree of hopelessness (amplified, no doubt, by his advancing cancer) in Harrison's words that undermines this interpretation: his assertion that "you've no idea what I've been through" points to an experience so horrendous as to surpass any rational understanding. Musically, the bright, acoustic backing and casual vocal detract from the overwhelmingly somber theme, to make "Looking for My Life" one of Harrison's more disquieting songs.

If the previous track presents a desperate reaction to terrifying circumstances, "Rising Sun" seeks to provide its optimistic counterpart. Harrison begins by painting a depressing picture of a world in which the streets are populated by "villains" and "sinners," and the truth is obscured by "guilt" and "disguise." Yet all of us have the ability to overcome such obstacles: the "rising sun" inside ourselves will provide light, clarity, and understanding. The song effectively restates the advice he had offered in "Within You Without You" thirty-five years earlier, when he had urged his audience to "realise it's all within yourself." "Rising Sun" is also the first track on the album to bear the stamp of the production techniques used by Lynne with ELO: reverberating guitar passages, descending riffs, and multiple string sections. Perhaps because its message is a familiar one, the song lacks an immediate impact and is a pleasant, if slightly bland, example of Harrison's faith in an innate spiritual morality. The possibility that the "rising sun" also refers to the son of God, who rose from the dead and whose love resides within us all, cannot be discounted; certainly, the reference to a "messenger from inner space," rather than the more familiar messengers from "outer space," demonstrates Harrison's conviction that the problems we face and the solutions we seek are not externally, but internally, generated.

The instrumental track "Marwa Blues" is built around Harrison's shimmering slide guitar, which reinterprets the traditional Indian melodic form within a more accessible Western framework. A raga typically has five, six, or seven notes, in separate ascending and descending structures, and its own recognizable feature or theme. Furthermore, each raga is associated with a particular time of the day or night.[8] "Raga Marwa," a traditional twilight or evening raga with six notes in the ascent and descent, was one of Harrison's favorite Indian pieces, and "Marwa Blues" is his homage to it, and to those musicians and composers who had exerted such an influence on his own musical career. Performed with a translucent purity, augmented by a sympathetic string arrangement, Harrison coaxes an exquisite melody that somehow manages to be spiritual, erotic, and descriptive at the same time. The absolute precision of his playing suggests that recording was a painstaking process, but the result is a tranquil and delicate composition that glides effortlessly around its harmonic theme. In 2004, Harrison was posthumously, and deservedly, rewarded with the Grammy for Best Pop Instrumental Performance for this track.

"Stuck Inside a Cloud" returns to the misery and isolation inflicted by his illness. Rather than a consistent narrative, Harrison's lyrics offer a series of disjointed observations, which create the impression of a man at his wit's end, frantically searching for the right words to convey his situation: he regrets the loss of his "concentration," and fears that he might also lose his "touch"; later, after remembering that he has visited "some exhibition," he adds that he has lost the "will to eat." And there is no prospect of a "cure" at hand. In the final verse, he fears an imminent parting from a loved one—but this is a parting caused not by the vagaries of romance, but by death itself. It is a bleak and unforgiving picture of a man in torment. But, just as in "Looking for My Life," the pervasive gloom of the words is lightened by the music—in this case, a clean, bright melody performed on guitars, piano, and Wurlitzer organ, with none of Lynne's occasional liking for musical melodrama.

"Run So Far" had appeared on Clapton's best-selling *Journeyman* album in 1989. Harrison had contributed guitar and harmony vocals to the track, which was another example of the Elton John–derived commercial rock he was writing at the time. A decade later, his own recording, here on *Brainwashed*, removes a verse or two, but is otherwise a close copy of Clapton's version. Presented as an intimate conversation with a friend, it is an addition to the long list of songs that examine the vicissitudes of the life of a professional musician. Like Simon and Garfunkel's "Homeward Bound" and John Denver's "Leaving on a Jet Plane," it considers the lonely existence of those touring performers obliged to leave friends and family behind as they prepare for the next date. Harrison realizes that there is "no escape" from the "mess" in which his companion finds himself, and he finds it difficult to give any advice other than to offer his sympathy and understanding. His own dislike of touring stemmed from his concerns over a range of issues—safety and security, deteriorating musical standards, a lack of privacy, physical and mental exhaustion—but here, his emphasis is on the personal unhappiness and frustrations that such a life can produce. The graceful regret in his description of the performer who has to keep going, while his "smile wears thin," has a note of inevitability about it: like it or not, there is "no way out." The relaxed tempo and Harrison's pensive, occasionally double-tracked, voice add to the sorrowful mood created by a gentle melody. Had the song been written in the 1970s, Harrison's attitude would have been one of anger; here, it has been replaced by a reluctant acquiescence.

Unsurprisingly for the man who composed "Something," the love song—either celebratory or reflective—had been a persistent choice throughout Harrison's songwriting career. *Brainwashed* departs from that tradition by locating the treatment of romantic love within the context of human mortality, and "Never Get over You" is the album's only unashamed love song, which sets out to speak unequivocally of the feelings between a man and a woman. As in other songs inspired by, and dedicated to, Olivia, including "Beautiful Girl" and "Dark Sweet Lady," his lyrics imply that he has been waiting for her arrival. However, finding fresh ways in which to write about love is a problem faced by all composers, and some of Harrison's vocabulary is immediately familiar (her "eyes," her "smile," her "touch," her "face"). The exception is his unexpected statement that "you warm the coldest feet"; by rooting his description of their affection in such a mundane reality, the song presents, for a moment at least, a touching and intimate example that is not only distinctive but entirely believable. It recalls very closely the kind of personal, often confessional, lyrics found in the songs of female singer-songwriters such as Joni Mitchell, Alanis Morissette, and Aimee Mann. Indeed, Mitchell's observation in the lyrics of "My Old Man" that, without her lover, "the bed's too big, the frying pan's too wide" contains exactly the same kind of diary-like detail that characterizes Harrison's words. His voice possesses an evident maturity, but is constrained by a curious lack of emotion. Musically, the track is brought to life by some lovely interludes of slide guitar that decorate a rather incomplete and unremarkable melody.

After his previous interpretations of songs by Cole Porter and Hoagy Carmichael, it is entirely appropriate that Harrison's final album should also include a song from the pre-rock 'n' roll era of North American show tunes. Harold Arlen and Ted Koehler had written "Between the Devil and the Deep Blue Sea" in the early 1930s, and Harrison provides a relaxed and uncomplicated version that also highlights his ability on the ukulele. An interesting feature of Koehler's lyrics is the manner in which he introduces each verse with a self-deprecatory confession: "I don't want you, but I hate to lose you" and "I should hate you, but I guess I love you." This may well be the inspiration behind Smokey Robinson's celebrated couplet in "You Really Got a Hold on Me" in which he admits "I don't like you, but I love you"—and Robinson was, of course, one of Harrison's, and the Beatles', favorite songwriters.

The title of "Rocking Chair in Hawaii" seems to place it alongside songs like "Soft-Hearted Hana" and "Gone Troppo" as a paean to his overseas homes. But the title is deceptive, and the song is a busy compilation of (mainly) musical reference points in his life. The tune is a slowed-down pastiche of Hank Williams's "Love Sick Blues," introduced with an intimation of the yodeling style that Williams had borrowed from Jimmie Rodgers, two performers much admired by Harrison in his childhood.[9] The title may be seen as an acknowledgment to songs by two other significant influences: "Rockin' Chair" by Hoagy Carmichael (two of whose compositions had been covered by Harrison on *Somewhere in England*) and "Rockin' Chair Blues" by Big Bill Broonzy (named in "Wreck of the Hesperus"). The lyrics about "the Baba Sai" are a reference to Sai Baba of Shirdi, the nineteenth-century Indian guru regarded by Hindus and Muslims alike as "the saintly father" and believed by some to be a reincarnation of Shiva. The conscious similarity in intent between Harrison's "I'm going down to the river" and Robert Johnson's "I went down to the crossroads" (in his 1936 recording of "Cross Road Blues") points to a deliberate historical connection. And finally, the words "I love you" use the identical upward notation that was employed in the same phrase, thirty years earlier, on the Beatles' recording of "For You Blue."

Within this complex web of associations, Harrison considers the physical eroticism of human relationships (commenting on the "sideways glances" from the unnamed woman whose "shoulder" and "thigh" so excite him) and the perennial contradictions of human existence (warning us against "cruising backwards [to] some place you've already been"). The lazy, languid rhythms and his exaggerated Southern drawl succeed in evoking Harrison's planned scenario perfectly: the unhurried troubadour gently rocking in his chair, while his thoughts wander leisurely from one subject to another. In words and music, "Rocking Chair in Hawaii" represents a timeless, and tempting, portrayal of contentment.

The last of the twelve tracks is "Brainwashed," in which Harrison fuses the cold fury of Bob Dylan's "Masters of War," the antiauthoritarianism of Pink Floyd's "Another Brick in the Wall," and the defiant challenge of Lennon's "Give Peace a Chance" to produce his assessment of the agencies through which individual liberties are restricted and human growth is stunted. Few targets escape his accusations: the education system, the political system, the financial system, the military, and the media and communications industry are all indicted for the part they have played in replacing spiritual concerns with material concerns. As a result, we exist in a "wilderness," faced by the prospect of an "eternity of darkness." While each verse—delivered in short, staccato sentences—continues to add to the list of guilty parties, the chorus proclaims that there is a solution: "God God God," implores Harrison, repeatedly.

Many of Harrison's songs explore, with varying degrees of optimism or pessimism, the conflict between the divine and the worldly, but here it is couched in the starkest possible terms. There is an uncompromising desperation which shows that, despite his apparent mellowing in songs like "That's the Way It Goes," his contempt for those whose lies, threats, and manipulations condemn us to "ignorance" is as deep as ever. Harrison has never sounded more like Dylan, and his voice captures the caustic, sneering tone of the "cousin Bob" mentioned in the lyrics. And in the same way that Tom Petty resolved to "stand my ground" when faced by a "world that keeps on pushin' me round" (in the lyrics of "I Won't Back Down"), Harrison's own response is equally emphatic: "I just won't accept defeat."

To provide a temporary respite from this onslaught, and to illustrate the beauty of the alternative world to which we might aspire, the track includes a spoken extract from the two-thousand-year-old text *How to Know God: The Yoga Aphorisms of Patanjali*. Spoken by Isabela Borzymowska, the passage states: "The soul does not love; it is love itself. It does not exist; it is existence itself. It does not know; it is knowledge itself."

"Brainwashed" segues into the Sanskrit prayer "Namah Pavarti," chanted together by George and Dhani Harrison. It is a supplication to Shiva, the Hindu god regarded as the Destroyer who, with Brahma (the Creator) and Vishnu (the Preserver), is one of the three inseparable and simultaneous manifestations of the Absolute, or Brahman. Hindu scriptures teach that Shiva periodically destroys the world in order to cleanse it of ignorance and evil, so that it might be recreated in its pure form. Dhani Harrison's decision to close *Brainwashed* in this way—to make "Namah Pavarti" the final track on the final album—reminds us that this is the purity that his father strove to attain, to which he devoted so much of his time, energy, and music.

CONCERT FOR GEORGE

In the following months, a number of tribute albums were released; most were poorly conceived or frankly exploitative, and the versions (by various artists) of Harrison's songs did little to enhance his or their status.[10] In February 2002, the Liverpool City Council staged its Concert for George Harrison, a hastily organized and somewhat unrepresentative charity show, at the city's Empire Theatre. However, remembering the satisfaction Harrison had derived from his appearance in the Bob Dylan 30th Anniversary Concert in 1992, in which all the participating musicians had offered their own performances of some of Dylan's classic songs,[11] Eric Clapton set about organizing a similar event.

The Concert for George took place at London's Royal Albert Hall on November 29, 2002, one year to the day after his death, and the subsequent CD and DVD were released one year later. The involvement of some of his closest friends and their affectionate, sometimes surprising, interpretations of his words and music made *Concert for George* a memorable and moving tribute to his forty-year career.[12]

The first half of the concert, on disc 1 of the album, features an extended program of music written by Ravi Shankar. It also includes a delicate, note-perfect duet between Jeff Lynne (on acoustic guitar) and Shankar's daughter, Anoushka (on sitar), of "The Inner Light," which does not appear at all out of place among the Indian folk and classical compositions that surround it. After the second half has been introduced by members of Monty Python performing "Sit on My Face" and "The Lumberjack Song," the assembled house band of familiar collaborators (including Ray Cooper, Dhani Harrison, Andy Fairweather-Low, Gary Brooker, Klaus Voormann, Henry Spinetti, Tom Scott, Jim Keltner, Albert Lee, Billy Preston, Tessa Niles, and Katie Kissoon) provides instrumental and vocal backing for the featured vocalists.

Disc 2 opens with three Beatles songs that had featured on *Live in Japan*. As might be expected, Lynne's performance of "I Want to Tell You" departs very little from the original; although John Lennon's songs are commonly regarded as the definitive blueprint for his career, Lynne's convincing imitation of Harrison's vocal inflections shows the extent to which he has absorbed influences from the whole Beatles' catalogue. Clapton's treatment of "If I Needed Someone" is equally straightforward. And although Brooker's version of "Old Brown Shoe" is given a more contemporary arrangement through the addition of a brass section and backing vocals, it too is a close copy of the track from the 1960s.

The first post-Beatles track is "Give Me Love (Give Me Peace on Earth)," and both Lynne's vocal and Clapton's instrumental re-creations of Harrison's style are in keeping with the song's gentle plea for peace and love. Similarly, "Beware of Darkness" is performed by Clapton in a way that captures the thoughtful intent of the original. The appearance of Joe Brown to sing "Here Comes the Sun" represents the album's first real surprise. Along with singers like Tommy Steele, Marty Wilde, Adam Faith, Billy Fury, and Cliff Richard, Brown was one of the United Kingdom's earliest rock 'n' roll stars. However, his gruff voice, Cockney accent, and cheery persona had led him away from a career in rock and established him instead in the tradition of English stage and music-hall entertainers. He and Harrison had become close friends (Harrison had been the best man at Brown's second marriage in 2000), but his attempt to reproduce the purity and elegance demanded by "Here Comes the Sun" is more than a little unexpected. His second song is far more successful: the casual tone and relaxed outlook of "That's the Way It Goes" are much better suited to Brown's informal, sing-along style.

This is followed by three songs from Tom Petty and the Heartbreakers. "Taxman" reprises the version found on *Revolver* (with the original references to Wilson and Heath properly restored). Their performance of "I Need You" transforms Harrison's composition for the Beatles into an uncannily accurate reconstruction of the Byrds' style that exerted a major influence on his songwriting in the mid-1960s. Petty's approximation of the clipped vocal delivery of Roger McGuinn, the chiming twelve-string

Rickenbacker guitar, full harmonies, and a slowed tempo combine to make this the kind of plaintive ballad that would have been perfectly at home on the Byrds' albums (*Mr. Tambourine Man, Turn Turn Turn, Fifth Dimension*) of 1965–1966. On "Handle with Care," Lynne joins the band to trade lead vocals with Petty, as two of the three remaining Traveling Wilburys re-create the song that effectively led to the group's formation.

"Isn't It a Pity" features an emotional performance by Billy Preston that recasts Harrison's somber treatment of the song as an impassioned, and uplifting, soulful anthem. Preston had first met the Beatles in Hamburg in 1962, as a member of Little Richard's backing band, and had remained a personal friend and valued professional colleague.[13] Whereas Harrison's low-key vocal had emphasized his mournful observations about the human condition, Preston's spirited delivery introduces shades of anger, rebellion, and inspiration. As the song builds to a climax, his swirling organ solo gives way to Clapton's stirring guitar contribution (the album's first), which in turn gives way to the closing vocal chorus from "Hey Jude." In terms of musical intensity, "Isn't It a Pity" is one of the album's outstanding tracks. Its distance from the version on *All Things Must Pass* is reminiscent of the huge transformation that Joe Cocker's recording of "With a Little Help from My Friends" and Jimi Hendrix's reworking of "All along the Watchtower" brought to the original tracks by the Beatles and Dylan.

The appearance of Ringo Starr is given an extra poignancy by his choice of song. "Photograph" was not only written by the two former Beatles but, as he comments in his spoken preamble, "the meaning's changed now." His memories of "the places we used to go" and his realization that "you're not coming back any more" take on an added, more personal, significance in the context of this performance. Starr's second song is one of two non-Harrison compositions on the disc, Carl Perkins's "Honey Don't," which had been included on *Beatles for Sale* in 1964.

Sam Brown's performance of "Horse to the Water" is the only track on which a female vocalist takes the lead. Supported by Jools Holland and Jim Capaldi, she gives an up-tempo, soulful interpretation of the song Harrison had recorded for Holland shortly before his death (and to which she had contributed backing vocals). In a style that is clearly and convincingly derived from Aretha Franklin, Brown captures the raw excitement and sheer enjoyment that were understandably absent from Harrison's own recording. Although the track is included on the DVD, it is absent from the CD.

Paul McCartney takes the lead vocal on three tracks. "For You Blue" is close to Harrison's original version and features some fine bottleneck guitar from Marc Mann. "Something" is perhaps the most surprising performance of the whole concert. It begins with McCartney's ukulele providing the only accompaniment to his voice, but what could have been an embarrassing mismatch is, in fact, a tasteful and moving union. In the second verse, drums, piano, and guitars provide additional backing, before the chorus, when Clapton's electric guitar and Preston's keyboard make their entry. At this point, the song undergoes a sudden transformation: Clapton takes over on lead vocal (supported by Lynne) and the mood of the song changes from that of a wistful serenade to a dramatic ballad, underpinned by the introduction of a string section. The final chorus is forcefully sung by Clapton and McCartney together. In splicing together two competing interpretations of Harrison's composition, the performers demonstrate that the emotional impact of his words and music is equally powerful in simple or sophisticated settings. After that, "All Things Must Pass" is sung by McCartney honestly and compassionately, and the version does full justice to the song's obvious poignancy.

McCartney moves to the piano and allows Clapton to take the lead vocal for "While My Guitar Gently Weeps," a song with which he is permanently associated, having contributed to the versions released on *The Beatles*, *The Concert for Bangla Desh*, and *Live in Japan*. The extended, but restrained, guitar solo with which he closes the track is perhaps the most expressive of them all, conveying the pain and suffering of a world in which love is actively denied. His performance also illustrates the intention behind Harrison's decision to leave the expected accusation that follows "I look at you all . . . " unspoken in the final verse. It is as though, frustrated and sorrowful, he has run out of words; by saying nothing, he communicates much.

Preston's interpretation of "My Sweet Lord" wisely resists any temptation to alter its basic structure, and the song is performed with the calm assurance of Harrison's own version. It is followed, just as it was on *All Things Must Pass*, by "Wah-Wah." In a move designed to illustrate the democratic nature of the tribute, its lead vocal switches among Clapton, Lynne, and Preston, but the result is somewhat uneven; Lynne's voice, in particular, is noticeably ragged and tries too hard to match the excitement generated by the all-star band. The final track is "I'll See You in My Dreams," sung and performed by Joe Brown on ukulele. Written in the 1920s by Isham Jones and Gus Kahn, the song had been recorded by such performers as Louis Armstrong, Ella Fitzgerald, and Doris Day, but is perhaps best known in the memorable instrumental version by Django Reinhardt. Here, its nostalgic mood and simple lyrics make it a touching finale.

Cover versions of songs can take one of two forms: a rendition, which is a straightforward copy of the original, or a transformation, involving innovative or significant alteration.[14] On *Concert for George*, the overwhelming majority of the twenty Harrison songs are relatively faithful renditions; only "I Need You," "Isn't It a Pity" and "Something" depart substantially from the original versions. This is very different from the interpretations of songs at the Bob Dylan 30th Anniversary Concert, where performers seemed at times to be in competition with each other to produce the most startling variation. This has little to do with the internal properties of the compositions themselves, and more to do with the context in which they are to be presented. In Dylan's case, the concert was staged to honor his continuing presence as a songwriter and recording artist; in Harrison's, the concert was organized to allow those there—audience and performers—to engage in a retrospective celebration of the man and his music.

Let It Roll: Songs by George Harrison

Finally, in June 2009, the first compilation to span Harrison's entire solo career was released. It contained nineteen tracks, chosen by Olivia Harrison and digitally remastered by Giles Martin (the son of George Martin). In 2006, the two Martins had coproduced *Love*, a synergistic reworking of more than thirty Beatles songs and the inspiration for the Cirque du Soleil's show that opened at the Mirage in Las Vegas earlier that year. One of the highlights of *Love* was George Martin's sensitive addition of strings to Harrison's original acoustic demo of "While My Guitar Gently Weeps," which transformed the song into a plaintive and delicate ballad. While *Let It Roll* presents no such metamorphoses, the enhanced production does bring a brightness and clarity to the songs and distinguishes the album as far more than a mere collection of old tracks.

However, what is of more interest is the selection of material, which reflects Olivia's (and presumably, George's) estimation of his music. There are no tracks from the trio of albums released between 1974 and 1976 (*Dark Horse*, *Extra Texture*, and *Thirty Three & ⅓*) nor from *Gone Troppo*. Perhaps unsurprisingly, it is his first and last albums from which the greatest number of individual songs are taken: five from *All Things Must Pass* ("Ballad of Sir Frankie Crisp (Let It Roll)," "My Sweet Lord," "All Things Must Pass," "What Is Life," and "Isn't It a Pity") and three from *Brainwashed* ("Any Road," "Marwa Blues," and "Rising Sun"). Within this symmetry, there are two relatively unfamiliar tracks: Dylan's "I Don't Want to Do It," from the soundtrack of *Porky's Revenge*, and "Cheer Down," cowritten with Petty, which featured in the soundtrack of *Lethal Weapon 2* and was also included on *Best of Dark Horse, 1976–1989*. Of course, the presence of these two songs (and also "This Is Love," written with Lynne) may be acknowledgments of their friendships as much as musical decisions.

It is equally significant that, notwithstanding Harrison's aversion to a solo career spent in the shadow of the achievements of the Beatles, *Let It Roll* includes three songs he wrote and recorded with the group. The live performances of "While My Guitar Gently Weeps," "Something," and "Here Comes the Sun" are taken from *The Concert for Bangla Desh*, which enables the inclusion of music that was created in, but not performed by, the group (and which also finds a place for a sustained contribution by Clapton to the album).

Any attempt to distill an illustrative sample of Harrison's solo output from three decades, ten studio albums, and two live albums into one compact disc is a formidable task, inevitably leading to disagreements about its omissions, oversights, and lost opportunities. But, while one might regret the exclusion of songs like "Don't Let Me Wait Too Long," "You," "Crackerbox Palace," "Handle with Care," and "Pisces Fish," the track listing of *Let It Roll* does allow for some plausible observations to be made about Harrison's personal preferences. In particular, one way to explore his own assessment of his music is to look for consistent patterns of choice across the four live or compilation albums in which he helped to determine the final selection of songs: *The Concert for Bangla Desh*, *Best of Dark Horse, 1976–1989*, *Live in Japan*, and *Let It Roll*. No less than seven songs are present on three of the four albums: "While My Guitar Gently Weeps," "Something," "Here Comes the Sun" (all written during the twelve-month period between August 1968 and July 1969, when Harrison gloriously demonstrated that the depth of his songwriting skills was no less impressive than that of Lennon and McCartney), "My Sweet Lord," "All Those Years Ago," "Got My Mind Set on You," and "Cheer Down." While this is in no way conclusive, it does suggest that Harrison recognized the importance of a small number of songs that might begin to form the nucleus of a coherent and representative body of his work, both within and without the Beatles, and by which he might wish to be remembered.

Conclusion

As a member of the Beatles, George Harrison wrote and recorded less than twenty-five songs; as a solo performer, he wrote and recorded well over a hundred. And yet, to many listeners, it is the body of work he created with the group that defines his enduring reputation. While this remained a permanent source of irritation to him, it was inevitable. Despite his protestations, he never left the Beatles. How could he? Economically, the group was largely responsible for the evolution of popular music in Britain from a small branch of the domestic entertainment business into one of the country's most profitable exports. Musically, the Beatles introduced innovative elements into the creation of their songs that served as examples for others to follow. Industrially, they demonstrated assertions of independence that helped to free them, and others, from the restrictive and paternalistic patterns of management and organization that had characterized the business in Britain. Historically, the group existed, and continues to exist, as one of the key moments in the narrative of the twentieth century. Politically, they demonstrated that entertainers might also be permitted to step into the role of intellectuals. Socially, their unprecedented global popularity was achieved in part by the capacity that they, and their music, possessed to overcome traditional distinctions of age, social class, and gender among communities of fans. Culturally, they shifted the consumption, discussion, and analysis of popular music into settings from which it had been previously excluded. To have contributed to just one of these achievements would represent a considerable accomplishment. To have played a part in all of them is, quite simply, staggering. This is why George Harrison could never leave the Beatles and why descriptions of him as a "former Beatle" are inaccurate. Whatever else he became, Harrison—like John Lennon, Paul McCartney, and Ringo Starr—remained, and will always remain, a Beatle.

But in an objective sense, of course, the unit that had been the Beatles did come to an end in 1970, and for the last thirty years of his life, Harrison worked to construct a personal musical legacy that would stand alongside the collective output of the group and by which he would be judged. His first musical mentors were those performers who had influenced thousands of British teenagers to take up the guitar, and to switch from music-listening to music-making, in the 1950s: Elvis Presley, Buddy Holly, Carl Perkins, Little Richard, Lonnie Donegan, and others. During his years with the Beatles, he absorbed influences from an eclectic range of contemporary sources that included the Byrds, Smokey Robinson, and the Band. Then, as a solo artist, he frequently returned to the songs and styles of those prewar composers who had provided the backdrop to his childhood in the 1940s, such as Cole Porter, Hoagy Carmichael, Cab Calloway, and George Formby. All these impressions certainly helped to shape, and reflect, the creative context in which Harrison's distinctive musical signature developed. However, within his forty-year career, there were five definitive musical liaisons which gave that signature its momentum and determined its direction: these were his working attachments with John Lennon, Bob Dylan, Ravi Shankar, Eric Clapton, and Jeff Lynne.

Harrison's relationship with Lennon was perhaps the most complex. When Harrison first met him, through McCartney in early 1958, he was regarded as something of a hanger-on—even a nuisance—by the seventeen-year-old Lennon, for whom the two-and-a-half-year difference in their age was, at times, a severe social embarrassment.[1] When Harrison was deported from Germany in November 1960 during the Beatles' spell at Hamburg's Top Ten Club, for not possessing the appropriate adult work permit, his youth temporarily threatened the continued existence of the group itself.[2] And yet, despite these difficulties, he possessed a tenacious determination that was helped by the unbroken presence and continuous encouragement of his family.

The significance of this stable and supportive family background is often overlooked in biographies of the group and discussions of Harrison's position within it. Lennon's parents had separated in his childhood; his mother was killed in a traffic accident in 1958, and he had no contact with his father for a period of eighteen years, until his sudden reappearance in 1963. From the age of five, he had been brought up by his Aunt Mimi, whose disapproval of her nephew's love for rock 'n' roll has passed into folklore: "The guitar's all very well, John, but you'll never make a living from it." McCartney's mother had died in 1956 and, while his father never actively opposed his musical ambitions, he hoped that he would gain sufficient academic qualifications to pursue a career as a teacher.[3] Starr's parents had separated when he was just three years old, and at the age of six, he had spent more than a year in the hospital, recovering from the effects of appendicitis and peritonitis. And the group's first regular drummer, Pete Best, had an equally unsettled domestic background: his parents' marriage effectively ended in the early 1950s (although they were never divorced), and in 1962, just a few weeks before he was replaced by Starr, his thirty-eight-year-old mother gave birth to a child fathered by the Beatles roadie and Best's close friend, nineteen-year-old Neil Aspinall.[4]

In contrast, Harrison's childhood and adolescence were years of security and calm, creating an environment in which he was able to concentrate time and energy on efforts to improve his ability as a guitarist. The readiness with which the Harrisons made their home available to the group for its rehearsals was an unexpected benefit, and his status was confirmed by the choice of "In Spite of All the Danger" as the first original Beatles composition to be recorded. From that point on, his role within the Beatles was assured. For the next few years, Harrison quietly put to one side any serious thoughts of songwriting, but the daily inspiration provided by the example of Lennon and McCartney—which he readily acknowledged[5]—made it almost inevitable that he would return to it. And when he did (with "Don't Bother Me"), it was quite clear that of the two, it was Lennon who was his principal musical role model.

Harrison's lyrical preference for Lennon's tough cynicism ("Run for Your Life," "Not a Second Time," "You Can't Do That") against McCartney's overall sweetness ("And I Love Her," "Things We Said Today," "I've Just Seen a Face") was matched by his musical imitation of the buried melodies in Lennon's songs ("This Boy," "If I Fell," "Nowhere Man") rather than McCartney's tumbling modulations ("Can't Buy Me Love," "I'll Follow the Sun," "Another Girl"). He often cited "I Am the Walrus"—with its surrealistic tone, challenging vocabulary, and interpretive balance between the serious and the humorous—as a model for the sort of music he wished to emulate.[6]

The truth behind Lennon's claims that he would often help Harrison to complete his songs may be a matter for debate, but it explains the former's disappointment at not being given the credit he felt he deserved in the pages of Harrison's *I Me Mine*.[7] In addition, Lennon also harbored a deep resentment for what he saw as Harrison's hostility toward Yoko Ono.[8] And he not only challenged, but ridiculed, Harrison's religious beliefs, in songs like "God" (in which he poured scorn on the Bible, Jesus, Buddha, mantra, Gita, and yoga) and "I Found Out" (which compared Hare Krishna with "pie in the sky" and taunted that "there ain't no guru who can see through your eyes").

Yet despite these tensions, Harrison rarely reciprocated any ill feeling. From his public declaration in the 1970s that he would eagerly accept any opportunity to play with Lennon to the belief he expressed in the 1990s that Lennon would have readily participated in the Traveling Wilburys, it is clear that Harrison maintained a genuine artistic admiration for him, which was often absent from his musical relationship with McCartney.[9] Indeed, the determination with which Harrison organized the Concert for Bangla Desh was, in many ways, derived from Lennon's strength of political purpose. When, in the lyrics of "All Those Years Ago," Harrison sang "I always looked up to you," he was simply stating a historical fact.

Harrison first met Clapton in December 1964, during the weeklong run of the Beatles' Christmas shows at London's Hammersmith Odeon, when the Yardbirds (along with Elkie Brooks, Sounds Incorporated, and Freddie and the Dreamers) were among the supporting acts. In March 1965, Clapton left the Yardbirds to join John Mayall's Bluesbreakers, and a year after that, coinciding with the "Clapton Is God" graffiti that began to appear in and around London, he left Mayall and formed Cream. His technical virtuosity, free-flowing style, and ability to translate the blues traditions of Robert Johnson into a form that could be appreciated by white audiences made him popular music's first guitar hero. The two spent increasing amounts of time in each other's company, and the collaborations in 1968 on "While My Guitar Gently Weeps" and "Badge" were the beginning of a musical partnership that would continue over the next three decades.

While there is little doubt that Harrison's professional commitment to the guitar intensified as a result of their friendship—even to the point of adopting the Gibson SG Standard model favored by Clapton[10]—it is important to point out that Clapton's role was that of a facilitator rather than a mentor. Harrison never aspired to play the guitar like Clapton. Nor did he regard him as a competitor: on the few occasions when they did engage in a "guitar duel," it was inevitably Clapton who emerged victorious.[11] But, crucially, he did enable Harrison to construct a sense of his own worth as a musician. Just as Clapton felt honored to have been asked to assist in the recording of "While My Guitar Gently Weeps," so too Harrison's invitation to record with Cream was a welcome indication of his prestige within rock's musical hierarchy, at a time when the Beatles' internal divisions were beginning to undermine his self-confidence.[12]

From that point on, Clapton was a constant and reliable presence in Harrison's career. In addition to their numerous recording collaborations, it was he who encouraged Harrison to tour with Delaney and Bonnie in 1969, who stood alongside him on stage at the Concert for Bangla Desh in 1971, who engineered his return to live performance on the 1991 tour of Japan, and who organized the Concert for George in 2002. The fact that their friendship remained unaffected by the personal complications stemming from their marriages to Pattie Boyd is a testament to the depth of their mutual affection.

Given their overlapping histories, it may appear surprising that Clapton and Harrison managed to compose only a handful of songs together, but in fact, their differing musical backgrounds prevented any significant writing activity. Harrison's life in popular music had been ignited by rock 'n' roll, Clapton's by the blues. While the two styles were not incompatible, they contained sufficient distinctions in approach, execution, and emphasis to make joint compositions an unlikely proposition. In addition, Clapton never shared the spiritual impetus that informed a major part of Harrison's songwriting in the post-Beatles years. Their relationship is, therefore, best understood as one of parallel development: separate trajectories that crossed common ground, and occasionally merged, but which remained essentially independent.

Although the Beatles did not meet Dylan until August 1964, each had been aware of the other's music for some time before that.[13] Individually, both Lennon and McCartney were quick to incorporate lyrical and melodic patterns from his music into their own existing styles (on tracks like "I'm a Loser," "I've Just Seen a Face," "It's Only Love," "I'm Looking through You," and "You've Got to Hide Your Love Away"). However, at that point, Harrison's career as a songwriter was barely beginning, and for him the impact of Dylan's songs was that much more profound, helping to define his evolving style. To describe a songwriter as "socially conscious" has become something of a cliché, but the major lesson that Harrison learned from Dylan was that he could move away from the conventions of the two- or three-minute love song and begin to engage with the political as well as the personal in his music. While early signs of this were evident in several of his Beatles songs ("Taxman," "I Want to Tell You," "Piggies"), it was after he was freed from the constraints of group membership that he used his newfound independence to dramatically expand the range of his songwriting activities, often in unpredictable and idiosyncratic ways.

Harrison's association with Clapton may have included many more shared appearances, but in terms of creative output, it is his relationship with Dylan that has been the more productive. Their joint authorship of "I'd Have You Anytime" (and the still unreleased "Every Time Somebody Comes to Town") in the late 1960s was repeated twenty years later in the multiple compositions of the Traveling Wilburys. In the intervening years, Harrison covered several of Dylan's songs ("If Not for You," "I Don't Want to Do It") and wrote and recorded numerous tracks whose lyrical references, rhyming structures, and thematic concerns were clearly derived from Dylan's examples.

Of course, given the enormity of Dylan's contribution to popular music, it would be surprising if there were no signs of his influence on his fellow musicians. Just as the Beatles themselves provided new musical templates to which others could refer, so too Dylan created theoretical and substantive models for those wishing to explore alternative routes. What makes the connections between the two unusual is that they were reciprocated in equal measure. After Dylan, the Beatles' music was collectively character-ized by an overtly political stance, while at the same time the individual members began to develop quite distinctive artistic traits. After the Beatles, Dylan's music shifted from acoustic, folk-based compositions to electric rock 'n' roll, and he began to replace his solo performing style with the onstage companionship of the Band.

Harrison was never in any doubt about his debt to Dylan, and he remained a loyal and devoted admirer. Over the years, other performers have been colloquially depicted in ways that seem to elevate and preserve their status—Elvis Presley, as "the King"; James Brown, "the Godfather of Soul"; Bruce Springsteen, "the Boss"; Michael Jackson, "the King of Pop"—but to Harrison there was only one "gaffer"; no one else came close.[14] In 2007, an appropriate legacy of their personal and professional friendship was included on the compilation album *Instant Karma: The Amnesty International Campaign to Save Darfur*. Aimed at raising funds to alleviate the humanitarian crisis caused by the civil war in western Sudan, the album featured interpretations of Lennon's songs by a wide-ranging collection of musicians, including R.E.M. ("Number 9 Dream"), Youssou N'Dour ("Jealous Guy"), U2 ("Instant Karma"), and Jackson Browne ("Oh My Love"). Also included was a contemporary, and persua-sive, reworking of "Gimme Some Truth," performed by Jakob Dylan and Dhani Harrison.

Harrison's close relationship with Shankar has often been used to sup-port the claim that he was the first musician to incorporate elements of In-dian music—particularly the sitar—into Western rock. While this may be hard to prove, it is certainly true that he popularized it and generated enormous interest among performers and audiences alike. His enthusiasm was initially triggered after interludes of sitar music had been added to the soundtrack of *Help!* to add to the Indian identification of the cult followers of the goddess Kaili. However, he was not entirely alone in his eagerness to investigate the instrument and the styles of music with which it was associated. In 1965, the raga-like drone of the Kinks' "See My Friends" and the Yardbirds' "Heart Full of Soul" had both preceded Harrison's first credited use of the sitar on "Norwegian Wood"; the following year, the Rolling Stones' "Paint It Black" and the Byrds' "Eight Miles High" would introduce more audiences to East–West musical syntheses. When Harrison met Shankar, in London in June 1966, it was therefore at a time when the implications of fusing the two separate musical traditions which they represented were already under consideration.

Nonetheless, the immediate friendship between the two and Harrison's earnest desire to learn the sitar from Shankar set him apart from those con-temporary musicians for whom the instrument was, if not a new toy, cer-tainly only a temporary distraction. After a few preliminary lessons at his home in Esher, Harrison traveled to Bombay in September 1966, the first of many visits to the country, during which he would supplement his dedication to the country's music with an equally determined approach to understanding its religion and philosophies. Shankar's gift to him of Paramhansa Yogananda's *Autobiography of a Yogi* cemented his spiritual commitment and directed him along a path that would continue to influence his musical output for the next thirty-five years. Thus, although the overt use of the sitar largely disappeared from his recorded music after *Wonderwall Music* and "The Inner Light" in 1968, the themes of devotion, humility, sacrifice, and self-scrutiny emphasized by his Indian gurus remained ever-present in the lyrics of his songs.[15]

And far from being simply friends, the two were fellow musicians. Shankar's appearances at the Concert for Bangla Desh in 1971, the Dark Horse Tour in 1974, and the Concert for George in 2002 reminded Western audiences of the key part he played in Harrison's musical history; similarly Harrison's role as producer of albums such as *Ravi Shankar and Ali Akbar Khan in Concert* (1972), *Shankar Family and Friends* (1974), *Ravi Shankar's Music Festival from India* (1976), *Ravi Shankar in Celebration: Highlights* (1996), and *Ravi Shankar: Chants of India* (1997) demonstrated his enduring love for the music, and musicians, of India. Harrison and Shankar both saw their relationship as a complex mixture of father–son, teacher–student, and close friends.[16] In one sense, they appeared to have nothing in common: the twenty-three-year difference in their ages, the gulf in their cultural, geographical, and religious backgrounds, and the gap in their social status (Harrison's father was a bus driver, Shankar's was the chief minister to the Maharajah of Jhalawar) would seem to rule out any basis for friendship. And yet, in another sense, those contrasting factors helped to prevent any personal or professional rivalries, produced spaces and separations that their music could fill, and ultimately created—from two very different beginnings—a partnership that was never competitive, but perfectly complementary.

From the mid-1970s onward, the concept of "world music"—broadly defined as music produced outside North America and Western Europe and sung in languages other than English—became a familiar category to rock and pop audiences, through the indigenous music of singer-songwriters such as Bob Marley and well-publicized collaborations with third world musicians by David Byrne, Paul Simon, Peter Gabriel, Ry Cooder, and others.[17] Although the term—initially, a marketing brand devised by the major record companies—was never formally applied to the music they produced, there is little doubt that, individually and in partnership, Harrison and Shankar (along with contemporary African performers such as Hugh Masakela and Miriam Makeba) were important pioneers in the erosion of traditional ethnic and geographical boundaries between musical forms.

When Harrison's collaborations with Lynne began in the mid-1980s, it was at a time when his professional status and musical enjoyment were at a particularly low point. *Somewhere in England* and *Gone Troppo* had, for different reasons, been disappointing albums, and his displeasure at their negative reception had kept him away from the recording studio for five years. In addition, the critical mauling given to *Shanghai Surprise* had damaged the reputation of Handmade Films, and there was a perception that Harrison's achievements might remain things of the past. By contrast, Lynne's reputation was at its highest point. With the Electric Light Orchestra, he had enjoyed multimillion sales figures and sellout stadium tours around the world, but was beginning to seek new challenges: thus, as producer and/ or writer, he had worked with performers as diverse as Dave Edmunds, Del Shannon, Helen Reddy, the Everly Brothers, and Agnetha Faltskog.

He and Harrison came from similar backgrounds. Born in the 1940s, both experienced their early musical socialization through the American rock 'n' roll that swept across the United Kingdom in the mid-1950s. Both were born into working-class homes, in large manufacturing conurbations whose distance from London facilitated the growth of distinctive local musical scenes: among the other musicians to have emerged from the "Black Country" around Birmingham—the name reflects the heavy industrial landscape and its legacy of smoke and soot—are the Moody Blues, the Spencer Davis Group, Slade, Led Zeppelin's John Bonham and Robert Plant, Black Sabbath, and Judas Priest.

Much of the music of Lynne's first group, the Beatles-inspired Idle Race, was marked by a whimsical, almost plaintive character that managed to combine McCartney's pop cuteness with Lennon's surreal meanderings. In ELO, those themes remained, but were surrounded by production techniques that brought together elements of orchestral backing, classical arrangements, and grandiose melodies to create a powerful commercial presence. In 1979, Harrison had created a plausible imitation of ELO's approach on "Faster," but had not repeated the experiment. Now, after the relative failures of *Somewhere in England* and *Gone Troppo*, he was aware that, while his recent music might have retained its personal, original, and idiosyncratic qualities, it had (notwithstanding the success of "All Those Years Ago") certainly lost its commercial edge. With Lynne's help, he rediscovered it.

As coproducer (and occasional cowriter) from *Cloud Nine*, through the detours of the Traveling Wilburys and the re-creations of "Free As a Bird" and "Real Love," to *Brainwashed*, Lynne effectively directed the last decade of Harrison's career. He never attempted to exercise a controlling influence, but, by sharing some of the responsibilities Harrison had previously shouldered alone, he gave him a freedom that allowed him to return to the sheer enjoyment of making, and playing, music. Under Lynne's guidance, and with a little help from his friends, Harrison's songs recaptured the positive, forceful exuberance that had gradually been eroded, producing mature and sophisticated examples of contemporary rock that were as much of their time as "Don't Bother Me," "Here Comes the Sun," and "My Sweet Lord" had been of theirs.

Although it would be perverse to cast it in terms of a musical collaboration, there was one more attachment in Harrison's life that exerted an equally profound influence on the music he created: his relationship with God. His rejection of Catholicism as a child effectively severed any ties with religion for years, but his decision was motivated less by a lack of interest in such matters than by his conclusion that many Western faiths, especially Roman Catholicism, were hypocritical institutions that recruited and controlled their members through fear.[18] When, in the mid-1960s, he visited India for the first time and discovered that Hinduism was not only a religion but also a way of life guided by principles of compassion, devotion, meditation, and inner consciousness, he was immediately drawn to it. Although he never formally became a Hindu, Harrison persistently incorporated elements of its beliefs into a humanitarian spirituality that illuminated his life and suffused his music.

Beginning with "Within You Without You" and "The Inner Light," Harrison embarked on a musical mission to refashion rock 'n' roll as a legitimate vehicle for religious debate. It was to remain one of his abiding practices. Furthermore, as the considerable number of biblical quotations and references to reincarnation in his songs attest, his was not a narrow, exclusive view of belief grounded in a particular church, but one which combined components of Hinduism, Christianity, and Buddhism.[19] The lexical similarity between "Christ" and "Krishna" (both derived from the Greek word *Christos*) was, to Harrison, an affirmation of the "oneness" of all religions. This is why so many of his songs, from *All Things Must Pass* to *Brainwashed*, refer not to a specific deity, but to "God" or "the Lord": a divine reality, known by different names across different faiths. And, for Harrison, the essence of this divinity was love. Indeed, his belief that human love and spiritual love were inseparable parts of the universal love explains the apparent ambiguity in many of his songs between romance and religion. From this perspective, the unresolved status of the nature of the love presented in the lyrics of "Long Long Long," "Isn't It a Pity," "Love Comes to Everyone," "Blow Away," and "Wake Up My Love" is irrelevant. The two kinds of love are, in fact, one.

His commitment to the divine nature of love was, of course, one of the characteristics that distinguished his solo career from those of Lennon and McCartney. As Beatles, all had written of its radical ability to transform our lives. Lennon's insistence that "all you need is love," McCartney's belief that "the love you take is equal to the love you make," and Harrison's claim that "with our love we could save the world" were cogent reflections of the zeitgeist of the late 1960s. But while his partners quickly moved on to other topics in their songs, Harrison's ongoing exploration of the theme within its religious framework was indicative of a constant and deliberate reflection on the role and function of his music. God was not just a character in a song, but the inspiration for much of his music.

In 1992, when Harrison attended the *Billboard* Music Awards ceremony to become the first recipient of its Century Award, which salutes the "creative achievement of an artist's still-developing body of work,"[20] he expressed surprise that he had been singled out for commendation.[21] It echoed his sentiments of three decades earlier, when the Beatles were awarded the MBE (Member of the Order of the British Empire), for services to industry.[22] While he retained a healthy cynicism about the credibility of such honors and the motivations of those giving them, they do nonetheless provide one indication of a performer's status and an overall sense of his or her position within the popular music community. It is, therefore, worth noting that in addition to the 1970 Academy Award for Original Music Score given to the Beatles for the soundtrack of *Let It Be*, Harrison's work was recognized on numerous occasions throughout his forty-year career, including eleven Grammys (as a Beatle, a Traveling Wilbury, and a solo performer), from Best New Artist (with the Beatles) in 1964 to Best Pop Instrumental Performance (for "Marwa Blues") in 2003, and two separate inductions into the Rock and Roll Hall of Fame (with the Beatles in 1988 and as a solo performer in 2004).[23] And in 2009, at a ceremony attended by McCartney, Petty, Lynne, Eric Idle, and Olivia and Dhani Harrison, the Hollywood Chamber of Commerce honored him by unveiling a star on the Hollywood Walk of Fame. Appropriately, his star is in front of the iconic, thirteen-story Capitol Records tower, where, in the 1960s, telephone callers were greeted by the words, "Capitol Records: Home of the Beatles."

Among the many hundreds of quotations attributed to Harrison, there are two that, while they may well be apocryphal, seem to sum up his attitude toward his musical career. The first was in response to an invitation to look back over his years as a Beatle: "Well," he reflected, "if you've got to be in a rock 'n' roll band, it might as well be the Beatles." The second was during a conversation with Michael Palin, who complained about being overshadowed by other members of the Monty Python team: "You should try being in a band with Lennon and McCartney," responded Harrison.

Both statements are lovely examples of the dry, self-deprecating strain of humor that distinguished Harrison throughout his life. But both also contain genuine insights into what it was like to be George Harrison. For all the achievements of his post-Beatles career, he knew that the most auspicious moment of his fifty-eight years was when he was invited by Lennon and McCartney to join the Quarry Men. Although the benefits of being a Beatle far outweighed the drawbacks of being perceived as a junior partner in the group, the task of trying to correct that imbalance was something he never fully accomplished. Lennon's frank assertion that he and McCartney would have succeeded with two other musicians, whereas Harrison and Starr would not, only made explicit what many others might have acknowledged implicitly.[24] But this does not disguise the fact that the magic of the Beatles lay in their unique combination of individual musical characteristics. Lennon's raw genius, McCartney's commercial polish, Harrison's precise craftsmanship, and Starr's robust adaptability gelled perfectly to create the most sublime popular music most of us will ever hear.[25] It is scarcely surprising that, like Lennon and McCartney, Harrison found it simply impossible to reproduce the same consistency of perfection and innovation in his post-Beatle music.

And yet, he never shirked from the challenge. *All Things Must Pass* was a stunning debut album and an intense spiritual statement; *The Concert for Bangla Desh* established the artistic legitimacy of the charity album; *Cloud Nine* represented one of rock's most successful "comebacks"; and the two *Traveling Wilburys* albums took the concept of the recording "supergroup" to new heights. Even on his less acclaimed albums, there are individual songs, often overlooked, of great charm, energy, and beauty: examples include "Grey Cloudy Lies" from *Extra Texture*; "Pure Smokey" from *Thirty Three & 1/3*; "Your Love Is Forever" from *George Harrison*; "Life Itself" from *Somewhere in England*; and "That's the Way It Goes" from *Gone Troppo*. Harrison's music could be irritatingly idiosyncratic ("His Name Is Legs," "I Don't Care Anymore"), written-to-order products ("Poor Little Girl," "That Kind of Woman"), or affectionate imitations of others' styles ("Learning How to Love You," "Hottest Gong in Town"). He engaged in philosophical discussions of the human condition ("The Art of Dying," "Circles") and searingly honest bouts of self-examination ("Just for Today," "Pisces Fish"). He wrote love songs ("Let It Down," "Dark Sweet Lady") and prayers ("Hear Me Lord," "Dear One"). His lyrics expressed his fondness for family ("Deep Blue," "Unknown Delight") and friends ("Miss O'Dell," "Behind That Locked Door") and his contempt for the self-styled leaders of politics and industry ("Save the World," "Brainwashed").

Harrison's music brought together elements from each of the five separate traditions whose synthesis in the early 1950s gave birth to rock 'n' roll. From the blues, he learned the ways in which a song can become a personal statement of reflection and melancholy; from gospel, he took not only the themes of redemption and religious salvation but also the structure of call and response between the lead vocalist and backing singers; from jazz, he incorporated displays of musical expertise and improvisation into his own development as a guitarist; from ballads, he absorbed the conventions of the love song; and from folk song (which includes country music), he understood the importance of music's narrative function and the ability of songs to tell stories. And although the majority of his compositions were songs, he also wrote memorable instrumental tracks. From "Cry for a Shadow" to "Marwa Blues," his determination to be recognized as a guitarist never deserted him.

The celebrated epigraph at the beginning of E. M. Forster's *Howard's End* states simply: "Only connect." It is a call, echoed across much of his writing, to seize the day and unite the spiritual and material aspects of life. This was, in essence, the goal that Harrison set himself: to understand the relationship between the two sides of his life and to see them not as competing, but as complementary, forces.

While the task of the man was to achieve that understanding, the task of the songwriter was then to communicate it to others. The mechanisms by which that communication might be accomplished, and the motivations that lie behind it, have been explained in different ways by singer-songwriters,[26] and when those (sometimes overlapping) classifications are applied to the body of work produced by Harrison, it quickly becomes apparent that his songs demonstrate his ability to utilize each of them within his overall songwriting strategy. The concept of music as magical communication sees music itself as a product whose inspiration comes from someplace other than the musician; whether this other source is divine ("Be Here Now," "It Is He") or drug induced ("It's All Too Much," "I Me Mine"), the songwriter is simply a vehicle through which it flows. To approach music as social/political communication is to recognize the way in which songs can function as commentaries about the actions of particular groups ("Taxman," "Devil's Radio") or draw attention to specific events ("Bangla Desh," "All Those Years Ago"). Music can also take the form of personal communication, where song composition becomes a form of private diary writing ("Sue Me Sue You Blues," "Stuck Inside a Cloud") or an opportunity for reflexive self-analysis ("So Sad," "Looking for My Life"). The concept of music as formal communication focuses on the texture of music and its constituent technologies; sounds (synthetic and natural) become more important than words, melodies, and harmonies (*Wonderwall*). Music as adult communication describes the transition from adolescent to adult themes that reflects the experiences and changed priorities of songwriters as they move into parenthood, marriage, and middle age ("Any Road," "Wreck of the Hesperus"). Harrison's capacity to draw from all these patterns, to switch between them, and to do so across a variety of styles and periods is, by any standards, an impressive achievement. It also illustrates the flexible, enlightened, and progressive qualities that run through his words and music.

He preferred to write alone, but he also composed with some of the most illustrious names in popular music. The decade-long presence of Lennon and McCartney as professional role models brought opportunities and restrictions, and although even his earliest compositions have a distinctive quality (most clearly in their preference for minor chords), it was not until the

Beatles' demise in 1970 that he began to move away from the group's collective songwriting consciousness.[27] Many of his songs were inspired by his two wives, Pattie and Olivia, but he had no desire to have them accompany him in the studio or support him on the stage. The private and public responsibility for his songs was always his own. To himself, and to countless others, his music was a source of enjoyment, a vehicle of exploration, and a register of experience. It was also his life, his profession, and his craft.

Discography

The following comprises a complete listing of George Harrison's albums and singles, in chronological order of release.

ALBUMS

Wonderwall Music

George Harrison; Ashish Khan, sarod; Mahapurush Misra, tabla and pakavaj; Sharad and Hanuman Jadev, shanhais; Shambu-Das, sitar; Indril Bhattacharya, sitar; Shankar Ghosh, sitar; Chandra Shakher, sur-bahar; Shiv Kumar Shermar, santoor; S. R. Kenkare, flute; Vinaik Vora, thar-shanhai; Rij Ram Desad, harmonium and tabla-tarang; John Barham, piano and flugel horn; Tommy Reilly, harmonica; Colin Manley, guitar and steel guitar; Tony Ashton, jangle piano and organ; Philip Rogers, bass guitar; Roy Dyke, drums. Produced by George Harrison. 33⅓ rpm phonodisc, Apple ST 3350 (1968); reissued on compact disc, Apple 7-98706-2 (1992).

"Microbes" (Harrison)
"Red Lady Too" (Harrison)
"Tabla and Pakavaj" (Harrison)
"In the Park" (Harrison)
"Drilling a Home" (Harrison)
"Guru Vandana" (Harrison)
"Greasy Legs" (Harrison)

"Ski-ing" (Harrison)
"Gat Kirwani" (Harrison)
"Dream Scene" (Harrison)
"Party Seacombe" (Harrison)
"Love Scene" (Harrison)
"Crying" (Harrison)
"Cowboy Music" (Harrison)
"Fantasy Sequins" (Harrison)
"On the Bed" (Harrison)
"Glass Box" (Harrison)
"Wonderwall to Be Here" (Harrison)
"Singing Om" (Harrison)

Electronic Sound

George Harrison. Produced by George Harrison. 33⅓ rpm phonodisc, Zapple ST 3358 (1969); reissued on compact disc, Apple 8-55239-2 (1996).

"Under the Mersey Wall" (Harrison)
"No Time or Space" (Harrison)

All Things Must Pass

George Harrison, guitar and vocals; Ringo Starr, drums and percussion; Jim Gordon, drums and percussion; Andy White, drums and percussion; Klaus Voormann, bass guitar; Carl Radle, bass guitar; Gary Wright, keyboards; Bobby Whitlock, keyboards; Billy Preston, keyboards; Gary Brooker, keyboards; Pete Drake, pedal-steel guitar; Dave Mason, guitar; Bobby Keys, tenor saxophone; Jim Price, trumpet; Badfinger, rhythm guitars and percussion. Produced by George Harrison and Phil Spector. 33⅓ rpm phonodisc, Apple STCH 639 (1970); reissued on compact disc, Capitol 46688 (1990).

"I'd Have You Anytime" (Harrison, Dylan)
"My Sweet Lord" (Harrison)
"Wah-Wah" (Harrison)
"Isn't It a Pity, Version One" (Harrison)
"What Is Life" (Harrison)
"If Not for You" (Dylan)
"Behind That Locked Door" (Harrison)
"Run of the Mill" (Harrison)
"Beware of Darkness" (Harrison)

"Apple Scruffs" (Harrison)
"Ballad of Sir Frankie Crisp (Let It Roll)" (Harrison)
"Awaiting on You All" (Harrison)
"All Things Must Pass" (Harrison)
"I Dig Love" (Harrison)
"Art of Dying" (Harrison)
"Isn't It a Pity, Version Two" (Harrison)
"Hear Me Lord" (Harrison)
"Out of the Blue" (Gordon, Radle, Whitlock, Clapton, Wright, Harrison, Price, Keys, Aronowitz)
"It's Johnny's Birthday" (Harrison, Evans, Klein)
"Plug Me In" (Gordon, Radle, Whitlock, Clapton, Mason, Harrison)
"I Remember Jeep" (Baker, Voormann, Preston, Clapton, Harrison)
"Thanks for the Pepperoni" (Gordon, Radle, Whitlock, Clapton, Mason, Harrison)

The Concert for Bangla Desh

George Harrison, guitar and vocals; Eric Clapton, guitar; Bob Dylan, guitar and vocals; Billy Preston, keyboards and vocals; Leon Russell, keyboards, bass guitar and vocals; Ringo Starr, drums, percussion, and vocals; Klaus Voormann, bass guitar; Jim Horn, saxophone; Carl Radle, bass guitar; Don Preston, guitar and vocals; Pete Ham, acoustic guitar; Ravi Shankar, sitar; Ali Akbar Khan, sarod; Alla Rakah, tabla; Kamala Chakravarty, tamboura; additional supporting vocalists and instrumentalists. Produced by George Harrison and Phil Spector. $33^1/_3$ rpm phonodisc, Apple STCX 3385 (1972); reissued on compact disc, Epic 468835-2 (1991).

"Bangla Dhun" (Shankar, Khan)
"Wah-Wah" (Harrison)
"My Sweet Lord" (Harrison)
"Awaiting on You All" (Harrison)
"That's the Way God Planned It" (Preston)
"It Don't Come Easy" (Starkey)
"Beware of Darkness" (Harrison)
"While My Guitar Gently Weeps" (Harrison)
"Jumpin' Jack Flash" (Jagger, Richards)
"Young Blood" (Lieber, Stoller, Pomus)
"Here Comes the Sun" (Harrison)
"A Hard Rain's Gonna Fall" (Dylan)
"It Takes a Lot to Laugh, It Takes a Train to Cry" (Dylan)
"Blowin' in the Wind" (Dylan)
"Mr Tambourine Man" (Dylan)

"Just Like a Woman" (Dylan)
"Something" (Harrison)
"Bangla Desh" (Harrison)

Living in the Material World

George Harrison, guitar and vocals; Nicky Hopkins, keyboards; Gary Wright, keyboards; Klaus Voormann, bass guitar; Jim Keltner, drums; Ringo Starr, drums; Jim Gordon, drums; Jim Horn, saxophone and flute; Zakir Hussein, tabla; John Barham, strings. Produced by George Harrison; "Try Some Buy Some" produced by George Harrison and Phil Spector. 33⅓ rpm phonodisc, Apple SMAS 3410 (1973); reissued on compact disc, Capitol 94110 (1992).

"Give Me Love (Give Me Peace on Earth)" (Harrison)
"Sue Me Sue You Blues" (Harrison)
"The Light That Has Lighted the World" (Harrison)
"Don't Let Me Wait Too Long" (Harrison)
"Who Can See It" (Harrison)
"Living in the Material World" (Harrison)
"The Lord Loves the One (That Loves the Lord)" (Harrison)
"Be Here Now" (Harrison)
"Try Some Buy Some" (Harrison)
"The Day the World Gets Round" (Harrison)
"That Is All" (Harrison)

Dark Horse

George Harrison, guitar and vocals; Ringo Starr, drums; Jim Keltner, drums and percussion; Nicky Hopkins, keyboards; Billy Preston, keyboards; Gary Wright, keyboards; Willie Weeks, bass guitar; Andy Newmark, drums; Klaus Voormann, bass guitar; Mick Jones, guitar; Alvin Lee, guitar; Tom Scott, horns; Roger Kellaway, piano; John Guerin, drums; Max Bennett, bass guitar; Robben Ford, guitar; Jim Horn, flute; Chuck Findley, flute; Lon and Derek Van Eaton, backing vocals. Produced by George Harrison. 33⅓ rpm phonodisc, Apple SMAS 3418 (1974); reissued on compact disc, Capitol 98079 (1992).

"Hari's on Tour (Express)" (Harrison)
"Simply Shady" (Harrison)
"So Sad" (Harrison)
"Bye Bye Love" (Felice and Boudeleaux Bryant)
"Maya Love" (Harrison)

"Ding Dong, Ding Dong" (Harrison)
"Dark Horse" (Harrison)
"Far East Man" (Harrison)
"It Is He (Jai Sri Krishna)" (Harrison)

Extra Texture

George Harrison, guitar and vocals; Jim Keltner, drums and percussion; Nicky Hopkins, keyboards; Billy Preston, keyboards; Carl Radle, bass guitar; Leon Russell, piano; Gary Wright, keyboards; David Foster, keyboards and strings; Jim Horn, saxophone; Paul Stallworth, bass guitar; Jim Gordon, drums; Jesse Ed Davis, guitar; Klaus Voormann, bass guitar; Chuck Findley, horns; Andy Newmark, drums; Willie Weeks, bass; Tom Scott, horns. Produced by George Harrison. 33⅓ rpm phonodisc, Apple SW 3420 (1975); reissued on compact disc, Capitol 98080 (2000).

"You" (Harrison)
"The Answer's at the End" (Harrison)
"This Guitar (Can't Keep from Crying)" (Harrison)
"Ooh Baby (You Know That I Love You)" (Harrison)
"World of Stone" (Harrison)
"A Bit More of You" (Harrison)
"Can't Stop Thinking about You" (Harrison)
"Tired of Midnight Blue" (Harrison)
"Grey Cloudy Lies" (Harrison)
"His Name Is Legs (Ladies & Gentlemen)" (Harrison)

Thirty Three & ⅓

George Harrison, guitar, synthesizers, percussion, and vocals; Gary Wright, keyboards; Billy Preston, keyboards; Alvin Taylor, drums; David Foster, guitar and clavinet; Emil Richards, marimba; Richard Tee, keyboards; Willie Weeks, bass guitar; Tom Scott, saxophone, flute, and lyricon. Produced by George Harrison. 33⅓ rpm phonodisc, Dark Horse DH 3005 (1976); reissued on compact disc, Capitol 94086 (2004).

"Woman Don't You Cry for Me" (Harrison)
"Dear One" (Harrison)
"Beautiful Girl" (Harrison)
"This Song" (Harrison)
"See Yourself" (Harrison)
"It's What You Value" (Harrison)
"True Love" (Porter)

"Pure Smokey" (Harrison)
"Crackerbox Palace" (Harrison)
"Learning How to Love You" (Harrison)

Best of George Harrison

33⅓ rpm phonodisc, Capitol ST 11578 (1976); reissued on compact disc, Apple PAS 10011 (1987).

"Something" (Harrison)
"If I Needed Someone" (Harrison)
"Here Comes the Sun" (Harrison)
"Taxman" (Harrison)
"Think for Yourself" (Harrison)
"For You Blue" (Harrison)
"While My Guitar Gently Weeps" (Harrison)
"My Sweet Lord" (Harrison)
"Give Me Love (Give Me Peace on Earth)" (Harrison)
"You" (Harrison)
"Bangla Desh" (Harrison)
"Dark Horse" (Harrison)
"What Is Life" (Harrison)

George Harrison

George Harrison, guitars and vocals; Steve Winwood, keyboards and backing vocals; Andy Newmark, drums; Willie Weeks, bass; Neil Larsen, keyboards; Ray Cooper, percussion; Emil Richards, marimba; Gayle Levant, harp; Gary Wright, synthesizer; Eric Clapton, guitar; Del Newman, strings and horns. Produced by George Harrison and Russ Titelman. 33⅓ rpm phonodisc, Dark Horse DHK 3255 (1979); reissued on compact disc, Capitol 94087 (2004).

"Love Comes to Everyone" (Harrison)
"Not Guilty" (Harrison)
"Here Comes the Moon" (Harrison)
"Soft-Hearted Hana" (Harrison)
"Blow Away" (Harrison)
"Faster" (Harrison)
"Dark Sweet Lady" (Harrison)
"Your Love Is Forever" (Harrison)
"Soft Touch" (Harrison)
"If You Believe" (Harrison, Wright)

Somewhere in England

George Harrison, guitars, synthesizer, and vocals; Ringo Starr, drums; Ray Cooper, percussion; Willie Weeks, bass guitar; Neil Larsen, keyboards; Gary Brooker, keyboards; Al Kooper, keyboards; Tom Scott, lyricon and horns; Jim Keltner, drums; Dave Mattacks, drums; Herbie Flowers, tuba and bass guitar; Mike Moran, keyboards; Alla Rakha, tabla; Paul and Linda McCartney and Denny Laine, backing vocals. Produced by George Harrison and Ray Cooper. 33⅓ rpm phonodisc, Dark Horse DHK 3492 (1981); reissued on compact disc, Capitol 94088 (2004).

"Blood from a Clone" (Harrison)
"Unconsciousness Rules" (Harrison)
"Life Itself" (Harrison)
"All Those Years Ago" (Harrison)
"Baltimore Oriole" (Carmichael, Webster)
"Teardrops" (Harrison)
"That Which I Have Lost" (Harrison)
"Writing's on the Wall" (Harrison)
"Hong Kong Blues" (Carmichael)
"Save the World" (Harrison)

Gone Troppo

George Harrison, guitars, mandolin, synthesizer, and vocals; Henry Spinetti, drums; Billy Preston, keyboards and backing vocals; Jon Lord, synthesizer; Herbie Flowers, bass guitar; Mike Moran, keyboards; Ray Cooper, percussion; Jim Keltner, drums; Willie Weeks, bass guitar; Neil Larsen, keyboards; Gary Brooker, synthesizer; Dave Mattacks, drums; Alan Jones, bass guitar; Joe Brown, mandolin and backing vocals; Vicki Brown, Syreeta, Sarah Ricor, Willie Greene, Bobby King, Pico Pena, and Rodina Sloan, backing vocals. Produced by George Harrison, Ray Cooper, and Phil McDonald. 33⅓ rpm phonodisc, Dark Horse 1-23734 (1982); reissued on compact disc, Capitol 94089 (2004).

"Wake Up My Love" (Harrison)
"That's the Way It Goes" (Harrison)
"I Really Love You" (Swearingen)
"Greece" (Harrison)
"Gone Troppo" (Harrison)
"Mystical One" (Harrison)
"Unknown Delight" (Harrison)
"Baby Don't Run Away" (Harrison)

"Dream Away" (Harrison)
"Circles" (Harrison)

Cloud Nine

George Harrison, guitars, keyboards, and vocals; Jeff Lynne, guitar, bass guitar, and keyboards; Eric Clapton, guitar; Elton John, piano; Gary Wright, piano; Ringo Starr, drums; Jim Keltner, drums; Ray Cooper, percussion; Jim Horn, saxophone; Bobby Kok, cello. Produced by Jeff Lynne and George Harrison. 33⅓ rpm phonodisc, Dark Horse DH 25643-1, and compact disc, Dark Horse DH 25643-2 (1987).

"Cloud 9" (Harrison)
"That's What It Takes" (Harrison, Lynne, Wright)
"Fish on the Sand" (Harrison)
"Just For Today" (Harrison)
"This Is Love" (Harrison, Lynne)
"When We Was Fab" (Harrison)
"Devil's Radio" (Harrison)
"Someplace Else" (Harrison)
"Wreck of the Hesperus (Harrison)
"Breath Away from My Heaven" (Harrison)
"Got My Mind Set on You" (Clark)

Traveling Wilburys, Volume 1

George Harrison, guitars and vocals; Jeff Lynne, keyboards, guitars, and vocals; Tom Petty, acoustic guitar and vocals; Roy Orbison, acoustic guitar and vocals; Bob Dylan, acoustic guitar and vocals; Jim Keltner, drums; Jim Horn, saxophone; Ray Cooper, percussion; Ian Wallace, tom-toms. Produced by Jeff Lynne and George Harrison. 33⅓ rpm phonodisc, Wilbury Records 25796-1, and compact disc, Wilbury Records 25796-2 (1988).

"Handle with Care" (Harrison, Lynne, Petty, Orbison, Dylan)
"Dirty World" (Harrison, Lynne, Petty, Orbison, Dylan)
"Rattled" (Harrison, Lynne, Petty, Orbison, Dylan)
"Last Night" (Harrison, Lynne, Petty, Orbison, Dylan)
"Not Alone Any More" (Harrison, Lynne, Petty, Orbison, Dylan)
"Congratulations" (Harrison, Lynne, Petty, Orbison, Dylan)
"Heading for the Light" (Harrison, Lynne, Petty, Orbison, Dylan)
"Margarita" (Harrison, Lynne, Petty, Orbison, Dylan)
"Tweeter and the Monkey Man" (Harrison, Lynne, Petty, Orbison, Dylan)
"End of the Line" (Harrison, Lynne, Petty, Orbison, Dylan)

Best of Dark Horse, 1976–1989

George Harrison, guitar, banjo, and vocals; Jeff Lynne, bass guitar, keyboards, and backing vocals; Ian Paice, drums; Jim Horn, saxophone; Richard Tandy, piano; Ray Cooper, percussion. "Poor Little Girl," "Cockamamie Business," and "Cheer Down" produced by Jeff Lynne and George Harrison. 33⅓ rpm phonodisc, Dark Horse DH 25985-1, and compact disc, Dark Horse DH 25985-2 (1989).

"Poor Little Girl" (Harrison)
"Blow Away" (Harrison)
"That's the Way It Goes" (Harrison)
"Cockamamie Business" (Harrison)
"Wake Up My Love" (Harrison)
"Life Itself" (Harrison)
"Got My Mind Set on You" (Clark)
"Crackerbox Palace" (Harrison)
"Cloud 9" (Harrison)
"Here Comes the Moon" (Harrison)
"Gone Troppo" (Harrison)
"When We Was Fab" (Harrison)
"Love Comes to Everyone" (Harrison)
"All Those Years Ago" (Harrison)
"Cheer Down" (Harrison, Petty)

Traveling Wilburys, Volume 3

George Harrison, acoustic and electric guitars, mandolin, sitar, and vocals; Jeff Lynne, acoustic guitar, bass guitar, keyboards, and vocals; Tom Petty, acoustic guitar and vocals; Bob Dylan, acoustic guitar, harmonica, and vocals; Jim Keltner, drums; Ray Cooper, percussion; Jim Horn, saxophone; Gary Wright, guitar. Produced by George Harrison and Jeff Lynne. 33⅓ rpm phonodisc, Wilbury Records 26324-1, and compact disc, Wilbury Records 26324-2 (1990).

"She's My Baby" (Harrison, Lynne, Petty, Dylan)
"Inside Out" (Harrison, Lynne, Petty, Dylan)
"If You Belonged to Me" (Harrison, Lynne, Petty, Dylan)
"The Devil's Been Busy" (Harrison, Lynne, Petty, Dylan)
"7 Deadly Sins" (Harrison, Lynne, Petty, Dylan)
"Poor House" (Harrison, Lynne, Petty, Dylan)
"Where Were You Last Night" (Harrison, Lynne, Petty, Dylan)
"Cool Dry Place" (Harrison, Lynne, Petty, Dylan)
"New Blue Moon" (Harrison, Lynne, Petty, Dylan)

"You Took My Breath Away" (Harrison, Lynne, Petty, Dylan)
"Wilbury Twist" (Harrison, Lynne, Petty, Dylan)

Live in Japan

George Harrison, guitar and vocals; Eric Clapton, guitar; Steve Ferrone, drums; Ray Cooper, percussion; Greg Phillinganes, keyboards; Chuck Leavell, keyboards; Nathan East, bass guitar; Andy Fairweather-Low, guitar and backing vocals; Tessa Niles and Katie Kissoon, backing vocals. Produced by George Harrison. Compact disc, Dark Horse DH 26964-4 (1992).

"I Want to Tell You" (Harrison)
"Old Brown Shoe" (Harrison)
"Taxman" (Harrison)
"Give Me Love (Give Me Peace on Earth)" (Harrison)
"If I Needed Someone" (Harrison)
"Something" (Harrison)
"What Is Life" (Harrison)
"Dark Horse" (Harrison)
"Piggies" (Harrison)
"Got My Mind Set on You" (Clark)
"Cloud 9" (Harrison)
"Here Comes the Sun" (Harrison)
"My Sweet Lord" (Harrison)
"All Those Years Ago" (Harrison)
"Cheer Down" (Harrison, Petty)
"Devil's Radio" (Harrison)
"Isn't It a Pity" (Harrison)
"While My Guitar Gently Weeps" (Harrison)
"Roll Over Beethoven" (Berry)

Brainwashed

George Harrison, guitars and vocals; Jeff Lynne, guitars, keyboards, and vocals; Dhani Harrison, acoustic guitar and backing vocals; Bikram Ghosh, tabla; Jon Lord, piano; Jim Keltner, drums; Jane Lister, harp; Jools Holland, piano; Mark Flanagan, acoustic guitar; Herbie Flowers, bass guitar and tuba; Ray Cooper, drums; Joe Brown, acoustic guitar; Sam Brown, backing vocals. Produced by George Harrison, Jeff Lynne, and Dhani Harrison. Compact disc, Dark Horse/Capitol C2-41969 (2002).

"Any Road" (Harrison)
"P2 Vatican Blues (Last Saturday Night)" (Harrison)

"Pisces Fish" (Harrison)
"Looking for My Life" (Harrison)
"Rising Sun" (Harrison)
"Marwa Blues" (Harrison)
"Stuck Inside a Chord" (Harrison)
"Run So Far" (Harrison)
"Never Get over You" (Harrison)
"Between the Devil and the Deep Blue Sea" (Arlen, Koehler)
"Rocking Chair in Hawaii" (Harrison)
"Brainwashed" (Harrison)

Concert for George

Anoushka Shankar, sitar; Eric Clapton, guitar and vocals; Jeff Lynne, guitar and vocals; Dhani Harrison, acoustic guitar and backing vocals; Gary Brooker, keyboards and vocals; Joe Brown, guitar, ukulele, and vocals; Tom Petty, guitar and vocals; Billy Preston, keyboards and vocals; Ringo Starr, drums and vocals; Paul McCartney, guitar, ukulele, and vocals; additional supporting vocalists and instrumentalists. Produced by Jeff Lynne. Compact disc, Warner Bros. 0349702412 (2003).

"Sarve Shaam" (traditional), concert chorus
"Your Eyes" (Ravi Shankar), Anoushka Shankar
"The Inner Light" (Harrison), Jeff Lynne and Anoushka Shankar
"Arpan" (Ravi Shankar), Anoushka Shankar
"I Want to Tell You" (Harrison), Jeff Lynne
"If I Needed Someone" (Harrison), Eric Clapton
"Old Brown Shoe" (Harrison), Gary Brooker
"Give Me Love (Give Me Peace on Earth)" (Harrison), Jeff Lynne
"Beware of Darkness" (Harrison), Eric Clapton
"Here Comes the Sun" (Harrison), Joe Brown
"That's the Way It Goes" (Harrison), Joe Brown
"Taxman" (Harrison), Tom Petty
"I Need You" (Harrison), Tom Petty
"Handle with Care" (Harrison, Lynne, Petty, Orbison, Dylan), Tom
    Petty, Jeff Lynne, and Dhani Harrison
"Isn't It a Pity" (Harrison), Billy Preston
"Photograph" (Harrison, Starr), Ringo Starr
"Honey Don't" (Perkins), Ringo Starr
"For You Blue" (Harrison), Paul McCartney
"Something" (Harrison), Paul McCartney and Eric Clapton
"All Things Must Pass" (Harrison), Paul McCartney
"While My Guitar Gently Weeps" (Harrison), Paul McCartney and
    Eric Clapton

"My Sweet Lord" (Harrison), Billy Preston
"Wah-Wah" (Harrison), Eric Clapton and Band
"I'll See You in My Dreams" (Jones, Kahn), Joe Brown

Let It Roll: Songs by George Harrison

Compact disc. Dark Horse/Capitol 65019 (2009).

"Got My Mind Set on You" (Clark)
"Give Me Love (Give Me Peace on Earth)" (Harrison)
"Ballad of Sir Frankie Crisp (Let It Roll)" (Harrison)
"My Sweet Lord" (Harrison)
"While My Guitar Gently Weeps" (Harrison)
"All Things Must Pass" (Harrison)
"Any Road" (Harrison)
"This Is Love" (Harrison, Lynne)
"All Those Years Ago" (Harrison)
"Marwa Blues" (Harrison)
"What Is Life" (Harrison)
"Rising Sun" (Harrison)
"When We Was Fab" (Harrison)
"Something" (Harrison)
"Blow Away" (Harrison)
"Cheer Down" (Harrison, Petty)
"Here Comes the Sun" (Harrison)
"I Don't Want to Do It" (Dylan)
"Isn't It a Pity" (Harrison)

SINGLES

"My Sweet Lord" (Harrison); "Isn't It A Pity" (Harrison). 45 rpm
    phonodisc, Apple 2995 (1970).
"What Is Life" (Harrison); "Apple Scruffs" (Harrison). 45 rpm
    phonodisc, Apple 1828 (1971).
"Bangla Desh" (Harrison); "Deep Blue" (Harrison). 45 rpm
    phonodisc, Apple 1836 (1971).
"Give Me Love (Give Me Peace on Earth)" (Harrison); "Miss
    O'Dell" (Harrison). 45 rpm phonodisc, Apple 1862 (1973).
"Dark Horse" (Harrison); "Hari's on Tour (Express)" (Harrison). 45
    rpm phonodisc, Apple 1877 (1974).
"Ding Dong, Ding Dong" (Harrison); "I Don't Care Anymore"
    (Harrison). 45 rpm phonodisc, Apple 1879 (1974).
"You" (Harrison); "World of Stone" (Harrison). 45 rpm phonodisc,
    Apple 1884 (1975).

"This Guitar (Can't Keep from Crying)" (Harrison); "Maya Love" (Harrison). 45 rpm phonodisc, Apple 1885 (1975).

"This Song" (Harrison); "Learning How to Love You" (Harrison). 45 rpm phonodisc, Dark Horse DRC 8294 (1976).

"Crackerbox Palace" (Harrison); "Learning How to Love You" (Harrison). 45 rpm phonodisc, Dark Horse DRC 8313 (1977).

"Blow Away" (Harrison); "Soft-Hearted Hana" (Harrison). 45 rpm phonodisc, Dark Horse DRC 8763 (1979).

"Love Comes to Everyone" (Harrison); "Soft Touch" (Harrison). 45 rpm phonodisc, Dark Horse DRC 8844 (1979).

"All Those Years Ago" (Harrison); "Writing's on the Wall" (Harrison). 45 rpm phonodisc, Dark Horse DRC 49725 (1981).

"Teardrops" (Harrison); "Save the World" (Harrison). 45 rpm phonodisc, Dark Horse DRC 49785 (1981).

"Wake Up My Love" (Harrison); "Greece" (Harrison). 45 rpm phonodisc, Dark Horse 7-29864 (1982).

"I Really Love You" (Swearingen); "Circles" (Harrison). 45 rpm phonodisc, Dark Horse 7-29744 (1983).

"I Don't Want to Do It" (Dylan); Dave Edmunds "Queen of the Hop" (Woody Harris). 45 rpm phonodisc, Columbia 38-04887 (1985).

Songs by George Harrison. "Sat Singing" (Harrison); "Lay His Head" (Harrison); "Flying Hour" (Harrison); "For You Blue" (Harrison). Limited edition 45 rpm extended play (EP) phonodisc, Genesis Publications/Ganga Distributors SGH 777 (1988).

"Got My Mind Set on You" (Clark); "Lay His Head" (Harrison). 45 rpm phonodisc, Dark Horse 7-28178 (1987).

"When We Was Fab" (Harrison); "Zig Zag" (Harrison, Lynne). 45 rpm phonodisc, Dark Horse 7-28131 (1988).

"This Is Love" (Harrison, Lynne); "Breath Away from Heaven" (Harrison). 45 rpm phonodisc, Dark Horse 7-27913 (1988).

[Traveling Wilburys] "Handle with Care" (Harrison, Lynne, Petty, Orbison, Dylan); "Margarita" (Harrison, Lynne, Petty, Orbison, Dylan). 45 rpm phonodisc, Wilbury Records 27732-7 (1988).

[Traveling Wilburys] "End of the Line" (Harrison, Lynne, Petty, Orbison, Dylan); "Congratulations" (Harrison, Lynne, Petty, Orbison, Dylan). 45 rpm phonodisc, Wilbury Records 27637-7 (1989).

"Cheer Down" (Harrison, Petty); "That's What It Takes" (Harrison). 45 rpm phonodisc, Warner Bros. 22807-7, and compact disc single, Warner Bros. 09P3-6191 (1989).

[Traveling Wilburys] "Wilbury Twist" (Harrison, Lynne, Petty, Orbison, Dylan); "New Blue Moon" (Harrison, Lynne, Petty,

Orbison, Dylan). Cassette single, Wilbury Records 19443-4 (1991).

Songs by George Harrison 2. "Life Itself" (Harrison); "Tears of the World" (Harrison); "Hottest Gong in Town" (Harrison); "Hari's on Tour (Express)." Limited edition 45 rpm EP phonodisc, Genesis Publications/Ganga Distributors SGH 778 (1992).

Notes

INTRODUCTION

1. Other successful U.K.-based skiffle performers included the Vipers, Johnny Duncan and the Bluegrass Boys, and the Chas McDevitt Skiffle Group with Nancy Whiskey.

2. Jim O'Donnell, *The Day John Met Paul* (New York: Hall of Fame Books, 1994).

3. In one of his first media interviews, Harrison named Duane Eddy (and Chet Atkins) as his favorite musician. "Lifelines of the Beatles," *New Musical Express*, February 15, 1963, 9.

4. In addition to those performers mentioned, the Beatles' live repertoire in 1957–1959 included their versions of songs by Gene Vincent, Eddie Cochran, Jerry Lee Lewis, Lloyd Price, the Coasters, Fats Domino, and Ray Charles. Mark Lewisohn, *The Beatles Live!* (London: Pavilion, 1986), 12–26.

5. See, for example, Simon Frith, Andrew Goodwin, and Lawrence Grossberg, eds., *Sound and Vision: The Music Video Reader* (New York: Routledge, 1993); Steve Jones and Martin Sorger, "Covering Music: A Brief History and Analysis of Album Cover Design," *Journal of Popular Music Studies 11/12* (1999/2000): 68–102; Ian Inglis, "Nothing You Can See That Isn't Shown: The Album Covers of the Beatles," *Popular Music* 20, no. 1 (2001): 83–97; and Carol Vernallis, *Experiencing Music Video: Aesthetics and Cultural Context* (New York: Columbia University Press, 2004).

CHAPTER 1

1. Numerous comparisons have been made between the characteristics of these roles and those of other quartets that preceded or followed the Beatles. Consider, for example, the common lineage from the Marx Brothers through the Beatles to the Monkees: Groucho Marx–John Lennon–Micky Dolenz; Chico Marx–Paul McCartney–Davy Jones; Harpo Marx–Ringo Starr–Peter Tork; Zeppo Marx–George Harrison–Mike Nesmith.

2. Bob Neaverson, *The Beatles Movies* (London: Cassell, 1997), 11–46.

3. Marc Shapiro, *All Things Must Pass: The Life of George Harrison* (New York: St. Martin's Press, 2002), 24.

4. Alan Smith, "Close-Up on a Beatle: George Harrison," *New Musical Express*, August 16, 1963, 2.

5. Mark Lewisohn, *The Complete Beatles Chronicle* (London: Pyramid, 1992), 63.

6. Bob Spitz, *The Beatles: The Biography* (New York: Little, Brown, 2005), 285–87.

7. Hunter Davies, *The Quarrymen* (London: Omnibus, 2001), 73–74.

8. Although formally credited to Harrison and Lennon, drummer Pete Best recalls that it was created largely by Harrison alone and identifies it as an early example of his songwriting talent. See Pete Best and Patrick Doncaster, *Beatle! The Pete Best Story* (London: Plexus, 1985), 104–5.

9. For an analysis of the ingenuity brought by the Beatles to the traditional sentiments and vocabulary of the love song, see Guy Cook and Neil Mercer, "From Me to You: Austerity to Profligacy in the Language of the Beatles," in *The Beatles, Popular Music and Society: A Thousand Voices*, ed. Ian Inglis (New York: St. Martin's Press, 2000), 86–104.

10. Derek Johnson, "Shadows Sing with the Beatles." *New Musical Express*, April 12, 1963, 3.

11. George Harrison, *I Me Mine* (London: W. H. Allen, 1982), 84.

12. Brian Southall and Rupert Perry, *Northern Songs: The True Story of the Beatles Song Publishing Empire* (London: Omnibus, 2006), 45–46.

13. Alan Clayson, *The Quiet One: A Life of George Harrison* (London: Sidgwick & Jackson, 1990), 125.

14. Walter Everett, *The Beatles as Musicians: The Quarry Men through "Rubber Soul"* (New York: Oxford University Press, 2001), 284–85.

15. An account of the events that took place at that first meeting is presented by Peter Brown and Steven Gaines, *The Love You Make* (New York: McGraw-Hill, 1983), 134–36.

16. Ian Inglis, "Synergies and Reciprocities: The Dynamics of Musical and Professional Interaction between the Beatles and Bob Dylan," *Popular Music and Society* 20, no. 4 (1997): 53–79.

17. Geoffrey Giuliano, *Dark Horse* (London: Bloomsbury, 1989), 54.

18. Wilfrid Mellers, *Twilight of the Gods: The Beatles in Retrospect* (London: Faber, 1973), 61.

19. Matthew Bannister, "The Beatle Who Became a Man: 'Revolver' and George Harrison's Metamorphosis," in *Every Sound There Is*, ed. Russell Reising (Burlington, VT: Ashgate, 2002), 183–93.

20. Hunter Davies, *The Beatles* (London: Heinemann, 1968), 341.

21. Allan Kozinn, *The Beatles* (London: Phaidon, 1995), 144.

22. Ravi Shankar, *Raga Mala: An Autobiography* (New York: Welcome Rain, 1999), 189–203.

23. Allan F. Moore, *The Beatles: Sgt. Pepper's Lonely Hearts Club Band* (Cambridge, UK: Cambridge University Press, 1997), 45–46.

24. For an assessment of Harrison's ability as a sitar player, see Sandy Loewenthal, "Instruments in Combination," in *Making Music*, ed. George Martin (London: Pan, 1983), 196–204.

25. There seems to have been general agreement within the Beatles' inner circle that "Only a Northern Song" was a disappointing composition of inferior quality. Geoff Emerick, *Here, There and Everywhere* (New York: Gotham Books, 2006), 165–66.

26. Davies, *The Beatles*, 232.

27. Harrison, *I Me Mine*, 106.

28. For a detailed account of the time spent in Rishikesh by the Beatles, their wives/girlfriends, and friends (including Donovan, Mia Farrow, and Mike Love), see Paul Saltzman, *The Beatles in Rishikesh* (New York: Viking Studio, 2000).

29. Ed Whitley, "The Postmodern White Album," in Inglis, *Beatles, Popular Music and Society*, 105–25.

30. Mark Brown, "Here Comes the Song," *Guardian*, May 9, 2009, 12.

31. Hunter Davies, "The Week in Books: George Harrison's Teenage Angst," *Guardian Saturday Review*, May 16, 2009, 5.

32. See, for example, Vincent Bugliosi and Curt Gentry, *Helter Skelter: The True Story of the Manson Murders* (New York: W. W. Norton, 2001); and Tommy Udo, *Charles Manson: Music Mayhem Murder* (London: Sanctuary, 2002).

33. Harrison, *I Me Mine*, 128.

34. Nicholas Schaffner, *The Beatles Forever* (New York: McGraw-Hill, 1977), 125.

35. Pattie Boyd, *Wonderful Today: George Harrison, Eric Clapton and Me* (London: Headline, 2007), 116.

36. Emerick, *Here, There and Everywhere*, 303–4.

37. Alan Smith, "Beatle Single by George," *New Musical Express*, November 1, 1969, 3.

38. Simon Leng, *While My Guitar Gently Weeps* (Milwaukee, WI: Hal Leonard, 2006), 50–51.

39. George Martin, *All You Need Is Ears* (New York: St. Martin's Press, 1979), 177–89.

40. Ian Peel, *The Unknown Paul McCartney: McCartney and the Avant-Garde* (London: Reynolds & Hearn, 2002), 36–37.

41. There is no shortage of books that seek to explain the extent of the decade's cultural transformations. See, for example, Christopher Booker, *The Neophiliacs: The Revolution in English Life in the Fifties and Sixties* (London: Collins, 1969); Bernard Levin, *The Pendulum Years: Britain and the Sixties* (London: Jonathan Cape, 1970); Jonathon Green, *Days in the Life* (London: Heinemann, 1988); Roger Hutchinson, *High Sixties* (Edinburgh: Mainstream, 1992); and Michka Assayas and Claude Meunier, *The Beatles and the Sixties* (New York: Henry Holt, 1996).

42. See, for example, Shapiro, *All Things Must Pass*, 90–91; Clayson, *Quiet One*, 174.

43. Bernie Krause, who was present at the recording of "No Time or Space," has claimed that the track is nothing more than an edited version of an introductory synthesizer lesson. Elliott J. Huntley, *Mystical One: George Harrison* (Toronto: Guernica, 2004), 30.

44. Brown and Gaines, *Love You Make*, 333–39.

45. For an appreciation of Harrison's importance to the Beatles as a guitarist, see Robbie McIntosh, "Twelve Strings That Changed the World," *Mojo* 98 (January 2002): 43.

46. "Sing One for the Lord" appeared on Preston's 1970 album *Encouraging Words* alongside early, and overlooked, versions of "All Things Must Pass" and "My Sweet Lord."

CHAPTER 2

1. The first triple album in popular music history was *Woodstock*, released in August 1970, just a few months before *All Things Must Pass*.

2. Robert Shelton, *No Direction Home: The Life and Music of Bob Dylan* (New York: Beech Tree, 1986), 422.

3. This element of Harrison's spiritual philosophy accords with the Hindu concept of *neo-Vedanta*, which insists that there is one divine reality, who is known by different names across different faiths. Dale C. Allison, *The Love There That's Sleeping: The Art and Spirituality of George Harrison* (New York: Continuum, 2006), 6–23.

4. Marc Shapiro, *All Things Must Pass: The Life of George Harrison* (New York: St. Martin's Press, 2002), 105.

5. The extent of Lennon's and McCartney's persistent criticisms of Harrison's songs is exposed in Doug Sulphy and Ray Schweighardt, *Get Back: The Beatles' "Let It Be" Disaster* (New York: St. Martin's Press, 1998), 42–136.

6. Jonathan Gould, *Can't Buy Me Love: The Beatles, Britain, and America* (New York: Harmony Books, 2007), 127–28.

7. George Harrison, *I Me Mine* (London: W. H. Allen, 1982), 162.

8. Clinton Heylin, *Dylan: Behind the Shades* (London: Viking, 1991), 193.

9. Anthony DeCurtis, "The Return of George Harrison: Looking Back on the Beatles, LSD and the Sixties," in *Harrison by the Editors of* Rolling Stone, ed. Robert Love (New York: Simon & Schuster, 2002), 146.

10. Her suspicions about Harrison's infidelity are clarified in Pattie Boyd, *Wonderful Today: George Harrison, Eric Clapton and Me* (London: Headline, 2007), 148.

11. Harrison had produced, and sung on, the *Radha Krishna Temple* album in 1971. When rereleased in 1998, under the new title *Chant and Be Happy! Indian Devotional Songs*, it included extracts of conversations with Harrison, Yoko Ono, and John Lennon and was credited to Harrison and the London Radha Krishna Temple.

12. Stefan Granados, *Those Were the Days: An Unofficial History of the Beatles' Apple Organization, 1967–2002* (London: Cherry Red Books, 2002), 27.

13. Carole Bedford, *Waiting for the Beatles: An Apple Scruff's Story* (Poole, Dorset, England: Blandford, 1984).

14. John Blake, *All You Needed Was Love: The Beatles after the Beatles* (London: Hamlyn, 1981), 121–25.

15. Harrison, *I Me Mine*, 208.

16. Geoffrey Giuliano, *Dark Horse* (London: Bloomsbury, 1989), 81.

17. Walter Everett, *The Beatles as Musicians: "Revolver" through the Anthology* (New York: Oxford University Press, 1999), 284–85.

18. David Cavanagh, "George Harrison: The Dark Horse," *Uncut* 135 (August 2008): 36–48.

19. Chet Flippo, *McCartney: The Biography* (London: Sidgwick & Jackson, 1988), 320.

20. Keith Richards's affectionate and positive assessment of Harrison's ability as a guitarist is reported in Love, *Harrison*, 228–29.

CHAPTER 3

1. Stefan Granados, *Those Were the Days: An Unofficial History of the Beatles Apple Organization, 1967–2002* (London: Cherry Red Books, 2002), 197–212.

2. John Blake, *All You Needed Was Love: The Beatles after the Beatles* (London: Hamlyn, 1981), 127–28.

3. Geoffrey Giuliano, *Dark Horse* (London: Bloomsbury, 1989), 164–66.

4. David Sheff and G. Barry Golson, *The Playboy Interviews with John Lennon and Yoko Ono* (New York: Playboy Press, 1981), 142–43.

5. George Harrison, *I Me Mine* (London: W. H. Allen, 1982), 238.

6. George Martin, *Summer of Love: The Making of "Sgt. Pepper"* (London: Macmillan, 1994), 148–49.

7. See, for example, Spencer Leigh, *Drummed Out: The Sacking of Pete Best* (Bordon, Hants, England: Northdown, 1998); and Ian Inglis, "Pete Best: History and His Story," *Journal of Popular Music Studies* 11/12 (1999/2000): 103–24.

8. Phil Spector's determination to find another hit single for his wife Ronnie is discussed in Richard Williams, *Phil Spector: Out of His Head* (London: Omnibus Press, 2003), 161–62.

9. Harrison, *I Me Mine*, 214.

10. Jann Wenner, *Lennon Remembers* (London: Penguin, 1972), 160.

11. David Cavanagh, "George Harrison: The Dark Horse," *Uncut* 135 (August 2008): 36–48.

12. See, for example, Blake, *All You Needed Was Love*, 156; and Giuliano, *Dark Horse*, 148–49.

13. Pattie Boyd, *Wonderful Today: George Harrison, Eric Clapton and Me* (London: Headline, 2007), 174–77.

14. For a discussion of the urban myths and legends of rock music, see Ian Inglis, "Sex and Drugs and Rock 'n' Roll," *Popular Music and Society* 30, no. 5 (2007): 591–603.

15. Philip Norman, *Shout! The True Story of the Beatles* (London: Hamish Hamilton, 1981), 338.

16. Anthony Scaduto, *Bob Dylan* (London: W. H. Allen, 1972), 175–86.

17. Ben Fong-Torres, "The Troubled 1974 U.S. Tour," in *Harrison by the Editors of* Rolling Stone, ed. Robert Love (New York: Simon & Schuster, 2002), 125–29.

18. Kevin Howlett, *The Beatles at the BBC: The Radio Years, 1962–1970* (London: BBC Books, 1996), 49.

19. Mark Lewisohn, *The Beatles: 25 Years in the Life* (London: Sidgwick & Jackson, 1987), 161.

20. Alan Clayson, *Ringo Starr* (London: Sidgwick & Jackson, 1981), 181.

21. See May Pang and Henry Edwards, *John Lennon: The Lost Weekend* (New York: SPI Books, 1983).

Chapter 4

1. Jack Kerouac, *On the Road* (New York: Viking, 1957).

2. Mike Brocken, "Some Other Guys," *Popular Music and Society* 20, no. 4 (1996): 23–27.

3. Janet Wolff, *The Social Production of Art* (London: Macmillan, 1981), 95–116.

4. Chris Salewicz, *McCartney: The Biography* (London: Queen Anne Press, 1986), 188–89.

5. The term *conspicuous consumption* was introduced by sociologist Thorstein Veblen to describe the practice of purchasing and using items in order to increase one's visible prestige and produce admiration in others. See Thorstein Veblen, *The Theory of the Leisure Class: An Economic Study of Institutions* (New York: Macmillan, 1902).

6. Alan Lewens, *Walk On By: Soundtrack of the Century* (London: HarperCollins, 2001).

7. This claim was denied by Dylan in the interview he gave to Jann Wenner in *Rolling Stone*, November 19, 1969.

8. Ian Inglis, "Some Kind of Wonderful: The Creative Legacy of the Brill Building," *American Music* 21, no. 2 (2003): 214–35.

9. Ken Emerson, *Always Magic in the Air: The Bomp and Brilliance of the Brill Building Era* (London: Fourth Estate, 2005).

10. Michael Brocken, *Bacharach* (London: Chrome Dreams, 2003).

11. Bill Harry, *The Ultimate Beatles Encyclopedia* (London: Virgin, 1992), 90.

12. Simon Frith, "Backward and Forward," in *The Beat Goes On*, ed. Charlie Gillett and Simon Frith (London: Pluto, 1996), 4–5.

13. Serge Dutfoy, Dominique Farran, and Michael Sadler, *The Cartoon History of Rock and Roll* (London: Elm Tree Books, 1986).

14. George Melly, *Revolt into Style* (London: Allen Lane, 1970).

15. Dick Hebdige, *Subculture: The Meaning of Style* (London: Methuen, 1979).

16. Alistair Taylor, *A Secret History* (London: John Blake, 2001), 154.

17. Ian MacDonald, *Revolution in the Head* (London: Fourth Estate, 1994), 175.

18. George Harrison, *I Me Mine* (London: W. H. Allen, 1982), 370.

19. Sara Cohen, "Sounding Out the City: Music and the Sensuous Production of Place," *Transactions of the Institute of British Geographers* 20 (1995): 434–46.

20. Geoffrey Giuliano and Brenda Giuliano, eds., *The Lost Beatles Interviews* (London: Virgin, 1995), 158.

21. Denny Somach and Ken Sharp, eds., *Meet the Beatles . . . Again!* (Havertown, PA: Musicom, 1995), 30.

22. Ray Coleman, *John Lennon* (London: Futura, 1985), 490.

23. Harrison's first involvement with film production had come some years earlier, when he financed the production of *Little Malcolm and His Struggle against the Eunuchs* (dir. Stuart Cooper, 1974) adapted from David Halliwell's stage play.

24. Norma Coates, "If Anything, Blame Woodstock," in *Performance and Popular Music: History, Place and Time*, ed. Ian Inglis (Aldershot, England: Ashgate, 2006), 58–69.

25. Ian Inglis, "The Road Not Taken," in Inglis, *Performance and Popular Music*, 41–51.

26. See, for example, Fred Fogo, *I Read the News Today: The Social Drama of John Lennon's Death* (Lanham, MD: Littlefield Adams, 1994); and Anthony Elliott, *The Mourning of John Lennon* (Berkeley: University of California Press, 1999).

27. See, for example, Hanif Kureishi, "Boys Like Us," *Weekend Guardian*, November 3/4, 1991, 4–7.

28. Hunter Davies, *The Beatles* (London: William Heinemann, 1968), 341–43.

29. Barry Miles, *Paul McCartney: Many Years from Now* (London: Secker & Warburg, 1997), 593–95.

30. Peter Brown and Steven Gaines, *The Love You Make* (London: Macmillan, 1983), 28–29.

31. Joshua M. Greene, *Here Comes the Sun: The Spiritual and Musical Journey of George Harrison* (New York: Wiley, 2006), 287–88.

32. Harrison, *I Me Mine*, 28.

33. The full components of Epstein's managerial strategy are discussed in Ian Inglis, "Conformity, Status and Innovation: The Accumulation and Utilisation of Idiosyncrasy Credits in the Career of the Beatles," *Popular Music and Society* 19, no. 3 (1996): 41–74.

34. Richard DiLello, *The Longest Cocktail Party* (London: Charisma, 1972), 10.

35. Geoffrey Giuliano, *Dark Horse* (London: Bloomsbury, 1989), 208.

36. Marc Shapiro, *All Things Must Pass: The Life of George Harrison* (New York: St. Martin's Press, 2002), 151.

37. For an insight into the mutual economic benefits that music and film can bring to each other, see Lee Barron, "Music Inspired By: The Curious Case of the Missing Soundtrack," in *Popular Music and Film*, ed. Ian Inglis (London: Wallflower, 2003), 148–61.

CHAPTER 5

1. The Prince's Trust is the United Kingdom's leading youth charity, working with disadvantaged young people between the ages of 14 and 30. It was established by the Prince of Wales in 1976.

2. See, for example, Ian MacDonald, *Revolution in the Head* (London: Fourth Estate, 1994), 175; and Philip Norman, *John Lennon: The Life* (London: HarperCollins, 2008), 770.

3. The distinctions between gossip and rumor are discussed in Kenelm Burridge, "Cargo," in *Mythology*, ed Pierre Maranda (Harmondsworth, England: Penguin, 1972), 127–35.

4. Yoko Ono, *Grapefruit* (London: Sphere, 1970).

5. Anthony DeCurtis, "George Harrison Gets Back," in *Harrison by the Editors of* Rolling Stone, ed. Robert Love (New York: Simon & Schuster, 2002), 134–41.

6. Ian Inglis, "The Politics of Nomenclature," *Journal of Popular Music Studies* 18, no. 1 (2006): 3–17.

7. Tom Petty, "Remembering George," in Love, *Harrison*, 223–25.

8. Alan Clayson, *The Quiet One: A Life of George Harrison* (London: Sidgwick & Jackson, 1990), 300.

9. Dale C. Allison, *The Love There That's Sleeping: The Art and Spirituality of George Harrison* (New York: Continuum, 2006), 17–18.

10. See, for example, Peter Wicke, "The Role of Rock Music in the Political Disintegration of East Germany," in *Popular Music and Communication*, ed. James Lull (Newbury Park, CA: Sage, 1992), 196–206.

11. See, for example, Leon Rosselson, "Pop Music: Mobiliser or Opiate," in *Media, Politics and Culture: A Socialist View*, ed. Carl Gardner (London: Macmillan, 1979), 40–50.

12. Mitchell Axelrod, *Beatletoons: The Real Story behind the Cartoon Beatles* (Pickens, SC: Wynn, 1999).

13. Marc Shapiro, *All Things Must Pass: The Life of George Harrison* (New York: St. Martin's Press, 2002), 127.

14. Bill Harry, *The George Harrison Encyclopedia* (London: Virgin, 2003), 250–52.

15. See, for example, Jeff Beck's comments in *Performance and Popular Music*, ed. Ian Inglis (Aldershot, England: Ashgate, 2006), xiii–xvi.

16. Mark Hertsgaard, *A Day in the Life: The Music and Artistry of the Beatles* (New York: Delacorte, 1995), 252–54.

17. This is, however, a perception that has been rigorously challenged by Paul McCartney. See, for example, Barry Miles, *Paul McCartney: Many Years from Now* (London: Secker & Warburg, 1997); and Ian Peel, *The Unknown Paul McCartney: McCartney and the Avant Garde* (London: Reynolds & Hearn, 2002).

18. In April 1992, Harrison gave a onetime benefit concert for the Natural Law Party at London's Royal Albert Hall. Supported by many of the musicians who had appeared on the previous year's tour of Japan, he performed "I Want to Tell You," "Old Brown Shoe," "Taxman," "Give Me Love (Give Me Peace on Earth)," "Something," "What Is Life," "Piggies," "Got My Mind Set on You," "Cloud 9," "Here Comes the Sun," "My Sweet Lord," "All Those Years Ago," "Cheer Down," "Isn't It a Pity," and "Devil's Radio."

19. George Harrison, *I Me Mine* (London: W. H. Allen, 1982), 45.

20. Shapiro, *All Things Must Pass*, 174–75.

CHAPTER 6

1. Marc Shapiro, *All Things Must Pass: The Life of George Harrison* (New York: St. Martin's Press, 2002), 181.

2. George Harrison, *I Me Mine* (London: W. H. Allen, 1982), 59.

3. See, for example, Lisa A. Lewis, ed., *The Adoring Audience: Fan Culture and Popular Media* (London: Routledge, 1992); Matthew Hills, ed., *Fan Cultures* (New York: Routledge, 2002); and Cornel Sandvoss, *Fans: The Mirror of Consumption* (Malden, MA: Polity Press, 2005).

4. The Beatles, *Anthology* (London: Cassell, 2000), 216.

5. The origins and repercussions of the inconsistencies between belief and behavior—as expressed in the theory of cognitive dissonance—have long been explored by psychologists; see, for example, Leon Festinger, *A Theory of Cognitive Dissonance* (Stanford, CA: Stanford University Press, 1957).

6. Alan Clayson, *The Quiet One: A Life of George Harrison* (London: Sidgwick & Jackson, 1990), 8.

7. Joshua M. Greene, *Here Comes the Sun: The Spiritual and Musical Journey of George Harrison* (New York: Wiley, 2006), 329.

8. Ravi Shankar, *Raga Mala: An Autobiography* (New York: Welcome Rain, 1999), 320–21.

9. Harrison, *I Me Mine*, 53–54.

10. They included *He Was Fab: A Loving Tribute to George Harrison* (2002); *Songs from the Material World: A Tribute to George Harrison* (2003); and *Thanks for the Pepperoni: A Tribute to George Harrison* (2004).

11. The appearance of Sinead O'Connor provided the only variation. When prevented, by prolonged booing, from performing Dylan's "I Believe in You," she responded by delivering an impromptu version of Bob Marley's "War." For a full discussion, see Emma Mayhew, "The Booing of Sinead O'Connor," in *Performance and Popular Music: History, Place and Time*, ed. Ian Inglis (Aldershot, England: Ashgate, 2006), 172–87.

12. The one notable absentee in the cast of performers was Bob Dylan. Unable to be in London on November 29, he paid a personal tribute to Harrison by performing "Something" at his Madison Square Garden concert on November 13. His only other performance of the song was at the Liverpool Echo Arena on May 1, 2009; while in Liverpool, he also visited Lennon's childhood home, which had been bought by Yoko Ono and donated to the National Trust in 2003.

13. The Beatles, *Anthology*, 78.

14. Dai Griffiths, "Cover Versions and the Sound of Identity in Motion," in *Popular Music Studies*, ed. David Hesmondhalgh and Keith Negus (London: Arnold, 2002), 51–64.

CONCLUSION

1. Cynthia Lennon, *John* (London: Hodder & Stoughton, 2005), 42–43.

2. Bob Spitz, *The Beatles* (New York: Little, Brown, 2005), 229–31.

3. Ross Benson, *Paul McCartney: Behind the Myth* (London: Victor Gollancz, 1992), 33–35.

4. While Aspinall remained a key member of the Beatles' inner circle (and chief executive of Apple) until his death in 2008, Best had no further contact with any of the Beatles. See Roag Best (with Pete Best and Rory Best), *The Beatles: The True Beginnings* (Ipswich, England: Spine, 2002), 151.

5. Elliot J. Huntley, *Mystical One: George Harrison* (Toronto: Guernica, 2004), 12.

6. Hunter Davies, *The Beatles* (London: William Heinemann 1968), 351.

7. David Sheff and G. Barry Golson, *The Playboy Interviews with John Lennon and Yoko Ono* (New York: Playboy Press, 1981), 126–28.

8. Jann Wenner, *Lennon Remembers* (London: Penguin, 1972), 67–68.

9. Geoffrey Giuliano and Brenda Giuliano, eds., *The Lost Beatles Interviews* (London: Virgin, 1995), 156.

10. Andy Babiuk, *Beatles Gear* (San Francisco: Backbeat, 2002), 182.

11. Pattie Boyd, *Wonderful Today: George Harrison, Eric Clapton and Me* (London: Headline, 2007), 175–76.

12. Things came to a head for Harrison during the recording of *Let It Be*, in January 1969, when, frustrated by continuous disagreements with McCartney and Lennon, he announced that he was quitting the group and was absent from the studio for several days. For a full account, see Doug Sulphy and Ray Schweighardt, eds., *Get Back: The Unauthorized Chronicle of the Beatles' "Let It Be" Disaster* (New York: St. Martin's Press, 1997).

13. Ian Inglis, "Synergies and Reciprocities: The Dynamics of Musical and Professional Interaction between the Beatles and Bob Dylan," *Popular Music and Society* 20, no. 4 (1997): 53–79.

14. Geoffrey Giuliano, *Dark Horse* (London: Bloomsbury, 1989), 55.

15. Harrison was not alone in the Beatles in his desire to incorporate Indian influences into his compositions. It has been claimed, for example, that as many as twenty of the group's songs, including Lennon–McCartney compositions such as "Tomorrow Never Knows," "Rain," "I Am the Walrus," "Dear Prudence," and "Blackbird" contain musical and/or lyrical references to Indian sources. See David Reck, "The Beatles and Indian Music," in *Sgt. Pepper and the Beatles*, ed. Olivier Julien (Aldershot, England: Ashgate, 2008), 63–73.

16. Ravi Shankar, *Raga Mala: An Autobiography* (New York: Welcome Rain, 1999), 6–7, 230.

17. For useful overviews of the history and development of world music, see, for example, Francis Hanly and Tim May, *Rhythms of the World* (London: BBC Books, 1989); and Terry E. Miller and Andrew Shahriari, *World Music: A Global Journey* (New York: Routledge, 2006).

18. Steve Turner, *The Gospel According to the Beatles* (Louisville, KY: Westminster John Knox Press, 2006), 38–41.

19. See, for example, Dale C. Allison, *The Love There That's Sleeping: The Art and Spirituality of George Harrison* (New York: Continuum, 2006), 56–57, 79–80. Among those songs whose lyrics are derived from biblical passages are "The Day the World Gets Round," "Love Comes to Everyone," and "Lay His Head"; among those that consider reincarnation are "The Answer's at the End," "Life Itself," and "Heading for the Light."

20. Subsequent winners of the *Billboard* Century Award have included Buddy Guy, Billy Joel, Joni Mitchell, Carlos Santana, Chet Atkins, James Taylor, Emmylou Harris, Randy Newman, John Mellencamp, Annie Lennox, Sting, Stevie Wonder, and Tom Petty.

21. Joshua M. Greene, *Here Comes the Sun: The Spiritual and Musical Journey of George Harrison* (New York: Wiley, 2006), 302.

22. Alan Clayson, *The Quiet One: A Life of George Harrison* (London: Sidgwick & Jackson, 1990), 136.

23. Since its creation in 1986, only a handful of performers have been inducted twice into the Rock and Roll Hall of Fame (as a solo artist and as a group member). In addition to Harrison, the list includes Jeff Beck (the Yardbirds), Michael Jackson (the Jackson Five), John Lennon (the Beatles), Sam Cooke (the Soul Stirrers), Paul Simon (Simon and Garfunkel), Clyde McPhatter (the Drifters), Paul McCartney (the Beatles), Curtis Mayfield (the Impressions), and Neil Young (Buffalo Springfield). Eric Clapton (the Yardbirds and Cream) is the only musician to have been inducted three times.

24. Sheff and Golson, *The Playboy Interviews With John Lennon & Yoko Ono*, 141.

25. In his autobiography, Brian Epstein predicted that nothing like the Beatles could ever happen again. He drew attention to McCartney's glamour, Lennon's command, and Starr's quaintness, and he described Harrison as the boy next door, the business Beatle, and a young man with a genuine interest in the outside world. Brian Epstein, *A Cellarful of Noise* (London: Souvenir Press, 1964), 92.

26. Stan W. Denski, "Music, Musicians and Communication: The Personal Voice in a Common Language," in *Popular Music and Communication*, ed. James Lull (Newbury Park, CA: Sage, 1992), 33–48.

27. Terence J. O'Grady, *The Beatles: A Musical Evolution* (Boston: Twayne, 1983), 172–74.

Annotated Bibliography

Allison, Dale C. *The Love There That's Sleeping: The Art and Spirituality of George Harrison*. New York: Continuum, 2006.

> Written by a Christian scholar, this is a perceptive and informed account of the spiritual components of Harrison's music. While it occasionally exaggerates the extent of the religious references in his lyrics, it presents an intriguing analysis of many familiar songs.

Assayas, Michka, and Claude Meunier. *The Beatles and the Sixties*. New York: Henry Holt, 1996.

> The authors attempt, with some success, to locate the achievements of the Beatles within their specific historical period.

Barrow, Tony. *John, Paul, George, Ringo and Me*. London: Sevenoaks, 2005.

> Candid revelations from the Beatles' press officer.

Beatles, The. *The Beatles Anthology*. London: Cassell, 2000.

> An indispensable, firsthand version of the Beatles' story by the group members and their closest associates. Made to accompany the television documentary series, this is probably the closest thing to a genuine autobiography.

Bedford, Carole. *Waiting for the Beatles: An Apple Scruff's Story.* New York: Sterling, 1984.

Immortalized in Harrison's song on *All Things Must Pass,* this is one "scruff's" account of the small group of female fans who were a permanent fixture outside Apple's offices in the late 1960s and early 1970s. The author claims a special closeness with Harrison, and much of the book is about that relationship.

Best, Pete, and Patrick Doncaster. *Beatle! The Pete Best Story.* London: Plexus, 1985.

The former drummer's first published account of his time with the Beatles.

Best, Pete, and Bill Harry. *The Best Years of the Beatles.* London: Headline, 1996.

Subjective and sensationalized anecdotes from the group's years in Hamburg and Liverpool.

Black, Johnny, ed. *Q The Beatles: Band of The Century.* London: Bauer, 1999.

This collection of feature articles, interviews, and photographs is *Q*'s tribute to the Beatles.

Blake, John. *All You Needed Was Love: The Beatles after the Beatles.* London: Hamlyn, 1981.

Includes frank assessments of Harrison's fall into musical mediocrity in the 1970s.

Boyd, Pattie. *Wonderful Today: George Harrison, Eric Clapton and Me.* London: Headline, 2007.

An intimate account of her years with Harrison and Clapton, by the woman who inspired "Something." Short on musical detail, but full of fascinating and surprising glimpses into their daily lives.

Bramwell, Tony. *Magical Mystery Tours.* New York: Thomas Dunne, 2005.

The author was a childhood friend of Harrison who became one of the permanent staff in the NEMS and Apple organizations. His presence throughout the Beatles' career and his close relationship with Harrison make this one of the more relevant "insider" accounts.

Braun, Michael. *Love Me Do: The Beatles' Progress.* London: Penguin, 1964.

Of all the books about the early Beatles, this is the most valuable. It observes, in straightforward terms, the growth of Beatlemania and the group's reaction to it. Written before the full extent of their global achievements could be even imagined, Braun's portrait of four young men struggling to comprehend the world in which they find themselves is a superb piece of factual reporting.

Brown, Peter, and Steven Gaines. *The Love You Make*. London: Macmillan, 1983.

Another insider account of the Beatles' story, from the man who began as manager of Brian Epstein's NEMS record shop in Liverpool and ended as executive director of Apple.

Cavanagh, David. "George Harrison: The Dark Horse." *Uncut* 135 (August 2008): 36–48.

Retrospective evaluation of Harrison's career, featuring an interview with Paul McCartney.

Clayson, Alan. *The Quiet One: A Life of George Harrison*. London: Sidgwick & Jackson, 1990.

Clayson has published individual biographies of all four Beatles. Thoroughly researched, but written in a self-consciously "hip" style.

Davies, Hunter. *The Beatles*. London: Heinemann, 1968.

Originally published more than forty years ago, Davies has updated and revised this book on several occasions. Although dismissed as "bullshit" by Lennon, it remains the only authorized biography, written with the cooperation of Epstein and the Beatles.

DiLello, Richard. *The Longest Cocktail Party*. London: Charisma Books, 1973.

Anecdotal memories of the author's time as "house hippie" at Apple.

Emerick, Geoff. *Here, There and Everywhere*. New York: Gotham Books, 2006.

From 1963 to 1969, Emerick was the Beatles' recording engineer. His recollections of those sessions, particularly the routine lack of importance given by the others to Harrison's songs, do much to explain Harrison's increasing frustration within the group.

Epstein, Brian. *A Cellarful of Noise*. London: Souvenir Press, 1964.

A well-meaning, if rather formal, description of the early years of Beatlemania and Epstein's relationship with the four Beatles.

Everett, Walter. *The Beatles as Musicians: "Revolver" through the Anthology*. New York: Oxford University Press, 1999. *The Beatles as Musicians: The Quarrymen through "Rubber Soul."* New York: Oxford University Press, 2001.

Substantial and impressively detailed assessments of the group's musical progression.

Frontani, Michael R. *The Beatles: Image and the Media*. Jackson: University Press of Mississippi, 2007.

Scholarly analysis of the Beatles' transformation from pop stars to cultural spokesmen.

Gentle, Johnny. *Johnny Gentle and the Beatles' First Ever Tour*. Runcorn, Cheshire, England Merseyrock, 1998.

An affectionate account of the group's tour of Scotland in 1960 as the backing band for British singer Johnny Gentle.

Giuliano, Geoffrey. *Dark Horse: The Secret Life of George Harrison*. London: Bloomsbury, 1989.

An unremarkable biography that tracks Harrison through his Beatles career and solo years. Olivia and George Harrison took great exception to the expert status and insider knowledge claimed by the author.

Gould, Jonathan. *Can't Buy Me Love: The Beatles, Britain, and America*. New York: Harmony Books, 2007.

Unusually thoughtful and serious biography of the Beatles.

Granados, Stefan. *Those Were the Days: An Unofficial History of the Beatles Apple Organization, 1967–2002*. London: Cherry Red Books, 2002.

Quite informative about the circumstances behind the early solo recordings of the four ex-Beatles.

Greene, Joshua M. *Here Comes the Sun: The Spiritual and Musical Journey of George Harrison*. New York: Wiley, 2006.

Essentially a standard biography of Harrison that manages to devote a little more space than usual to his spiritual beliefs.

Harrison, George. *I Me Mine*. London: W. H. Allen, 1982.

With a little help from Derek Taylor, these are Harrison's own reflections on his life and music up to and including the songs on *George Harrison*. What emerges is a picture of a private, thoughtful man, for whom his songs are a profoundly satisfying means of expression.

Harry, Bill. *The George Harrison Encyclopedia*. London: Virgin, 2003.

A veteran of the Liverpool scene of the 1950s and '60s, Harry presents an informative collection of entries pertaining to all aspects of Harrison's personal and professional life.

Hertsgaard, Mark. *A Day in the Life: The Music and Artistry of the Beatles*. New York: Delacroix, 1995.

Limited attempt to tell the story of the Beatles through their music.

Heylin, Clinton. *The Act You've Known for All These Years*. Edinburgh: Canongate, 2007.

The author assesses the importance of *Sgt. Pepper* by placing it alongside other groundbreaking albums of the period.

Howlett, Kevin. *The Beatles at the BBC: The Radio Years, 1962–1970*. London: BBC Books, 1996.

Song-by-song history of their radio performances in the 1960s.

Huntley, Elliot J. *Mystical One: George Harrison*. Toronto: Guernica, 2004.

Poorly written and sloppily edited account of Harrison's solo years.

Inglis, Ian, ed. *The Beatles, Popular Music and Society: A Thousand Voices*. New York: St. Martin's Press, 2000.

Academic writers from a variety of disciplines—sociology, linguistics, musicology—present their observations on the Beatles.

Julien, Olivier, ed. *Sgt. Pepper and the Beatles: It Was Forty Years Ago Today*. Burlington, VT: Ashgate, 2008.

Fascinating and informative reflections on the album's historical impact and influence.

Kane, Larry. *Ticket to Ride*. Philadelphia: Running Press, 2003.

A journalist's account of the Beatles' historic visits to the United States in 1964 and 1965.

Kozinn, Allan. *The Beatles*. London: Phaidon Press, 1995.

Unremarkable account of the group's musical evolution.

Kruger, Ulf, and Ortwin Pelc, eds. *The Hamburg Sound*. Hamburg: Ellert & Richter Verlag, 2006.

Published to accompany an exhibition at the Museum of Hamburg History, the book presents a series of articles that consider the presence of the Beatles (and others) in Germany in the early 1960s.

Leach, Sam. *The Rocking City*. Liverpool: Pharaoh Press, 1999.

Memories of the formative Beatles, from one of Liverpool's first pop promoters.

Leigh, Spencer. *Twist and Shout!* Liverpool: Nirvana, 2004.

Anecdotes and recollections from those present at the birth of the Mersey Beat.

Leng, Simon. *While My Guitar Gently Weeps: The Music of George Harrison.* Milwaukee, WI: Hal Leonard, 2006.

Exhaustive record of the key places, dates, and personnel in Harrison's recording career.

Lewisohn, Mark. *The Complete Beatles Chronicle.* London: Pyramid Books, 1992.

A purely factual historical record of the Beatles' performances and recording dates.

Loescher, Greg, ed. *Goldmine: The Beatles Digest.* Iola, WI: Krause, 2000.

Fascinating and wide-ranging compilation of articles from the pages of *Goldmine*. Charles Reinhart's pieces on the Beatles' instrumental tracks and Harrison's Dark Horse record label are especially interesting.

Love, Robert, ed. *Harrison by the Editors of* Rolling Stone. New York: Simon & Schuster, 2002.

Published as a tribute to Harrison after his death, this brings together a compilation of interviews, articles, and photographs from the pages of *Rolling Stone*.

Macdonald, Ian. *Revolution in the Head: The Beatles' Records and the Sixties.* London: Fourth Estate, 1994.

A much-praised, track-by-track analysis of the group's songs that succeeds in placing them—individually and collectively—in their sociohistorical context.

Martin, George. *All You Need Is Ears.* New York: St. Martin's Press, 1979.

Autobiography of the Beatles' producer, with extended sections about his personal and professional involvement with the group.

Martin, George. *Summer of Love: The Making of "Sgt. Pepper."* London: Macmillan, 1994.

Contains a detailed discussion of Harrison's desire to bring Indian influences into his music, along with an assessment of his songwriting ability.

McCabe, Peter, and Robert D. Schonfeld. *Apple to the Core: The Unmaking of the Beatles.* London: Sphere, 1972.

Depressing account of the managerial and financial difficulties that led to the disintegration of the Beatles.

Mellers, Wilfrid. *Twilight of the Gods: The Beatles in Retrospect*. London: Faber, 1973.

The first sustained musicological assessment of Beatles songs, written at a time when serious investigations of popular music were still regarded as inappropriate. From *Please Please Me* to *All Things Must Pass*, Mellers offers interesting accounts of some of Harrison's more memorable compositions.

Moore, Allan F. *The Beatles: Sgt. Pepper's Lonely Hearts Club Band*. Cambridge, UK: Cambridge University Press, 1997.

A meticulous analysis of the group's iconic album by a leading musicologist.

Neaverson, Bob. *The Beatles Movies*. London: Cassell, 1997.

A valuable overall history of the Beatles on screen, including insights into Harrison's frame of mind during the filming of *Let It Be*.

Norman, Philip. *Shout!* London: Hamish Hamilton, 1981.

One of the better Beatles biographies.

O'Dell, Denis. *At the Apple's Core*. London: Peter Owen, 2002.

Contains numerous examples of the frustration felt by Harrison during the Apple years.

O'Grady, Terence J. *The Beatles: A Musical Evolution*. Boston: Twayne.

Important attempt to refocus attention firmly on the group's music, which, the author believes, is often overlooked in the many histories and explanations of the Beatles' success.

Peel, Ian. *The Unknown Paul McCartney: McCartney and the Avant-Garde*. London: Reynolds & Hearn, 2002.

Although ostensibly about McCartney, the book provides useful information about the way in which Lennon and Harrison also became increasingly interested in "experimental" approaches to music-making in the late 1960s.

Quantick, David. *Revolution: The Making of the Beatles' White Album*. London: Unanimous, 2002.

Rather simplistic attempt to contextualize the creation of *The Beatles*.

Rayl, A. J. S., and Curt Gunther. *Beatles '64: A Hard Day's Night in America*. London: Sidgwick & Jackson, 1989.

Rayl's text and Gunther's photographs depict the contrast between the unprecedented momentum of Beatlemania and the down-to-earth attitude of the Beatles themselves.

Reising, Russell. *Every Sound There Is*. Burlington, VT: Ashgate, 2002.

Detailed scholarly analysis of *Revolver*, with ample space given to Harrison's contributions to the album.

Saltzman, Paul. *The Beatles in Rishikesh*. New York: Viking Studio, 2000.

The author was one of the guests at the Maharishi Mahesh Yogi's ashram in 1968, when the Beatles, at Harrison's insistence, arrived for several weeks of meditation and spiritual exploration. This is his written and photographic record of that time.

Sandercombe, W. Fraser. *The Beatles Press Reports*. Burlington, ON: Collector's Guide, 2007.

Compilation of Beatles-related articles and interviews from the British weekly music press (*Record Mirror, Disc & Music Echo, Melody Maker, Mersey Beat*) between 1961 and 1970.

Schaffner, Nicholas. *The Beatles Forever*. New York: McGraw-Hill, 1977.

Among the very best of the hundreds of books that examine the history of the Beatles. Intelligently written, it also covers their solo careers until 1977.

Shankar, Ravi. *Raga Mala: An Autobiography*. New York: Welcome Rain, 1999.

An invaluable and honest account of Shankar's musical and spiritual journey. The lengthy sections on his relationship with Harrison demonstrate the depth of their friendship and testify to their shared musical commitment.

Shapiro, Marc. *All Things Must Pass: The Life of George Harrison*. New York: St. Martin's Press, 2002.

Superficial and predictable biography, written in the wake of Harrison's death.

Sheff, David, and G. Barry Golson, eds. *The Playboy Interviews with John Lennon and Yoko Ono*. New York: Playboy Press, 1981.

Transcript of a series of candid and revealing interviews carried out three months before Lennon's death. His comments contain frank assessments of Harrison's music, and the often difficult relationship between the two men.

Somach, Denny, and Ken Sharp, eds. *Meet the Beatles . . . Again!* Havertown, PA: Musicom, 1995.

Compilation of interviews, mainly from the 1980s, including Harrison's press conference to promote *George Harrison* in 1979 and an interview with his sister, Louise.

Somach, Denny, Kathleen Somach, and Kevin Gunn, eds. *Ticket to Ride.* New York: William Morrow, 1989.

Transcripts of Scott Muni's WNEW-FM radio shows, including an interview with Harrison in 1987 to promote *Cloud Nine* in which he talks freely about his new partnership with Jeff Lynne.

Southall, Brian. *Abbey Road.* Cambridge, England: Patrick Stephens, 1982.

A history of the studios made famous by the Beatles, with a useful summary of the group's early activities there.

Southall, Brian, and Rupert Perry. *Northern Songs: The True Story of the Beatles Song Publishing Empire.* London: Omnibus, 2006.

Two music industry insiders provide a detailed history of the tangled legal and financial disputes that beset the Beatles' song catalogue.

Spitz, Bob. *The Beatles.* New York: Little, Brown, 2006.

The most detailed biography of the Beatles to date.

Sulphy, Doug, and Ray Schweighardt. *Get Back: The Unauthorized Chronicle of the Beatles' "Let It Be" Disaster.* New York: St. Martin's Press, 1997.

Day-by-day reconstruction of the events in January 1969 that included the recording of *Let It Be*, the rooftop concert in London's Savile Row, and Harrison's temporary departure from the group.

Sutherland, Steve, ed. "The Beatles: The Complete Story." London: IPC Ignite, 2002.

Year-by-year reproduction of Beatles-related articles, reviews, interviews, and photographs, originally published in the *New Musical Express* between 1962 and 1970.

Taylor, Alistair. *A Secret History.* London: John Blake, 2001.

The Beatles-related memoirs of Brian Epstein's personal assistant, prompted by an exaggerated sense of injustice. It reveals far more about the person who wrote it than it does about the people against whom it is directed.

Taylor, Derek. *It Was Twenty Years Ago Today.* New York: Bantam, 1987.

Retrospective analysis of the Summer of Love, *Sgt. Pepper*, and the Beatles' search for spiritual enlightenment.

Thompson, Phil. *The Best of Cellars.* Liverpool: Bluecoat Press, 1994.

A history of the Cavern Club, where the Beatles made 274 appearances between February 1961 and August 1963.

Trynka, Paul, ed. *The Beatles: Ten Years That Shook the World*. New York: Dorling Kindersley, 2004.

This is *Mojo*'s tribute to the Beatles. Many of the feature articles, interviews, and photographs were previously published in three separate "limited edition" magazine compilations: *1,000 Days of Beatlemania: The Early Years, 1962–1964* (2002); *1,000 Days That Shook the World: The Psychedelic Beatles, 1965–1967* (2002); and *1,000 Days of Revolution: The Beatles' Final Years, 1968–1970* (2003).

Turner, Steve. *The Gospel According to the Beatles*. Louisville, KY: Westminster John Knox Press, 2006.

Detailed account of the Beatles' involvement with religious and philosophical ideas.

Turner, Steve. *A Hard Day's Write*. London: Carlton, 1994.

Very superficial attempt to understand and explain the inspiration behind the Beatles' songs.

Vollmer, Jurgen. *The Beatles in Hamburg*. Munich: Schirmer/Mosel, 2004.

Photographs and memories of the young Beatles by one of their German friends.

Wenner, Jann, ed. *Lennon Remembers*. London: Penguin, 1971.

Rolling Stone interviews in which Lennon speaks frankly about his relationship with the other Beatles.

Williams, Allan, and William Marshall. *The Man Who Gave the Beatles Away*. London: Elm Tree Books, 1975.

Voyeuristic recollections of the early Beatles, written by their first manager.

Woffinden, Bob. *The Beatles Apart*. New York: Proteus, 1981.

A general overview of the Beatles' achievements through the first decade of their solo careers.

Womack, Kenneth, and Todd F. Davis. *Reading the Beatles: Cultural Studies, Literary Criticism, and the Fab Four*. Albany: State University of New York Press, 2006.

A useful addition to the increasing number of academic studies of the Beatles.

Index

About the Author

IAN INGLIS is Reader in Popular Music Studies at Northumbria University, Newcastle upon Tyne, United Kingdom. His books include *The Beatles*, *Popular Music and Society*, *Popular Music and Film*; *Performance and Popular Music: History, Place and Time*; and *Popular Music on British Television*.